Creative Writing

Creative Writing

A Beginner's Manual

Anjana Neira Dev
Anuradha Marwah
Swati Pal

BA Programme Committee
University of Delhi

Pearson

ISBN: 978-81-317-1984-8

First Impression, 2009
Twentieth Impression, 2025
Twenty One Impression

Published by Pearson India Education Services Pvt. Ltd, CIN: U72200TN2005PTC057128.

Head Office: 1st Floor, Berger Tower, Plot No. C-001A/2, Sector 16B, Noida - 201 301, Uttar Pradesh, India.
Registered Office : Featherlite, 'The Address' 5th Floor, Survey No 203/10B, 200 Ft MMRD Road, Zamin Pallavaram, Chennai – 600044.
Website :in.pearson.com;Email:companysecretary.india@pearson.com

Printed in India by Pushp Print Services

Contents

Preface and Acknowledgements ix
Introduction: How to Use the Manual xi
Credits xiii

Unit 1: What is Creative Writing? 1
Defining Creativity 1
Measuring Creativity 2
Inspiration and Agency 4
Creativity and Resistance 6
Art and Propaganda 8
Creativity and Madness 8
What is Creative Writing? 9
Imagination and Writing 10
Restrictions of an Open Field 11
Can Creative Writing be Taught? 12
The Importance of Reading 13
Summary 14
References 16
Websites 16

Unit 2: The Art and Craft of Writing 17
Tropes and Figures 19
Style and Register 32
Formal and Informal Usage 32
Varieties of English 34
Language and Gender 36
Disordered Language 37
Playing with Words 39
Grammar and Word Order 40
Tense and Time 41
Grammatical Differences 42
Summary 43
References 44

Unit 3: Modes of Creative Writing 45
Writing to Communicate: The Writer and the Reader 45

SECTION I: POETRY 48
Writing Poetry 48
Definitions of Poetry: What is a Poem? 49
The Four Functions of Language 50
What to Write About and How to Start 50
Poetry and Prose 52
Shape, Form and Technique 54
Rhyme and Reason 59
Fixed Forms and Free Verse 61
Dominant Modes of Poetry—Lyrical, Narrative and Dramatic 67
Voices in the Poem 74
Some Indian English Poets and their Works 76
A Conversation with a Creative Writer 78
Writing Verse for Children 83
The Problem with Writing Poetry 89
Getting Down to Writing Poetry 90
Workshop 1: Practice 92
Workshop 2: Share and Learn 93
Workshop 3: Create 93

SECTION II: FICTION 94
Fiction 94
Non-fiction 95
Fiction and the 20th Century 96
The Importance of History 97
Literary and Popular Fiction 99
The Short Story and the Novel 101
Sweet Rice 105
Character 111
Plot 112
Point of View (Modes of Narration) 114
Setting (Milieu) 115
A Conversation with a Creative Writer 116
Writing Fiction for Children 117
What is Children's Literature? 119
The Sword of Dara Shukoh 120
A Conversation with a Creative Writer 131
Create a Person 132
Workshop 4 132
Workshop 5: Tutorial Format 133
Workshop 6 133
Workshop 7 (Optional) 134

SECTION III: DRAMA 134
What is Drama? 134
The Concept and Characteristics of Drama 134
The Plot in Drama or Dramatic Structure 139
Characterization in Drama 144

Verbal and Non-Verbal Elements in Drama 147
A Brief Overview of English Language Theatre in India 151
Some Different Styles of Contemporary Theatre in Indian English 153
Some Well-known Practising Indian English Playwrights and their Plays 155
A Conversation with a Creative Writer 157
Writing for Films 158
Writing a Screenplay 165
The World of Children Through Film and Theatre 167
Scripting for Children's Theatre 167
Developing as a Playwright and Evaluating Your Script 170
Workshop 8: How to Develop a Situation 171
Workshop 9: Create a Sequence of Events 173
Workshop 10: Put the Sequence of Events into a Scene for a Play 173
References 174
Websites 175

Unit 4: Writing for the Media 177
Introduction 177
The Print Media 180
The Broadcast Media 188
The New Media 192
Advertising 196
References 204

Unit 5: Preparing for Publication 205
Revising and Rewriting 205
Proof Reading 207
Editing 208
Submitting Your Manuscript for Publication 213
Summary 215
References 215

Index 217
About the Authors 225

Preface and Acknowledgements

Whenever you read something that touches a chord in you, we are sure you wonder how the writer knew that this is what you have always felt in your innermost being. Whenever you read something that astounds you, don't you celebrate the widening of your intellectual horizons? While reading an extraordinarily beautiful work, don't you feel like a player in the grand drama of humanity?

Words are important. 'In the beginning was the Word' and thus begins the story of creation. The saga of humanity, a variety of thinking and feeling persons, starts with our ability to speak to others and share life with them, through the medium of language. This book is especially designed for all those who love the written word and are awed by its power to create magic.

What is it that writers do with words that invests them with so much power? This is one of the primary questions addressed by this book. We will take you 'backstage' to witness all that goes into the writing of poems, stories, plays, travelogues, newspaper reports and features, writing for the electronic and new media, etc., and attempt to motivate you to try your hand at translating your ideas and feelings into words and on to the printed page.

This is not a course about English Literature. Although framed under the broad rubric of literature in English, and by teachers of English, this course attempts something different. We aim to make students *write*, poems, stories, plays and journalistic articles. To facilitate this journey into the world of creative writing we have tried to look at writing from the inside, from the point of view of craft rather than from historical and theoretical perspectives. We are primarily concerned with an exploration into creativity, genres and language.

To demonstrate the flexibility of English that allows it to express a multitude of cultural identities, we have drawn extensively from Indian English literature that carries with it the flavour of our plural traditions. We hope to instil confidence in our students to enable them to use our own unique English assertively. We aim at increased sensitivity to all aspects of literature and we believe this would come from retracing the journeys made by the masters and by trying to chart one's own course. As Mark Twain has said, 'Training is everything … cauliflower is nothing but cabbage with a college education.'

We have given you all the ingredients and also samples of how these have been put together in a number of ways. While we hope you will savour the explorations, we also hope that this will only be the beginning of your engagement with the creative process. For ultimately, what you write should have your unique signature on it. We hope you will use this book as a starting point for your journey and as you embark on the lexical route, may inspiration be your constant companion.

The conception, nurturing and execution of this book has been enriched in myriad ways by: Prof. Rajiva Verma, Prof. Ramesh Gautam, Prof. R. Parthasarathy, Mr. Mahesh Dattani, Ms. Subhadra Sen Gupta, Mr. Arvind Joshi, Dr. Syamala Kallury, Dr. Angelie Multani, Ms. Sampurna Chattarji, Mr. Sanjay Kumar, Mr. Somnath Batabayal, Mr. Uttam Sinha, Ms. Sanam Khanna, Ms. Saloni Sharma and Mrs. Kamal Dev. A special note of appreciation for Mr. Jaideep Krishnan whose creative inputs gave the book its final shape.

Introduction: How to Use the Manual

This is a creative writing manual for beginners for all those who want to empower themselves with creativity. Creativity cannot be imposed on unwilling students; nor can it be encapsulated within the covers of a book. Creativity is learnt in the school of life; this manual is merely an aid.

It is written with a view to group activity. The manual uses the workshop format assuming that there would be a facilitator\mentor\teacher who would conduct a series of structured activities with a group of learners; and provide advice and encouragement. However, we do not rule out self-study. In the absence of a facilitator\teacher and other like-minded learners the manual may be used as a guide. The student would in such a case be advised to find a mentor who s/he could visit occasionally or correspond with periodically and to whom s/he could submit her/his drafts for advice and encouragement.

The manual could also be used productively within a creative writing group without a permanent facilitator\mentor\teacher. Members of the group who have come together with the express purpose of discussing their work and getting feedback from other beginner-writers, would profit a great deal from the practical advice that the manual provides. It is suggested that they nominate a facilitator for each unit and do the activities provided in the manual as writing practice.

Whichever format—classroom, self-study, or writing group—the student employs, we strongly recommend that the Manual be used in the sequence it is written. Every section follows the preceding section and leads to the successive section. None should be plucked out of context especially as the exercises and activities are also arranged developmentally. It would not be a good idea, for instance, to scare oneself by trying to write an entire short story, poem or drama (Workshops of Unit 3) after going through only Unit 1.

The aim of the manual is focussed and, appropriately, a verb: writing. Writing is 'doing': it is active and the practitioners need to be proactive. Our second and equally strong recommendation is do more and more. We have provided a few activities in the manual but they should be taken as the basic minimum. By no means are they exhaustive. It would be a good idea for the facilitator or the learner to come up with many more activities on the lines of those already provided. In itself that would be an exercise in creativity. Ideally 80 per cent of the time spent on the manual should be in the 'doing'.

The 'doing' also includes reading creatively. A writer can never be a passive recipient of ideas. So, as suggested later in the book, a beginner-writer may need to read hungrily and even indiscriminately, but s/he should always read with a view to what s/he can use for her/his own purpose. For this, ideas need to be saved in the mind; dwelt upon; and transcended. We suggest keeping:

- A notebook to take down words, phrases, entire dialogue that strike the student.
- A file to preserve clippings from newspapers and journals.

This isn't all. Often reading sets one onto a course and the reader, consciously or subconsciously, continues to dialogue with the book long after it has been returned to the library or kept back on the shelf. We also suggest keeping:

- A slam book that the student has with her/him all the time to jot down ideas immediately as they occur (even at midnight).

All these will come in handy while doing the activities. It is our wish and hope that the users of the manual surprise their mentors and also themselves with their ideas and writing. Our minds are uncharted territories. The manual is designed to aid and guide the voyage into creativity.

Credits

26: 'Mirrors', *Crossing the Waters* by Sylvia Plath, with permission from Harcourt Brace Jovanovich Inc. and Thomson Learning. Copyright © Ted Hughes, 1971.

48: 'Ars Poetica', unpublished poem in typescript. Copyright © by R. Parthasarathy. Reprinted with permission of R. Parthasarathy.

53–54: Agha Shahid Ali, 'Postcard From Kashmir' from *The Half Inch Himalayas* © by Agha Shahid Ali and reprinted with permission of Wesleyan University Press.

71: 'Victim No 569', *Poem No. 24* , *Dispossessed Nest* (Nirula, 1986) by Jayanta Mahapatra, reproduced with permission of the author.

72: Poem 'Ordinary Things' reproduced with permission of the author, from Rukmini Bhaya Nair, *The Hyoid Bone* (Viking, 1993).

73: 'Homecoming' from *Rough Passage*, published by Oxford University Press. Copyright © by R. Parthasarathy. Reproduced with permission of R. Parthasarathy.

136–37: Extract from the play *Dance Like A Man*, reproduced with permission of the author, from Mahesh Dattani, *Final Solutions and Other Plays* (Manas, 1994).

103: Vilas Sarang, 'Notes of a Working Writer', *The Women in Cages* (Delhi: Penguin Books, 2006), reproduced with permission from Penguin Books.

120–30: 'The Sword of Dara Shukoh' by Subhadra Sen Gupta, reproduced with permission of Ratnasagar publishers.

140: Table, from Edwin Wilson, *The Theatre Experience*, 10th edition (McGraw-Hill, New York, 1980) with permission of McGraw-Hill Books.

150–51: *Harvest* (Kali for Women, 1998), reproduced with permission of Manjula Padmanabhan.

1

What is Creative Writing?

Defining Creativity

Creativity does not have an authoritative definition. However, most of us recognize creative acts, ideas and arts. When we visit the National Gallery of Modern Art; when we listen to Lata Mangeshkar; when we watch Shah Rukh Khan emote; or when we read Gabriel Garcia Marquez and Stephen King we know we are encountering creativity of different kinds. But creativity is not the preserve of the famous; it is not only limited to those who are celebrated as great artists or performers. We may also appreciate creativity in embroidery, cookery, or in an exceptionally beautiful flowerbed. Taking a walk through a DDA colony we may be struck by the transformation of an ugly staircase by a creative arrangement of earthen pots. Creativity is also an everyday phenomenon.

Creativity has become a catchword in modern industry. There is a big noise about creative ideas and solutions. It is commonplace in the echelons of management to spend lakhs organizing workshops to teach executives creative problem-solving. We know that more and more employers are concerned with identifying and fostering the creative potential of their employees.

These examples only serve to prove that creativity is a complex and varied phenomenon. Going by them, the painter Pablo Picasso was creative; so is Sabeer Bhatia, the founder of Hotmail; but so is the neighbourhood *chaiwallah*, who thought of sticking an omelette into a sweet bun and coming up with the widely popular *bunanda*. We intuitively recognize creativity but most of us would not be able to explain it. Let us try to find a working definition.

> *Creativity* (or *Creativeness*) is a mental process involving the generation of new ideas or concepts, or new associations between existing ideas or concepts. The products of creative thought (sometimes referred to as 'divergent thought' usually have both originality and appropriateness (Wikipedia).

We need to go further into the concepts of 'new', 'divergent thought', 'originality' and 'appropriateness'.

There are thinkers who believe that there can be nothing that is absolutely new in arts and ideas. Does that rule out creativity? Pablo Picasso, Sabeer Bhatia and the anonymous *chaiwallah*—all used pre-existing concepts, ideas and objects for their creations. Yet they extended the frontiers of human knowledge and experience. 'Creativity, it has been said, consists largely of re-arranging what we know in order to find out what we do not know', observed George Keller. The concept of 'new' is not universal or fixed in the definition. It is subjective and dynamic.

Creativity deals in subjectivity and emotion. It puts us in touch with the variety in human existence. *Divergent thinking* may be defined in opposition to convergent thinking. Convergent thinking involves aiming for a single, correct solution to a problem, whereas divergent thinking involves coming up with multiple answers to a given problem. Thus, creativity may be understood as the opposite of logical or analytical thought. Daniel Pink, in his book *A Whole New Mind*, argues that we are entering a new age where we will need to foster and encourage right-directed thinking (representing creativity and emotion) over left-directed thinking (representing logical, analytical thought). Other phrases to suggest creative thinking in current use are: thinking out of the box, lateral thinking and fluid intelligence.

Originality and appropriateness in the definition indicate two features of the product of creativity. We will try and understand them by comparing various kinds of creativity. There are obvious differences between the *bunanda* and Picasso's painting. Appropriateness is essential for the success of the *bunanda*: the taste, the pricing, the shelf life of the ingredients, the clientele. Similarly, the success of Hotmail is incumbent on the appropriateness of the technology. However, Picasso's art succeeds more due to its originality than its appropriateness. Works of art may sometimes flaunt their 'inappropriateness', their overturning of established conventions, as a defining feature.

Certain critics consider originality paramount in art and literature and argue that in other fields like everyday life, industry, architecture and design, creativity is qualitatively different as appropriateness of the product is as important as originality.

If we think more about it we realize that the continuum of creativity actually stretches from interpretation to innovation in art and literature as well. Classical dance and music or acting (the performing arts), for instance, would rely more on interpretation than painting and literature where there is greater scope to innovate or create 'new'. But even in literature and painting there are established genres that pull the practitioner towards the pole of interpretation. Alexander Pope is considered a great poet because he perfected the form of the 'heroic couplet' in English poetry. Picasso, too, both interpreted and innovated within cubism to attain his formidable reputation as the great modernist painter. Thus, lurking deep within what is startlingly new and original is an appropriate interpretation of the past and the present.

> Rather than look for a qualitative difference in kinds of creativity, or prioritize one over the other, it would be far better for our purpose to conclude that the manifestations of creativity are different in different fields. Originality and appropriateness may sometimes go hand in hand; at other times one may overtake the other, depending on the demands of the task at hand and the time and place.

Measuring Creativity

J. P. Guilford (1967) pioneered the modern *psychometric* approach to creativity. Taking a cue from the Guilford group many psychologists have developed tests to measure creativity. Although creativity is now accepted as an essential constituent of human intelligence, efforts to develop a reliable Creativity Quotient have met with little success.

The preceding discussion should give us a clue as to why it would be next to impossible to measure creativity objectively and across cultures. As we have seen, creativity dwells in subjectivity and variety. There are many kinds of creativity and the very definition of what constitutes a creative act is determined by its appropriateness to the context. Besides, most measures of creativity are dependent on the personal judgement of the tester, so a standardized measure is difficult to develop.

However, it would be instructive to know what psychologists measure in order to assess creativity. It may help us recognize highly creative people and acts. Tests of creativity may be scored on:

- **Fluency.** The total number of meaningful and relevant ideas generated in response to the test.
- **Flexibility.** The number of different categories of relevant responses.
- **Originality.** The rarity of the responses among the test subjects.
- **Elaboration.** The amount of detail in the responses.

Some psychologists favour a *social-personality approach*. To measure creativity, they assess personality traits such as independence of judgment, self-confidence, attraction to complexity, aesthetic orientation, risk taking and openness to experience.

Another way to assess creativity is to look at its various *dimensions*. Besides *originality* and *appropriateness* that have already been discussed, other related dimensions like the following may also be studied as indicators of creativity:

- **Intellectual leadership.** Creative thinkers are able to create new and promising theories or exciting trends which inspire others to follow; in essence starting a movement, a school of thought or a trend.
- **Sensitivity to problems.** The ability to identify problems that challenge others and open up a new field of thought is a mark of creative thinking.
- **Ingenuity.** Ingenious solutions that are able to solve problems in a neat and surprising way or reflect a new perspective of looking at the problem.
- **Unusualness.** Creative thinkers are able to see remote associations between ideas. When word association tests are given, people in highly creative literary fields like poets give a higher proportion of unique responses.
- **Usefulness.** Solutions or ideas that are also practical are considered more creative as the creator is able to meet the constraints of the problem while at the same time producing unusual and original solutions.

The above is from psychological literature that deals with all kinds of creativity. Measuring creativity would be especially useful in industry and education.

When we think of creative writing, the focus is slightly different from issues around recruitment or career choice. Through creative writing we are aiming at artistic achievement. The discussion that follows and the examples henceforth will deal specifically with creativity in art and literature.

Inspiration and Agency

> **Inspire** to infuse an animating, quickening or exalting influence into.
> **Inspiration** 1. an inspiring or animating action or influence. 2. *Theol.* A divine influence directly and immediately exerted upon the mind or soul of a man.
> (*Webster's Encyclopedic Unabridged Dictionary of the English Language* 1994)

Creativity, especially in art and literature, is often linked with inspiration. In definition no. 1 explained as a cause of the effect (creativity) the meaning of the word inspiration is easily understood. The problem arises in the theological definition (no. 2) where a supra human agency is assumed and is carried over into art and literature. The question that arises then is: if inspiration comes from a divine source, then are not human will and efforts irrelevant?

And all who heard should see them there,
And all should cry, Beware! Beware!
His flashing eyes, his floating hair!
Weave a circle around him thrice,
And close your eyes with holy dread,
For he on honey-dew hath fed,
And drunk the milk of Paradise.
—Coleridge (1974: 48–54)

This is Coleridge's description of the divinely inspired poet whom everybody regards with awe.

It is not up to the writers of this book to discount divine inspiration just as it is not up to them to challenge the existence of God. It would be sufficient to point out that Coleridge, the English Romantic poet, spoke in the idiom of the nineteenth century and that with the secularization of life in the twentieth and twenty-first centuries artists and writers have relocated inspiration to various other quarters: childhood experiences, works of other writers and artists, conscious or unconscious motivation, etc.

There is in the present time the strong conviction among a significant section that inspiration may be sought, fostered and learnt rather than merely awaited. This consciousness was not completely absent in the nineteenth century. Wordsworth, Coleridge's friend and the most famous of the English Romantics looked to Nature for inspiration:

Thanks to the human heart by which we live
Thanks to its tenderness, its joys and fears,
To me the meanest flower that blows can give
Thoughts that do often lie too deep for tears.
—Wordsworth (1977: 204–207)

Although the human heart is prioritized in this poem, Wordsworth invested Nature with awe-inspiring powers. Inspiration might have been sought deliberately but it was still a matter of mystical communication between the poet and Nature.

Modern poetry tends to be more self-reflective. The most important and perhaps the most quoted line in Wallace Stevens' *Of Modern Poetry* is the first, wrapping onto the second: 'The poem of the mind in the act of finding/What will suffice.'

Of Modern Poetry

The poem of the mind in the act of finding
What will suffice. It has not always had
To find: the scene was set; it repeated what
Was in the script.
Then the theatre was changed
To something else. Its past was a souvenir.

It has to be living, to learn the speech of the place.
It has to face the men of the time and to meet
The women of the time. It has to think about war
And it has to find what will suffice. It has
To construct a new stage. It has to be on that stage,
And, like an insatiable actor, slowly and
With meditation, speak words that in the ear,
In the delicatest ear of the mind, repeat,
Exactly, that which it wants to hear, at the sound
Of which, an invisible audience listens,
Not to the play, but to itself, expressed
In an emotion as of two people, as of two
Emotions becoming one. The actor is
A metaphysician in the dark, twanging
An instrument, twanging a wiry string that gives
Sounds passing through sudden rightnesses, wholly
Containing the mind, below which it cannot descend,
Beyond which it has no will to rise.
It must
Be the finding of a satisfaction, and may
Be of a man skating, a woman dancing, a woman
Combing. The poem of the act of the mind.

—Stevens (2006)

The poem of the act of the mind has to 'think' and find what will suffice. Not only has the focus shifted from the poet to the poem but also the purpose and agency are underscored as essential features of poetry.

Are we saying that modern poetry has stolen away all the 'awe' and 'mystery' associated with the poet? Is the creativity of the modern poet at a more pedestrian level than that of the one 'who on honey-dew hath fed'?

Even this poem of the mind generates the following image of creativity: 'The actor is\ A metaphysician in the dark, twanging\An instrument, twanging a wiry string that gives\Sounds passing through sudden rightnesses …'. It seems that no matter how close one might get to a rational explanation, creativity still seems to have a component that defies description and goes beyond the analytical mind. This is as it should be, as creativity is a product of divergent thought and is both subjective and original, and geared to extending knowledge.

We may conclude this discussion by inferring that inspiration refers to that element in creativity that is not completely understood by analytical thought. The tendency has been to demystify the process of creativity and psychological literature of the twentieth and twenty-first centuries provides valuable insight into the play of the conscious and unconscious motivation of the creator. One might sometimes complain that far from rejecting a supra human agency the twentieth century has created a new god for itself: 'psychology'. Just as ancient and medieval thinkers traced creativity to God, too many modern intellectuals explain away creative acts as arising from the subconscious mind of the artist. D.H. Lawrence's novel *Sons and Lovers* is often read and discussed as the expression of the 'Oedipal Complex'. If Coleridge was seen as possessed, isn't Lawrence's agency also undermined by seeing the novel only as a play of subconscious motivation?

However, the consensus in the present time seems to be that even though the process of creativity may not be 'fully understood' by the creator, even though inspiration may play a significant role, agency (human will and effort) cannot be undermined in the act of creation. Steven Stucky, a well-known composer, explains his creative process in the following words.

> In my line of work, I often overhear myself described as a 'creative person', yet I identify much more readily with those working stiffs who slug it out down in the trenches, day in and day out: with Thomas Edison and his '5 percent inspiration, 95 percent perspiration'; with Paul Hindemith, the great German composer, who, when asked where he got his ideas, simply held up his pencil, with Sir Harrison Birtwistle, the best English composer of our day, an authentic genius and gruff, no-nonsense bloke who, when asked by an interviewer some high-flown question about making art, replied, 'What preoccupies every working artist is simply how the hell you do it.'
>
> For me, composing means long, hard, unglamorous hours spent with pencil and paper and (especially) eraser, trying by hook or crook to tease something from nothing.

It isn't as though Stucky discounts inspiration totally. He acknowledges creative artists from other fields whose masterpieces often 'spark' his own work. He especially mentions 'the sly, lapidary prose style of Nabokov, which sparked my 1980 composition, *Transparent Things*. It's the brilliant textures and finely judged juxtapositions of Stravinsky's, *Petrushka*, which forms a backdrop for my own *Son et lumiere* of 1988. it is the humane, lyrical voice of poet Archie Ammons, who inspired my 1992 song cycle, *Four Poems of A.R. Ammons*.'

Creativity and Resistance

By now we have inferred that creativity being a profitable human attribute usually benefits society perceptibly and improves the quality of life. We may go on to assume that creative acts are always celebrated. That would be to overlook the subversive potential of creativity. As creativity involves the imagination and reaches out towards what is 'new' and 'original', it is by definition unconventional. It can challenge the norms and mores of society, upset the status quo and redistribute power. So, very often, authorities and power centres feel threatened and end up deriding and persecuting creative people.

The author Ayn Rand observed, '*The man who invented fire was probably burned at the stake.*' Closer to home, on Jan 1, 1989 Safdar Hashmi was chased by lathi-wielding political goons in Sahibabad and beaten to death. His only crime was that he was performing a play '*Halla Bol*' in support of striking industrial workers. Salman Rushdie's novel *Satanic Verses* raised a veritable storm of protest and a fatwa was issued against the author for an irreverent depiction of the Prophet. The painter M.F. Hussain was similarly threatened for his controversial depiction of Hindu goddesses. Film-maker Deepa Mehta's *Fire* was attacked for its taboo theme of lesbianism; her film *Water* could not be shot in India because a certain section objected to her portrayal of the plight of Hindu widows.

The artists mentioned above may not have deliberately or consciously intended to challenge established power structures. But there are scores who have been very direct in their criticism: Dalit writers like Daya Pawar and Omprakash Valmiki against caste oppression in India; Black writers in the USA against racism; Chernyavsky and others against Czarist Russia; Milan Kundera against the Communist regime in Czechoslovakia; and most recently Nobel Laureate Orhan Pamuk against Turkish policies, to name but a few. Most have had to face persecution in some form.

The above examples go to establish that creative expression has the potential to challenge the status quo and bring about a change in society. Those who threaten and persecute creative people are usually beneficiaries of the system and are interested that things remain as they are. They seek to inhibit creativity in various ways.

Censorship that involves banning of books and government control over art and literature has been found to be inimical to creativity, and so has the control of big and powerful capitalist institutions. Evolved and aware societies have to constantly come up with ways to protect 'freedom of expression.'

Sometimes, it may mean that creative artists collectively resist attempts to stifle expression. In 2001, the rich and powerful Mitchell Trust tried to stop the publication of a first novel by an African American writer that parodied the classic bestseller *Gone with the Wind.* Ever since it was published in the 1930's it has continued to hurt the sensibilities of the African American community by its stereotypical portrayal of black (nigger) characters. In 2001, a young African American writer Alice Randall finished writing its parody *The Wind Done Gone* in which she gave voice and subjectivity to Margaret Mitchell's cardboard characters. The Mitchell Trust swooped down and attempted to prohibit the publication of this novel. A number of writers, a lot of them African-Americans but many Whites, came together to oppose the move. We reproduce here portions from a news item quoting the famous African-American writer and Nobel laureate Toni Morrison as she makes a strong case in favour of Alice Randall and in opposition to white racism. Morrison argues in favour of artistic rights and praises Randall's efforts of attempting to assuage the historical damage done to the African American community in the USA:

> 'Considering the First Amendment rights properly accorded Gone with the Wind, in spite of the pain, humiliation, and outrage its historical representation has caused African Americans, it seems particularly odd for the Mitchell estate to deny this clever but gentle effort to assuage the damage Gone with the Wind has caused. That it has asked legal redress does not seem to have embarrassed it.' She continues, 'To crush the artistic rights of an African American writer seems to me not only reckless but arrogant and pathetic.'

In the same news item, Morrison also makes an important literary point about the difference between plagiarism and inspiration: '*The Wind Done Gone* neither "follows" nor copies nor exploits *Gone With the Wind.* What Miss Randall's book does is imagine and occupy narrative spaces and silences never once touched upon nor conceived of in Mrs. Mitchell's novel.... As to the form and quality of Miss Randall's novel (as it relates to charges of 'theft' and 'subliteracy'), her book is written in the form of a diary discovered among the papers of a deceased woman—a form with precedents far older than the novel genre.'

Art and Propaganda

Some critics argue that true creativity should not be tainted by politics or causes, as true art is universal. In practice, it would be very difficult to reject works only because they are associated with causes. Arthur Miller's drama is considered Left, as is Pablo Neruda's poetry; Toni Morrison argues the cause of African American women in novel after novel; Saul Bellow speaks for the Jews; all four are Nobel Laureates and their works are indisputably 'art'.

The concept of universal art, that is of an above 'causes', has been challenged repeatedly in the present times. What used to be called 'universal' perhaps expressed the value of the dominant section of society. Creativity is always subjective; which is not to say that all art is propaganda, or that there is no difference between art and propaganda. *We call a work of art 'propaganda'—irrespective of what it says—if artistic considerations are compromised because of ideology.*

However, merely ascribing motives or politics to the creator does not take away from the creativity of the work. Resistance to established norms is, in fact, a valuable function of creativity—one that is cherished by the under-privileged all over the world.

Creativity and Madness

We know that creative people are unusual. In the above section we discussed how they might sometimes be regarded with suspicion, even derided and persecuted. That is not all. There is also a more subtle way in which they are constantly marginalized: people often accuse them of being impractical, dreamy and cut-off from reality. It is no coincidence that from time immemorial, side by side with being deified as 'divinely inspired', creative people have also been compared with 'lunatics'.

In Shakespeare's immortal words:

The lunatic, the lover, and the poet
Are of imagination all compact [composed].

Shakespeare ascribes the propensity to hallucinate to all three:

One sees more devils than vast hell can hold,
That is the madman. The lover, all as frantic,
Sees Helen's beauty in a brow of Egypt.
The poet's eye, in a fine frenzy rolling,
Doth glance from heaven to earth, from earth to heaven;
And as imagination bodies forth
The forms of things unknown, the poet's pen
Turns them to shapes, and gives to airy nothing
A local habitation and a name.
—Shakespeare (1955)

The madman is traumatised by imaginary devils; the lover goes against the prevalent notion of beauty and images his dark mistress as the 'fairest of all'; and the poet creates imaginary beings.

Thus, we see that imagination in all three cases is accused of creating a wedge between the individual and society. This point of view is not restricted to literature. A lot of psychological research has been dedicated to finding a correlation between creativity on the one hand and psychoticism, schizophrenia and bipolar disorder on the other. Psychological studies of highly creative people have shown that many have a strong interest in apparent disorder, contradictions, and imbalances, which seem to be perceived as challenges. However, we must not draw hasty conclusions from the findings of such research. There may be a positive correlation between creativity and certain pathological traits but that correlation does not establish an ingredient of abnormality in creative acts per se; nor does it suggest that creativity is 'abnormal'.

Psychologists, anyway, no longer use the concepts of normal and abnormal as watertight compartments in the study of personality. Human traits are studied on a continuum. Social variables too are recognized as playing an important role in determining what is considered normal or abnormal behaviour.

Creativity may be seen to dwell with pathology only to the extent that it is unconventional but unlike pathology creativity is positive in its manifestations.

Since appropriateness is an essential ingredient of creativity, meaninglessly destructive acts, even if masquerading as social change, or pointlessly unconventional acts (as in the state of madness), would not be classified under 'creative'.

The march of human civilization from the Stone Age to the Cyber Age would have been impossible without creativity. We may safely conclude that creativity is necessary and essential for humankind even though it upsets the applecart now and then.

What is Creative Writing?

While discussing creativity in art and literature we have already noted many examples from creative writing. In this section we will try and work out which kind of writing comes under the umbrella term 'creative writing'.

Creative writing is associated with originality of thought and expression. A gloss on 'creative' in Oxford Advanced Learner's Dictionary of Current English (Sixth Edition) explains creative writing as writing stories, plays and poems. Defining the term, however, is not easy. As the adjective 'creative' and our preceding discussion of creativity imply, creative writing is of many different kinds. It would be difficult to trace a common source in them and next to impossible to deem other genres of writing 'non-creative' per se.

Some sources attempt to distinguish creative writing from technical, professional and journalistic writing on the basis of the primacy of imagination. Imagination is central to forms like poetry, drama, fiction, screenwriting and self-exploratory writing.

Other sources include imaginative non-fiction, writing for children, reviews, anecdotes and editorials also as forms of creative writing.

We can see that there is an overlap. Whereas some sources consider journalistic writing non-creative, others put only reporting under non-creative but editorials and reviews are considered forms of creative writing. Academic writing too depending on its kind may be classified under either category. Some educational material is highly creative whereas in writing a book on Maths the author might keep strictly to facts and figures.

Creative is a much bigger category than non-creative as far as writing is concerned. Only those works that purport to keep out imagination and subjectivity are non-creative. But facts too may sometimes be conveyed by using language creatively (that is, by using similes and metaphors). A book on Maths may be brought out in an extremely imaginative (or creative) format.

Nevertheless, non-creative is an important category, as there is sometimes need to put down things exactly as they are, without embroidery. In reporting a murder, a police inspector may need to strictly keep imagination out and aim at 'objectivity'.

We may conclude that rather than being separate genres, creative and non-creative refer to the purpose of different kinds of writing. As far as writing technique goes, there is a fair amount of overlap between both categories. Principles of form and structure are similar in both.

Imagination and Writing

We have seen that imagination is central to the concept of creative writing. Literally, imagination means 'the action of imagining, or of forming mental images, or concepts of what is not actually present to the senses' (Webster). Thus, imagination reaches out towards the 'new' and the 'original'.

Is there a way of training people to be more imaginative? There is a view that formal schooling stifles innate imagination.

The School Boy

I love to rise in a summer morn,
When the birds sing on every tree;
The distant huntsman winds his horn,
And the sky-lark sings with me.
O! what sweet company.

But to go to school in a summer morn,
O! it drives all joy away;
Under a cruel eye outworn,
The little ones spend the day,
In sighing and dismay.

Ah! then at times I drooping sit,
And spend many an anxious hour.
Nor in my book can I take delight,
Nor sit in learning's bower,
Worn thro' with the dreary shower.

How can the bird that is born for joy,
Sit in a cage and sing.
How can a child when fears annoy,
But droop his tender wing,
And forget his youthful spring.

O! father and mother, if buds are nip'd,
And blossoms blown away,
And if the tender plants are strip'd
Of their joy in the springing day,
By sorrow and cares dismay,

How shall the summer arise in joy.
Or the summer fruits appear,
Or how shall we gather what griefs destroy
Or bless the mellowing year,
When the blasts of winter appear.

—Blake (1976)

Imagination and poetry during most of the nineteenth century was supposed to dwell with *naturalness*. Children, peasants, hermits, gypsies—all who had not been 'corrupted' by civilization—were prioritized as repositories of 'natural' wisdom. Poets consciously modelled themselves after them and poetry was likened to the song of the nightingale and the skylark. Keats observed, 'That if Poetry comes not as naturally as the leaves to a tree it had better not come at all.'

Almost two hundred years later we still have not completely rejected the notion of naturalness being an essential attribute of literature and this is the reason we distinguish between writings that need formal training, research or factual information and creative writing.

There is considerable merit in locating creative writing with naturalness rather than with specializations. Marginalized sections of society, the underprivileged, and the exploited can make their voices heard effectively through stories, poems, novels, drama and autobiography. They may not have access to expensive or elite education so they may not be able to occupy the valorized positions in society; but everybody can tell a story.

However, the concept of naturalness should not be taken to undermine the importance of will and agency. Everybody may be able to tell a story but the telling requires sustained effort. It is interesting that many women in the nineteenth century in India used autobiography to liberate themselves from the chains of tradition. Rassundari Debi attained fame for writing her autobiography at a time when women were actively discouraged from reading and writing. Learning to read and write certainly did not come as easily as 'leaves to a tree' to her. *Amar Jeeban* describes the painful process by which she recalled the oral lessons she had overheard as a child and matched them with the written words of the book she would stealthily remove from the shelf after the men of the household left for work.

> '... please god, teach me how to read. If you don't, who else will?' [I prayed constantly]...[thinking that] even if I tried hard and somebody was willing to teach me, where was the time? [I got discouraged] ... [But then] I thought, of course I will. God has given me hope. ... Encouraged, I kept that sheet to myself. ... [held it] in my left hand while I ...[cooked], and glanced at it through the sari, which was drawn over my face. But ... I could not identify the letters.
>
> I decided to steal one of the palm leaves on which my eldest son [practised] his handwriting. One look at the leaf, another at the sheet, a comparison with the letters I already knew, and, finally a verification with the speech of others—that was the process I adopted for sometime. Furtively I would take out the sheet and put it back promptly before anybody could see it (Rassundari Debi).

Restrictions of an Open Field

Theoretically, imagination belongs equally to everybody. It is not the preserve of the highly literate and the privileged. Creative writing may bypass technical training and academic discipline and, as we have discussed, at times it is just as well that it does.

What does it take to become a writer? Can anybody wake up one summer morning and say, 'From today, I am a writer.'

Let us take the example of the following advertisement on the net for a course in creative writing that suggests the kind of person who has the potential to write:

> Do you like to write? Does answering letters come naturally to you? Do you often note down anecdotes or scraps of verse, or dream up plots for stories? Do you enjoy rewriting or improving experiences in your mind? Do you make up conversations or descriptions? Can you forecast what a character in a soapie serial is going to say or do next? If an acquaintance has an adventure, do you imagine it in detail? Do you think about how you would have reacted if it had been you? Do you think about other ways it might have turned out? Do you fall in love with book characters? Do you sometimes find them stiff or wooden?

No other qualifications except reading books and watching serials have been suggested as essential pre-requisites for becoming a writer.

If this is the case, then, becoming a writer must be the easiest thing in the world. Natalie Goldberg (2001), a famous teacher of creative writing, recounts:

> A student in a workshop walked up to me swinging his briefcase. 'Hi, I am an engineer. I make forty-six thousand dollars a year. How long do you think it will take me to earn that much with writing?'
>
> 'Keep your job,' I told him. Now I think if that student comes again, I'll screech in bloodcurdling syllables, 'No advances! No assurances! No credentials! No merit!'
>
> 'Know that you will eventually have to leave everything behind: the writing will demand it of you. Bareboned, you are on the path with no markers, only the skulls of those who never made it back.'

We must not assume that just because creative writing is associated with imagination and naturalness, it is child's play. No published writer would deny that creative writing needs extraordinary tenacity and perseverance. The five per cent inspiration and ninety five per cent perspiration formula mentioned earlier in the section 'Inspiration and Agency' holds good for most writers. Some writers complain that precisely because it is a non-specialized field, writing takes over lives as no other profession.

Creative writing imposes rigorous discipline on the practitioner. The kind of discipline may differ from writer to writer but we may be sure that ultimately writing demands that the writer attains a super-specialization of his or her own making by leaving everything that was known behind.

Can Creative Writing be Taught?

If the discipline of creative writing is different for everybody, what is it that we are trying to do in this course?

The debate whether creative writing can be taught at all is not new and has raged in various fora since the setting up of the first writing school in Iowa in the pre-war years. Practically, every US university now offers creative writing courses at various levels; and starting with the University of East Anglia (UEA) in 1970, many British Universities also teach creative writing. In India, IGNOU offers correspondence courses and JNU occasionally offers a course in creative writing at the post-graduate level.

It would be interesting to find out what such courses achieve. First of all comes the question whether creative writing schools actually produce writers. Responding to the charge that not many who go through these courses actually go on to get published, Richard Francis explains, 'You can't judge a course simply by the number of publishable authors it produces. You don't judge History or English courses by the number of History or English academics they produce. Obviously it's great when people go on to achieve within the discipline, but often the course is about giving people the creative and analytical skills they can use in other areas of their life.' (Crace, 2003).

Do the students who do get published acknowledge writing schools? Anna Davis, a published novelist, observes in the same article, 'It (creative writing course) also taught me how to read and edit my own work. You could argue that I would have got there anyway, but the concentrated time span certainly accelerated the process.' (ibid)

Generally the answer to the question whether creative writing can be taught is both no and yes. Creative writing courses may not be able to create a writer; but they can definitely help identify and hone writing skills; they can make students start off on the course of writing and to write better and faster than they would have otherwise.

The Importance of Reading

> 'What do you need in order to become a writer?'
>
> My reply is always the same, 'Read, especially in your genre, listen deeply and of course, write.'
>
> Why are so many people surprised by this answer? If we'd ask a coach, 'How do you become a basketball player? we'd expect him to reply, 'know the game inside out, study players, stay in good shape, practice.' But with writing we seem to leave common sense behind. I could say, 'Eat two croissants a day, collect spiders and hope your old aunt leaves you money,' and people would nod, affirmed in their belief that writing is a profound and mysterious thing (Goldberg 2001).

If there is consensus about anything as far as creative writing goes it is the absolute essentialness of not just reading but reading in a way that 'cracks open the writer's craft'. Students who are beginning to write often begin with assuming that as writing is about 'originality' they do not need to go into the works of other writers. Some even argue that they deliberately do not read in order to protect their pristine creativity. Nothing can be further from the truth.

We have already discussed that to be creative requires 'appropriateness' along with originality. In art and literature too there is the pole of interpretation along with innovation that approximates what we call 'appropriate' elsewhere. The writer needs to interpret what has been written before. Interpretation does not mean being derivative (or unoriginal). It implies intimate knowledge of other works. This would be equally essential if the writer is choosing to 'experiment'.

Paul Mills observes, 'One of the pleasures and aims of reading is to learn something more about how to write. I see writers as researchers of their craft, experimenters who learn most from practice, but who also know and understand what other writers have done and how they operate.' (Mills 1996).

Language or the raw material of creative writing too has to be learnt from other writers. From time immemorial, writers have been advised to go beyond the dictionary meaning. It is the way words are used that gives them special significance. Practitioners of creative writing quickly realize the importance of words.

In the following extract dating back to the twelfth century, the first-rate poet is seen to undertake a deep exploration within language.

> The speech of first-rate poets streaming forth that sweet content reveals clearly their extraordinary genius which is as unearthly as it is ever bright.
>
> It is not understood by a mere learning in grammar and in dictionary. It is understood only by those who have an insight into the true significance of poetry.
>
> That meaning, and that rare word which possesses the power of conveying it, only those two deserve the careful scrutiny of the first-rate poet. (*Dhvanyaloka* 1982).

Summary

- *Creativity* (or *creativeness*) is a mental process involving the generation of new ideas or concepts, or new associations between existing ideas or concepts. The products of creative thought (sometimes referred to as 'divergent thought' usually have both *originality* and *appropriateness*.
- Although creativity is now accepted as an essential constituent of human intelligence, efforts to develop a reliable *Creativity Quotient* have met with little success.
- Inspiration refers to the element in creativity (art and literature) that is not completely understood by analytical thought.
- Even though the process of creativity may not be 'fully understood' by the creator, even though inspiration may play a significant role, agency (human will and effort) cannot be undermined in the act of creation.
- Creativity has subversive potential. It can challenge the norms and mores of society, upset status quo and redistribute power.
- We call a work of art propaganda if the artistic considerations are compromised because of ideology. Merely ascribing motives or politics to the creator does not take away the creativity of the work.
- Creativity may be seen to dwell with pathology only to the extent that it is unconventional but unlike pathology creativity is positive in its manifestations.
- Some sources distinguish creative writing from technical, professional and journalistic writing on the basis of the primacy of imagination. Rather than being separate genres creative and non-creative refer to the purpose of different kinds of writing.
- There is a view that formal schooling stifles innate imagination.
- There is considerable merit in locating creative writing in imagination and *naturalness* rather than in specializations. Marginalized sections of society, the underprivileged, and the exploited can make their voices heard effectively through stories, poems, novels, drama and autobiography.
- Creative writing imposes a rigorous discipline on the practitioner.

- Creative writing courses may not be able to create a writer; but they can definitely help identify and hone writing skills; they can make students start off on the course of writing and to write better and faster than they would have otherwise.
- If there is consensus about anything as far as creative writing goes it is the absolute essentialness of not just reading but reading in a way that 'cracks open the writer's craft'.

ACTIVITY 1

1. Find 5 synonyms for 'creativity' from a thesaurus and create your own definitions with each.
2. List 10 instances of creativity you have encountered in the course of a single day.
3. Discuss the similarities and differences between the creativity of:
    - a film maker like Karan Johar
    - a designer like Ritu Kumar
    - a writer like R. K. Narayan
    - a painter like M. F. Hussain
    - a dancer like Yamini Krishnamurthy
4. On the basis of the defining criteria given in the text, try and work out an alternative definition for 'creativity'.
5. What role does 'inspiration' play in the creative process?
6. Do you think it is possible to fully understand creativity, or is it like other mysteries of the universe—tantalizing us to explore them in greater depth and detail?
7. What do you think is the revolutionary/reformist potential of art? Discuss with reference to the cartoons about politicians from newspapers.
8. Do you think it is possible to find a valid and reliable measurement for human CQ— creativity quotient?
9. Debate the proposition that 'creative writing can never be taught; only caught'.
10. Read this extract from a fictional diary. Do you think this differs from a real diary— maybe one that you have written?

    The Secret Diary of Adrian Mole, Aged 13 3/4

    Chapter One
    Thursday January 1st
    BANK HOLIDAY IN ENGLAND, IRELAND, SCOTLAND AND WALES

    These are my New Year's resolutions:
    I will help the blind across the road.
    I will hang my trousers up.
    I will put the sleeves back on my records.
    I will not start smoking.
    I will stop squeezing my spots.
    I will be kind to the dog.
    I will help the poor and ignorant.

(Contd.)

After hearing the disgusting noises from downstairs last night, I have also vowed never to drink alcohol. My father got the dog drunk on cherry brandy at the party last night. If the RSPCA hear about it he could get done. Eight days have gone by since Christmas Day but my mother still hasn't worn the green lurex apron I bought her for Christmas! She will get bathcubes next year.
Just my luck, I've got a spot on my chin for the first day of the New Year!

References

Anandavardhana, *Dhvanyaloka* translated by K. Krishnamoorthy (Delhi: Motilal Banarsidass 1974, 1982, Section I, 6 – 8.).

Blake, William, 'A schoolboy' in J. Broonowski, *William Blake: A Selection of Poems and Letters* (Penguin, 1976).

Coleridge, Samuel Taylor, 'Kubla Khan' in John Beer (ed), *Samuel Taylor Coleridge: Poems* (London: Dent 1974).

Crace, John, *The Guardian* (Tuesday February 18, 2003).

Goldberg, Natalie, *Thunder and Lightning: Cracking Open the Writer's Craft* (New York: Bantam Books, 2001).

Kennedy, X.J., *Literature: An Introduction to Fiction, Poetry and Drama* (New York: Harper Collins, 1991).

Mills, Paul, *Writing in Action* (London and New York; Routledge, 1996).

Oxford Advanced Learner's Dictionary of Current English, Sixth Edition, A.S Hornby (ed). (Oxford: OUP 2002)

Rassundari Debi, *Amar Jeeban* (translated by Enakshi Chatterji), (Kolkata: Writer's Workshop, 1991)

Shakespeare, William, *A Midsummer Night's Dream* in *The Comedies of Shakepeare*, Players Illustrated Edition, Vol I. (Chicago Spencer Press Inc. 1955).

Stevens, Wallace, *Collected Poems* (London: Faber, 2006).

Webster's Encyclopedic Unabridged Dictionary of the English Language (New York: Gramary Books 1994).

Wordsworth, William, in John O Hayden (Ed), *William Wordsworth; Poems* (London: Penguin, 1977).

Websites

http://en.wikipedia.org/wiki/Creative_writing

http://www.writing.upenn. edu/~afilreis/88/of-modern-poetry.html

http://www.amazon.com

http://www.arts.cornell.edu/newsletr/fall96

http://www.gc.maricopa.edu

http://www.guardian.co.uk/

http://www.arts.cornell.edu/newsletr/fall96/stucky.htm, Arts & Sciences Newsletter, Fall 1996, Vol. 18, No. 1.

http://www.houghtonmifflinbooks.com/features/randall_url/april16pr.shtml

http://www.writing.upenn.edu/~afilreis/88/of-modern-poetry.html

2
The Art and Craft of Writing

When we learn a language we may master its grammar and assume that we know the language. But does grammatical accuracy guarantee that we communicate our ideas, thoughts and feelings, whether spoken or written, with force and beauty? No. We often say that words began as an attempt to project the pictures in our mind. So, when we write, we are in a sense, painting with words. What we need to learn is that artistic/creative writing is a craft and one of the tools that can help the writer is the knowledge of the tropes and figures of speech that exist within the language. Though both, a trope and a figure of speech can be understood as a departure from literal language, as 'figurative language', there is a distinction between them. While tropes are regarded as figures of thought that change the meaning of words by turning their sense; figures of speech (also called 'schemes') merely involve a certain expression of words in a manner intended to impact the audience/reader. These devices only rearrange the usual order of words. Thus while 'metaphor', 'simile', 'metonymy', 'synecdoche', 'irony', 'personification', 'hyperbole', 'litotes' etc., can be called tropes; 'antithesis'; 'chiasmus', 'apostrophe', etc., can be called figures of speech. Yet another category of figures is referred to as 'figures of sound'. These achieve emphasis by a repetition of sounds as in 'alliteration', 'assonance', 'consonance', etc. What the student needs to pay attention to is whether the figure of speech/trope is being used to illustrate an idea or enrich meaning.

Mr Standout

The word 'figure' (from Latin *figura*) means primarily the form or shape of an object. When we refer to a fine figure of a person, we comment on the distinctiveness of the person's actions and personality, which make him/her stand out.

Similarly, in language, tropes and figures of speech present a departure from a dull, ordinary way of expression by using more creative modes of communication. They make an idea more 'outstanding'.

Mr Dull

Just as one kiss from the princess changed the frog into a prince in that well known fairy tale we read as children, the appropriate use of tropes and figures of speech can transform

the nature of a piece of writing. The poetic; the dramatic; the real; the popular, the horrific, the humorous; the persuasive; are only a few of the effects that can be achieved through the correct usage of tropes and figures of speech. Knowing these is thus a form of empowerment in that they help you to be confident about your creative expression.

Since the beginning of literary expression, writers have embellished their work with figures of speech.

While it is difficult to list all the figures of speech available to the contemporary writer, some of the more frequently used ones have been defined here. We have classified them along certain cluster headings depending upon their distinctive features:

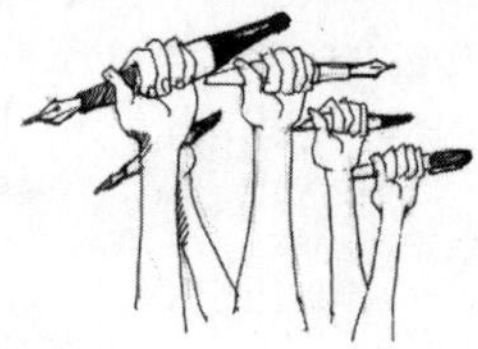

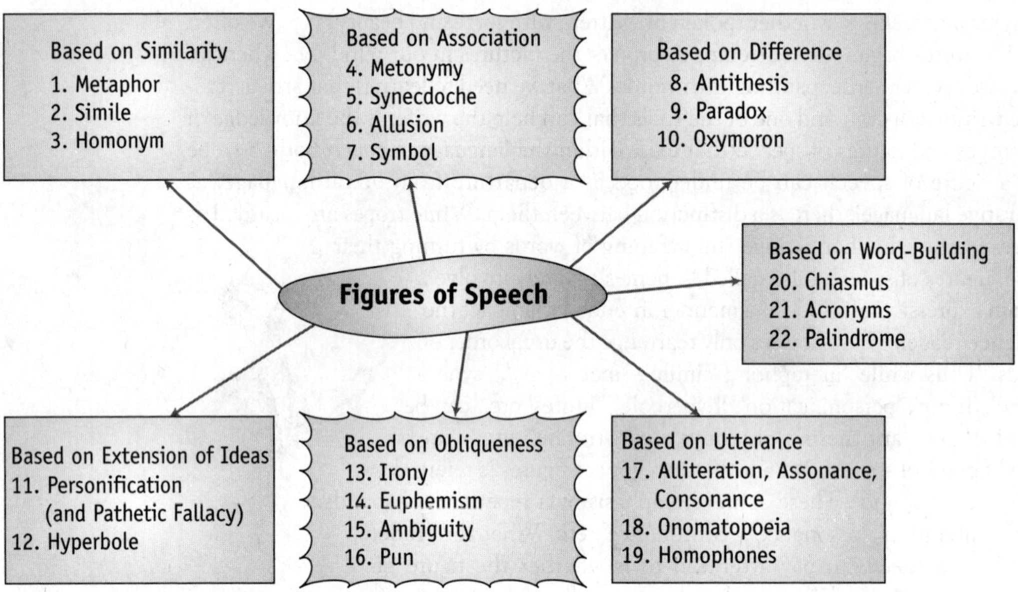

ACTIVITY 1

1. Define (a) Tropes (b) figures of speech
2. State in your own words the function of tropes and figures of speech
3. What are some of the effects of using tropes and figures of speech?

(Contd.)

Tropes and Figures

Based on Similarity

Metaphor (Greek, meaning 'a carrying over'): Two different things or ideas are fused together and one thing is described as being another, all its associations are thus also carried over. It is a figure of speech in which two dissimilar things are compared but only through implication. For example, to refer to a woman as 'that tigress' or say that 'she is a tigress' is metaphorical (if we say, she is like a tigress, we would be using a simile, this is explained later). Metaphors appear not just in the noun but also in the verb as well as adjectival forms. One of the most popularly quoted examples of metaphorical use are the lines from Shakespeare's *As You Like It*:

> **On a Clergyman's Horse Biting Him**
> *The steed bit his master;*
> *How came this to pass?*
> *He heard the good pastor*
> *Cry, 'all flesh is grass.'*
> *—Anon*

All the world's a stage,
And all the men and women merely players;
They have their exits and their entrances;
And one man in his time plays many parts…

Again, it may be used in the form of a long idiomatic phrase such as, 'a hard nut to crack'; 'a bird's eye view', and 'a dog-eared book'.

Because metaphors are able to create new and interesting combinations of ideas, object and sensations, they are used most effectively by writers, especially poets. However, metaphors also form part of our everyday speech as for example, when we say 'the tail end of the conversation'. Since these pass unnoticed, they do not carry a strong metaphorical element and so are called 'dead metaphors'.

> **Metaphors**
> *I'm a riddle in nine syllables/An elephant, a ponderous house/A melon strolling on two tendrils/ O red fruit, ivory, fine timbers!/This loaf's big with its yeasty rising/Money's new-minted in this fat purse/I'm a means, a stage, a cow in calf/I've eaten a bag of green apples/Boarded the train there's no getting off.*
> *—Sylvia Plath*

Simile (Latin, meaning 'like'): Simile, like metaphor is a means of comparing things that are essentially different. The distinction is that in simile the comparison is explicit and is expressed by the use of some word or phrase such as 'like', 'as', 'than', 'similar to', 'resembles', or 'seems'. For example, in a poem such as 'Harlem' by Langston Hughes (1902-1967), five out of the six images are similes.

Harlem

Does it dry up
Like a raisin in the sun?
Or fester like a sore-
And then run?
Does it stink like rotten meat?
Or crust and sugar over-
Like a syrupy sweet?
May be it just sags
Like a heavy load
Or does it explode?

P. G. Wodehouse used similes with panache to achieve some really comic effects. Consider the following lines from 'Uncle Fred in the Spring Time':

> The door of the Drones club swung open, and a young man in form fitting tweeds came down the steps and started to walk westwards. An observant passer-by, scanning his face, would have fancied that he discerned on it a keen, tense look, like that of an African hunter stalking a hippopotamus.

Homonym: (Greek, meaning 'same name'): It refers to a word that has two or more different meanings and derivations. For example the word 'pitch' which means (i) throw and (ii) tar; or 'date' which means (i) a calendar 'date' (ii) the fruit named 'date' and (iii) a colloquialism for two people going out together. Puns make use of homonyms and so often homonyms generate not just complexity but also humour.

Look at some of these funny rhymes that make use of Homonyms

of all the felt I ever felt, I
never felt a piece of felt
which felt the same as that
felt felt, when I first felt the
felt of that felt hat.

The two meanings of felt here are (a) the past tense of the verb feel; (b) a thick soft material.

In the following rhyme, there are four roles offered by the word 'Bob': your Bob, our Bob, bob as the old British coin 'shilling' and bob as a punch.

> *Remember: various figures of speech blend in to each other and it is sometimes difficult to classify a specific example as definitely metaphor or symbol, symbolism or allegory... (Perrine, 1978)*

Your Bob owes our Bob a bob. If your Bob doesn't give our Bob the bob your Bob owes our Bob, our Bob will give your Bob a bob in the eye. (Medgyes, 2002)

The context is British. Can you find an equivalent?

ACTIVITY 2

1. What is the difference between a metaphor and simile?
2. What are dead metaphors?
3. In each of the following quotations, identify and explain the comparison:
   (a) The pen is mightier than the sword.
   (b) I warmed both hands before the fire of life/it sinks; and I am ready to depart

(Contd.)

Landor (1775–1864)

(c) In the poem 'Harlem', identify the metaphor and explain it.

(d) It is with words as with sunbeams the more they are condensed, the deeper they burn.
Southey

(e) Like a Bridge over troubled waters I will lay me down.

4. What are homonyms? Try to recall some of the commonly used homonyms and make sentences to differentiate between then.

Based on Association

Metonymy: (Greek, meaning 'change of name'): In this figure of speech, the name of a thing is replaced by the name of an attribute of it or something else closely associated with it. For example, when we say 'from the cradle to the grave', the cradle stands for birth and the grave for death. One of the most popular metonymic saying is 'the pen is mightier than the sword', i.e., writing is more powerful/forceful than warfare. A word used in such metonymic expressions is sometimes called a 'metonym'. Metonymy is distinguished from metaphor in that metonymy involves establishing relationships of contiguity between two things and thus it works by plainer logical relationships; while a metaphor establishes relationships of similarity between two things. For example: Rachel De Quiroz says in *Metonymy, Or the Husband's Revenge*:

> A literary critic had scolded me because my hero went out into the night 'chest unbuttoned.'
> 'What deplorable nonsense!' wrote this eminently sensible gentleman. 'Why does she not say what she means? Obviously, it was his shirt that was unbuttoned, not his chest.'

Synecdoche (Greek, meaning 'taking up with, interpreting together'): This figure of speech is very similar to metonymy in that both substitute some significant detail or aspect of an experience for the experience itself. In a synecdoche, something is indirectly referred to by naming only a part or constituent of it to describe the whole of it; for example, when T. S. Eliot says in *The Love Song of J. Alfred Prufrock*:

> I should have been a pair of ragged claws scuttling across the floors of silent seas

he is speaking about the crab or lobster; the effect of a synecdoche in writing is thus somewhat like a cartoon, it creates an immediate visual picture of the most prominent aspect of something.

Again, in the poem 'The Naked and the Nude' Robert Graves says,

> Lovers without reproach will gaze
> On bodies naked and ablaze;
> The Hippocratic eye will see
> In nakedness, anatomy;
> And naked shines the Goddess when
> She mounts the lion among men.

The 'Hippocratic eye' in these lines refers to a doctor.

Allusion (Latin, meaning 'to play with, to touch lightly upon'): An allusion in a literary work is a means of suggesting far more than is said by a reference to something outside of itself. This could be to history, literary tradition, legends, personages, autographical details, etc. It relies upon the readers' familiarity and recognition of what is being mentioned so that the necessary connections are made. 'Topical allusions' refer to contemporary happenings; 'personal allusions' refer to the author's own life etc; 'imitative allusions' are made use of in parody and in 'structural allusions', one work reminds the reader of the structure of another. Allusions help to reinforce the emotion or the ideas of one's work with those of another work or occasion. For example, Shashi Tharoor, in his *The Great Indian Novel*, uses names of characters from the Mahabharata to refer to contemporary political personages. Or consider this short poem, *'Progress'* by Peter Meinke:

Rene Descartes (1596–1650) is regarded as the founder of modern philosophy. Line 1 recalls his famous phrase "I think therefore Iam".

This is a reference to Freudian psychoanalytic criticism; Freud speaks of desires, mainly sexual, in conflict with social norms that are repressed.

Progress

Man is mind
Cried old Descartes
And Wordsworth
answered
Man is heart
Down a new road
at last we come;
our cry: Libido ergo sum

The poet William Wordsworth believed that poetry is the spontaneous overflow of powerful feeling taking its origins from emotion recollected in tranquility.

Symbol (Greek, meaning 'mark, sign, token', originally 'put together'): A literary symbol is something that means more than what it is. Within a story, it is a person or an object or an event or an action or any other item that has a literal meaning but also suggests or represents other meanings by analogy or association. Symbols often exist by convention, such as a dove represents peace. These conventional symbols are used by writers but they also create their own. It is important to remember that a symbol may have more than one meaning but the area of these possible meanings is always controlled by the context.

The imprecision of a symbol make it both, one of the richest as well as one of the most difficult of figures used. Of course, it depends upon how directly the writer uses symbolism, as for example, in the poem A *White Rose* by John Boyle O'Reilly:

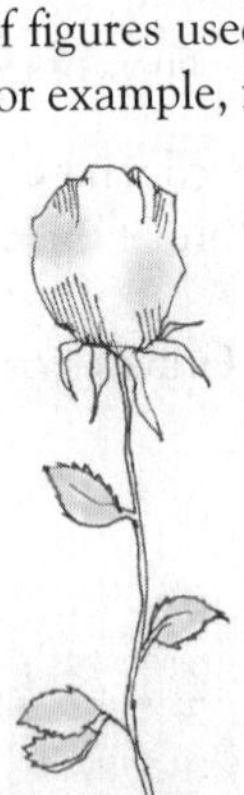

The red rose whispers of passion,
And the white rose breathes of love;
Oh, the red rose is a falcon,
And the white rose is a dove.

But I sent you a cream-white rosebud,
With a flush on its petal tips;
For the love that is purest and sweetest
Has a kiss of desire on the lips.

O'Reilly indicates clearly that the white rose is a symbol of spiritual attachment while the red rose is a symbol of physical desire or passion.

In the much performed play *Look Back in Anger*, John Osborne has shown the protagonist, Jimmy Porter constantly reading newspapers and drinking cups of tea; both acts are symbolic of the routine aspects of daily life. The ironing board used by the women has a similar symbolic value in the play.

ACTIVITY 3

1. What is the difference between Metonymy and Synecdoche? Give at least two examples of each from your own readings (these should be different from the ones given in this unit).
2. 'Gather ye rosebuds while ye may'

   Old Time is still a-flying;
   And this same flower that smiles today
   Tomorrow will be dying.

   The glorious lamp of heaven, the sun,
   The higher he's a-getting,
   The sooner will his race be run,
   And nearer he's to setting.
   —Robert Herrick

   What do the rosebuds symbolize in the first stanza? What does the course of day symbolize in Stanza 2?

Based on Difference

Antithesis (Greek, meaning 'opposite placing'): Philosophically speaking, this refers to the second of the two ideas that oppose each other, i.e., an argument that contradicts an original proposition or thesis. In terms of rhetoric, it serves to bring out contrasting ideas by using opposite forms of words. One of the most famous examples of Antithesis are the following lines from Shakespeare's *Hamlet*:

> To be, or not to be: that is the question
> Whether'tis nobler in the mind to suffer
> The slings and arrows of outrageous fortune,
> Or to take arms against a sea of troubles,
> And by opposing, end them?

Here, the idea of suffering or stoicism is placed against that of opposing or resistance. Again, we can see the use of antithesis in William Blake's *A Poison Tree*:

> I was angry with my friend
> I told my wrath, my wrath did end.
> I was angry with my foe:
> I told it not, my wrath did grow.
>
> And I watered it in fears,
> Night and morning with my tears;
> And I sunned it with smiles;

And with soft deceitful wiles.

Paradox (Greek, meaning 'beside-opinion'): A paradox is a situation or a statement that appears to be so self-contradictory that it startles the reader into attention. Behind the seeming impossibility, once all the conditions and circumstances involved in the paradox are understood, a meaning or truth can generally be discovered.

For example John Donne's challenging of the power of death in his poem entitled 'Death', is a striking example of the use of paradox.

Death

Death, be not proud, though some have called thee
Mighty and dreadful, for thou art not so;
For those whom thou think'st thou dost overthrow
Die not, poor Death; nor yet canst thou kill me.
From rest and sleep, which but thy pictures be,
Much pleasure; then from thee much more must flow;

And sooner our best men with thee do go-
Rest of their bones, and soul's delivery!
Thou'rt slave to fate, chance, kings, and desperate men,
And dost with poison, war, and sickness dwell;
And poppy or charms can make us sleep as well
And better than thy stroke. Why swell'st thou then?
One short sleep past, we wake eternally,
And Death shall be no more: Death, thou shalt die!

Death is an end to life but here the poet is talking about death itself coming to an end, i.e., death dying

The paradox most often quoted is that well know line by William Wordsworth, 'The child is father of the man'.

Oxymoron (Greek, 'pointedly foolish'): This figure of speech is a special variety of the paradox in which two opposing terms are brought together in what at first sight appears to be an impossible combination. There is nothing 'pointedly foolish' in the combination however and oxymorons have been used to convey serious human perceptions about a variety of subjects, especially by poets.

An oxymoron can occur in a phrase as well in a sentence. Shakespeare's Romeo [illegible] of his speeches:

I used to be indecisive: now I am not so sure.

Always remember you are unique, just like everyone else.

Why then, O brawling love, O loving hate,
O anything of nothing first create;
O heavy lightness, serious vanity,
Misshapen chaos of well-seeming forms,
Feather of lead, bright smoke, cold fire, sick health,
Still-waking sleep, that is not what it is

Based on Extension of Ideas

Personification (from Greek, meaning 'person making'): It consists in giving the characteristics of humans to animals, objects or concepts, i.e., to non-humans. It is a kind of metaphor in which the figurative term of the implied comparison is always a human

ACTIVITY 4

1. What is an antithesis? Write a 4–6 line poem using Antithesis.
2. … Where Ignorance is Bliss

   'Tis folly to be wise.
   —Thomas Gray

   Identify the figure of speech in this line and explain the use to which it is put.
3. Look at the following oxymora. What do they mean and what is the contradiction they contain?

   a plastic glass
   civil war
   a small fortune
   deafening silence
   an industrial park
   a sight unseen
   a working vacation
   loyal opposition
   an open secret
   old news
   a fresh frozen pizza
   cruel kindness
   liquid gas

being. For example, in his sonnet 'Composed upon Westminster Bridge, September 3, 1802', William Wordsworth personifies the city, the sun and the river so that they become protagonists in the drama of everyday life:

Earth has not anything to show more fair:
Dull would he be of soul who could pass by
A sight so touching in its majesty:
This city now doth like a garment wear
The beauty of the morning; silent, bare,
Ships, towers, domes, theaters, and temples lie
open unto the fields, and to the sky
All bright and glittering in the smokeless air.
Never did sun more beautiful steep
In his first splendour valley, rock or hill;
Ne'er saw I, never felt, a calm so deep!
The river glideth at his own sweet will.
Dear God! The very houses seem asleep;
And all that mighty heart is lying still!

Closely related to personification is the figure of speech called 'Pathetic fallacy', so called by Ruskin because it is a fallacy caused by an excited/overwrought state of feelings when the mind is borne away by emotions; it appears as if nature or inanimate objects echo the feelings of man or show interest in human action, either by sympathy or by antipathy.

The following lines by Pope serve as an apt example:

Her fate whisper'd by the gentle breeze,
And told in sighs to all the trembling trees;
The trembling trees, in every plain and wood,
Her fate remurmur to the silver flood,
The silver flood, so lately calm, appears
Swell'd with new passion, and o'er flows with tears.

Hyperbole (Greek, meaning 'throwing too far'): This refers to overstatement or exaggeration but with the purpose of expressing the truth. The effects vary from the funny to the grave, the imaginative to the practical and from the persuasive to the unbeliev-

ACTIVITY 5

1. Explain in your own words what you understand by Personification.
2. Read the following poem:

Mirror
I am silver and exact. I have no preconceptions.
Whatever I see I swallow immediately
Just as it is, unmisted by love or dislike.
I am not cruel, only truthful-
The eye of a little god, four cornered.
Most of the time I meditate on the opposite wall.
It is pink, with speckles. I have looked at it so long
I think it is a part of my heart. But it flickers.
Faces and darkness separate us over and over.

Now I am a lake. A woman bends over me,
Searching my reaches for what she really is
Then she turns to those liars, the candles or the moon.
I see her back, and reflect it faithfully.
She rewards me with tears and an agitation of hands.
I am important to her. She comes and goes.
Each morning it is her face that replaces the darkness.
In me she has drowned a young girl, and in me an old woman
Rises towards her day after day, like a terrible fish.
—Sylvia Plath

In what ways is the mirror like and unlike a person (first stanza)? In what ways is it like a lake (second stanza)?

3. Read the following lines:

There's been a death in the opposite house
As lately as today.
I know it by the numb look
Such houses have alway.

(Contd.)

The neighbours rustle in and out,
The doctor drives away,
A window opens like a pod
Abrupt, mechanically:
(Emily Dickinson, 'There's been a Death in the Opposite House)'

(a) Can you gauge what the speaker's attitude towards Death is on the basis of these lines?

(b) What is the figure of speech being used in these lines? Identify it.

4. 'To see her is but to love her,
And love but her for ever;
For Nature made her what she is,
And never made another'
Burns

What figure of speech is being employed to describe her? What do you think prompts this usage?

able. Such expressions are called 'bombast' when they appear as an inflated style of dramatic speech.

Based on Obliqueness

Irony (Greek, meaning 'dissembling'): This is a term with a range of meanings all of which involve a discrepancy between what is said and what is meant. It should not be confused with sarcasm, which is a crude form of irony intended to cause pain. There are broadly speaking, three kinds of irony.

The first, **verbal irony**, is a figure of speech in which the opposite is said from what is intended. It is used with great effect to expose the follies and vices of people. Generally the use of verbal irony implies that there is something in the speaker's tone and manner to show his/her real meaning. An example of such use of irony can be found in that noted speech of Mark Antony where he says

Yet Brutus says he was ambitious,
And Brutus is an honourable man!
—Julius Caesar

The reader/audience who has followed the play so far knows that Mark Antony means exactly the opposite of what he is saying.

*__Appreciation__..., Auntie did you feel no pain falling from that willow tree?
Will you do it, please, again?
'cos my friend here didn't see.*
Harry Graham

The second is **dramatic irony**, in which the contrast is between what a character says and what the reader knows to be true. The significance of this form of irony is that it serves as a comment upon the speaker or the speakers' expectations. In drama, especially in Greek tragedy from where dramatic irony stems, when the audience knows far more than a character, the irony in speech or action (within the story) becomes significant to that audience. An apt example is that moment in the Odyssey when the enemies of Ulysses wish a man good luck; the audience is aware that the man is actually Ulysses in disguise (Perrine).

In the third, **irony of situation**, the contrast occurs between appearance and reality, desire and its fulfillment or between what is and what should be. For example, consider the situation that the Mariner in Coleridge's poem 'The Rime of the Ancient Mariner' finds himself in the middle of the ocean:

Water, water, everywhere,
And all the boards did shrink;
Water, water, everywhere,
Nor any drop to drink.

Euphemism: (Greek, original meanning 'words of good omen'). Euphemisms alter the meaning and associations that people have for concepts. They hide nasty, embarrassing or scary facts and ideas by words that are more tempered and reduce the cruel or offensive or frightening effect considerably. For example, the use of 'pass away' instead of 'die', which makes the concept of death easier to accept or to call old people 'senior citizens' or 'elders', which imparts a certain sense of dignity or again to refer to house servants as 'domestic help', which gives the worker a better feeling about the job. Such euphemisms serve a fair purpose and are thus of 'good omen'.

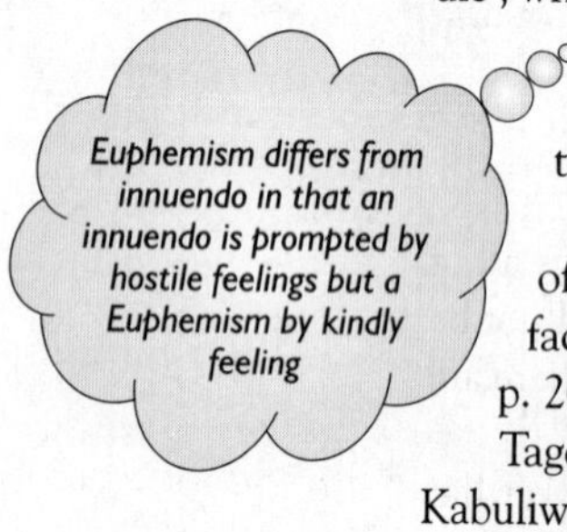

Sometimes euphemism simply obscures reality, as in references to the realities of war where a dead soldier is called a 'casualty' or a bomb is called an 'air to surface weapon' and indeed war itself is said to be 'a peace keeping action'. (Kolln, p. 208)

Tagore's short story 'Kabuliwallah' makes a touching use of euphemism. When the Kabuliwallah on being questioned by the little girl after he is arrested, says that he is going to his father-in-law's house, he is euphemistically referring to prison. Years later, after he is released and he comes to meet the little girl, he finds that it is her wedding day and he teases her about going to her in-laws' house.

Ambiguity (Latin, meaning 'doubtful, shifting'): It refers to the openness of language to different interpretations. In everyday speech, ambiguities are generally resolved by their context but in literature, they can be a source of rich meaning, often creating complex ideas and thoughts. In fact a piece of literature may be ambiguous in feeling as in the first stanza of Yeats' 'Sailing to Byzantium', where the tone seems to swing between celebration and condemnation:

That is no country for old men. The young
In one another's arms, birds in the trees
Those dying generations—at their song,
The salmon-falls, the mackerel-crowded seas,
Fish, flesh, or fowl, commend all summer long
Whatever is begotten, born, and dies.
Caught in that sensual music all neglect
Monuments of unageing intellect.

Pun: Possibly derived from the Italian, meaning 'fine point'. A pun is usually a play on words where two distinct meanings are suggested either by the same word or by two similar sounding words. The effect is generally witty though it could also be used to convey a serious context. For example, Christ punned on Peter's name, when he remarked that he, Peter, was the rock (Greek, Petra) on which he was going to build his church.

In Thomas Hood's 'Faithless Nelly Gray' the effect of the pun is semi-serious:

O, Nelly Gray! O, Nelly Gray!
Is this your love so warm?
The love that loves a scarlet coat,
Should be more uniform

Scarlet Coat here refers to the uniform of the British soldier.

ACTIVITY 6

1. The following lines form the first sentence of the novel *Pride and Prejudice* by Jane Austen:
   'It is a truth universally acknowledged that a single man in possession of a good fortune, must be in want of a wife'. What is the irony in this line?
   (For a fuller understanding, read the complete novel. Jane Austen is well known for the abundant use of irony in her novels.)
2. Why do we use euphemistic language? Can you think of five euphemisms that we use in ordinary speech?
3. John Keats uses ambiguity in the first line of 'Ode on a Grecian Urn' when he says 'Thou still unravish'd bride of quietness!' What is the ambiguity in this line?
4. Answer the following riddles; the answers are given below. (Medgyes, p. 52)
   1. What is the wettest animal?
   2. How did the sailor know there was a man on the moon?
   3. What do you call a very small mother?
   4. When a lemon asks for help, what does it want?
   5. Why couldn't the skeleton go to the dance?
   6. What do you call a sleeping bull?

(Contd.)

The answers are:

1. The rain deer = reindeer
2. He went to sea = see
3. A minimum = mini mum
4. Lemonade = lemon + aid
5. He had no body to go with = no + body
6. A bull-dozer = bulldozer

Based on Utterance

Very often units of sounds are repeated, especially by poets. Any unit, be it the vowel or the consonant sounds, the entire syllable or word or phrase or line or groups of lines, may be repeated. This serves a variety of purposes be it lending emphasis or sounding pleasant to the ears or giving structure to the writing.

Alliteration: (Latin, meaning 'move letters'): When the initial consonant sounds of a syllable (which consists of a vowel sound that is either preceeded or followed by consonant sounds) are repeated, it is called alliteration. The famous line from *Macbeth.* 'Double, double toil and trouble' is one such example of alliteration. As children, it was fun to repeat the alliterative language of Captain Haddock, the irascible character in Tintin comics; such as 'Billions of Blue Blistering Barnacles'.

Assonance: (Latin, meaning 'to answer to'): This involves the repetition of the vowel sounds at close intervals such as 'mad as a hatter' or 'free and easy'.

Consonance: (Latin, meaning 'sounding together'): The repetition of final consonant sounds is referred to as consonance such as in 'first and last', 'short and sweet' or the famous 'struts and frets' of Shakespeare.

Such repetitions may occur alone or in combination. Alliteration and assonance may be combined in such phrases as 'time and tide', 'kith and kin', 'fit as a fiddle' and 'thick and thin'. Again, alliteration and consonance are combined in phrases like 'last but not least'; 'good as gold' and 'crisscross'. The combination of assonance and consonance forms a rime. Limericks (or tongue twisters) make good use of all three repetitions; for example:

There's no need to light a night-light
On a light night like tonight,
For a night-light's a slight light
On a night like tonight.

Onomatopoeia (Greek, meaning 'name-making'): Onomatopoeia means the use of words whose sounds suggest their meaning such as 'hiss', 'snap' and 'bang'. Poets tend to use onomatopoeia more effectively than others. While pure onomatopoeia is rare and likely to be trivial, when combined with other devices that help convey meaning, it can achieve subtle and beautiful effects. Comic strips of course, use onomatopoeia most effectively.

Homophone (Greek, meaning 'same sound'): This refers to a word that is pronounced identically with another word but differs in spelling as well as in meaning. For example, wait/weight; sew/sow/so; maid/made; days/daze and so on. Homophones also help to create puns.

ACTIVITY 7

1. Find any three popular limericks in English. Create one of your own.
2. What are the three repetitions that one uses in a limerick.
3. Name some onomatopoeic words used in everyday speech; how would you use them in sentences of your own making?
4. What is the difference between a homophone and a homonym? Give four examples of homophones not given in the text and make sentences to show the difference in meaning between each set of homophone.

Based on Word Building

Chiasmus: is named after the Greek letter chi (x) indicating a crisscrossing arrangement of words; it means 'crossing over'. This is a figure of speech in which the word order of similar phrases in a sentence is reversed either by a repetition of the same words or a reversed parallel between two corresponding pairs of ideas. For example,

Zebra Question

I asked the zebra,
Are you black with white stripes?
Or white with black stripes?
And the zebra asked me,
Are you good with bad habits?
Or are you bad with good habits?
Are you noisy with quiet times?
Or are you quiet with noisy times?
—Shel Silverstein

Acronyms: An acronym is a word where each letter of the word is the first letter of some other complete word. This is a form of abbreviation and the interesting aspect is that the origins of such a word are forgotten and the acronym becomes in itself a new and independent word. For example, the commonly used TV for television or ID for various forms of identity cards or a word like 'LASER', which derives from 'Light Amplification (by) Stimulated Emission (of) Radiation'. Perhaps the most used acronym is 'ok' or 'okay' which derives, according to one theory, from 'oll korrect', a parody spelling of 'all correct'.

Palindrome: (Greek, meaning 'running back again'): When a word or a group of words reads the same, backwards or forwards, it is called a palindrome. For example 'MALAYALAM' or 'Madam, I'm Adam'.

These tropes and figures of speech should not be seen as the only formulae for good writing; the ones defined here are only the tip of the iceberg, there are so many others. However, to any writer, whether poet, dramatist or novelist, a knowledge and application of such tropes and figures of speech allows the fuller expression of sense impressions. In turn, they evoke corresponding emotions in the reader. Thus it is vital for a good writer to read and understand such literary tropes and figures of speech and use them appropriately while writing.

ACTIVITY 8

1. What do you understand by Chiasmus? In the poem 'Zebra Question', comment on how the sentence reversal changes the meaning/idea completely.
2. Find out what the following acronyms stand for:
   (a) AIDS
   (b) POSH
   (c) CAT
   (d) AIR
   (e) KISS
   (f) SWOT
   (g) ADD

Style and Register

Human language is neither uniform nor unchanging. It differs not just from culture to culture but also from one speaker to another whether in terms of pronunciation or choice of words or even the meaning of the words used. It is important to recognize these language variations; while writing, it lends authenticity to characterization.

Formal and Informal Usage

ASPECTS OF FORMAL & INFORMAL LANGUAGE

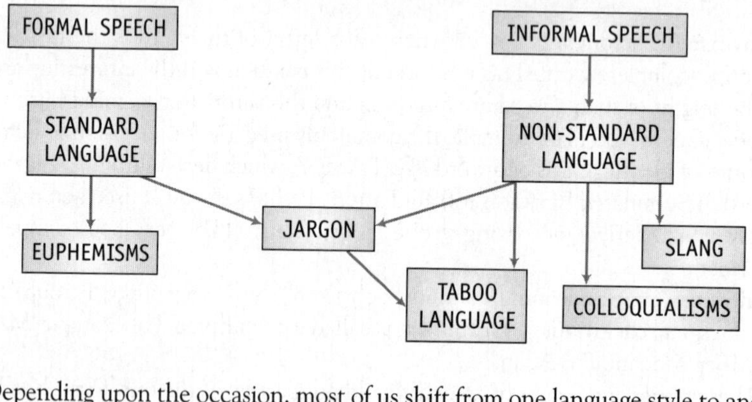

Depending upon the occasion, most of us shift from one language style to another, automatically and unconsciously. In other words, the social context decides the nature of the speech, i.e., whether one should use **formal** or **informal speech**.

So if the social context is in a way official or serious or governed by relationships of formality, where you are aware that not only what but also how you speak is of some importance; where there is a certain sense of consciousness about language, there formal speech occurs. Some examples of situations involving formal speech would be: facing an interview, especially for a job; speaking to an important person (in the Indian context; speaking to elders or distant relatives and acquaintances); addressing a formal meeting (as in Parliament, though Parliamentary language can be notoriously informal, indeed even foul, if a verbal fight ensues!); or speaking in a court of law.

On the other hand, **informal speech** occurs when the social situation is casual, friendly and relaxed (in such situations people are more at ease than in formal ones). Language tends to be spontaneous, rapid, uncensored, not always strictly grammatically correct and often involves abbreviations, shortening, contraction and deletion, in informal contexts. Example of such social settings would include chatting with an intimate friend; a close knit family environment and other such situations.

Most often, formal speech is equated with standard language while informal speech is regarded as a deviation or non-standard language or even, slang. **Standard language** refers to language that follows a certain 'standard' of correctness or purity in what and how something is spoken. **Non-standard language** is generally considered to be irregular due to its lack of conformity with a 'prescribed' format. It is vital to remember that such distinctions are only a reflection of social attitudes; no form of language is superior or inferior to another. In fact **slang**, which is part of informal speech, is one of the most creative uses of language in spite of the negative connotations that are associated with the term. Like any other fad, slang changes frequently and to use slang words that are outdated is regarded as being unfashionable. While some slang terms inform the vocabulary of a particular social group, such as teenagers or the underworld or drug culture or pop/remix culture, others are **colloquialisms** i.e., generalized terms of informal speech. In a certain sense, slang that caters to a particular social group is like **jargon**, which can be defined as a specialized vocabulary that grows out of the special needs of a particular profession/subject. So one may use legal jargon; medical jargon; academic jargon and even jargon related to jazz or rock and roll etc.—it all depends upon the field one is interested in. Sharing the same jargon promotes a feeling of solidarity within a group (and excludes the 'outsider' who is unable to speak or understand the jargon being used). Jargon then, is both a part of formal as well as informal speech.

In addition to slang and jargon, a number of words (that often arise from slang) are taboo words. **Taboo language** is one that is better avoided, at least in polite circles. It is a form of verbal abuse and includes swear words, insults, obscenities, profanities and name-calling. Sometimes euphemisms (see section I) replace taboo words such as the use of the expression the 'F word' instead of directly using the word f* % of course, Taboo language is not always the language of obscenity; it refers also to language that is sacred and not used outside a certain religious or magical context.

ACTIVITY 9

In what category of speech would you place the following words/expressions? Can you make sentences using these?

1. Awesome
2. Chillax!
3. Damn it!
4. Paradigm shift

(Contd.)

5. Sound byte
6. Genre
7. 'Good morning. Please be seated'.
8. Long Time No See
9. Pass Away
10. Co-brother
11. Ok Tata
12. Party-sharty
13. Respected sir
14. Homely, convented girl
15. Crap.

Varieties of English

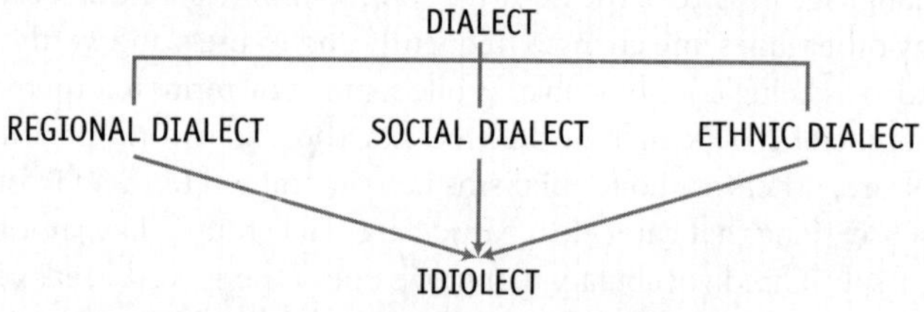

Americans, Australians, the Asians, the British—all speak English. Yet each of these groups differ noticeably in their speech. When groups of speakers differ perceivably in their language, they are said to speak different **dialects** of the language.

Dialects are governed by many factors, the regional, the social and the ethnic to name just a few. The **regional dialect** is the distinct form of a language spoken in a certain geographical area. For example, in England, one speaks of the Yorkshire dialect, on the ground that inhabitants of Yorkshire speak English that has certain linguistic features distinctly different from English in the other parts of England. The **social dialect** is the distinct form of language spoken by people belonging to a specific socio-economic class such as for example, the English spoken by the 'hands', or working class people in the Dickens novel *Hard Times* (as against the language spoken by the educated upper class elite). The **ethnic dialect** refers to the language used by a people hailing from a common ethnic origin such as Indian English which is historically associated with speakers of Asian (Indian) ancestry.

Certain dialects, in popular usage, are looked down upon as being 'substandard' or 'incorrect' or even 'impure' (refer to the section on standard and non-standard English, discussed a little earlier). Thus Black English or the English spoken by Black Americans (the very term is misleading for it denies linguistic variations among speakers of Black English) has been labelled as nonstandard and in fact, even called inaccurate. Once more, it would be pertinent to remember that it is social prejudices rather than linguistic judgments that lead to such viewpoints. Also, one should remember that, often language variations between speakers cannot be linked to a region, social class or ethnic group;

sometimes the term 'dialect' simply implies that speakers show some variations in the way they use elements of the language. In fact no two speakers of a language, even when using the same dialect, use language in the same way. Every individual has a distinct speech or language pattern which informs the identity of the speaker. This language followed by an individual is called **idiolect** and every speaker of a language has a distinguishable idiolect.

In spite of the experience of dialectical and idiolectical variations, the fact that we refer to English (in this case) as if it were a monolithic language, is due to the fact of **mutual intelligibility**. This means that speakers of English not only recognize that they are speaking the same (though not identical) language, but also comprehend each other.

Some language variants are understood by a smaller, more specialized group such as **pidgin**, which is an example of a language that comes into being when people who come into contact share no common language. This is typical of a colonial situation where one group politically and economically dominates over the other and desires trade with the subordinate group. The word pidgin is said to have originated from the English word business as pronounced in Chinese pidgin English. Pidgin languages have limited uses and reduced vocabularies and grammars, as they are drawn by the dominant language. However they are still used in highly expressive ways. Hawaiian pidgin English, Japanese Pidgin English and Filipino pidgin English are just some of the variations of pidgin English.

Sometimes when a pidgin begins to acquire native speakers who use it as their primary language, it is referred to as a **creole language**. This generally happens when the older people of a community rely on a pidgin to communicate with each other as they speak mutually incomprehensible native languages but their children acquire the pidgin as their first language. Thus we have such Creole languages as Gullah or the sea Island Creole spoken by descendants of African slaves living on the Sea Islands off the coast of Georgia and South Carolina; and Haitian Creole. When a pidgin is creolized, there is a definite expansion of vocabulary as well as grammar.

Language variations also occur in cases of **code switching** and **borrowing**. In code switching, the speaker uses a mixture of distinctive language varieties, whether for rhetorical effect or emphasis or fostering a feeling of community. In everyday speech this occurs when speakers of one language borrow words from another language; the foreign words come to be used not as substitutions but as regular parts of the vocabulary. The commonly used 'curry' and 'tandoori', which we recognize as words originally borrowed from Asia, are now vocabulary items listed in English dictionaries. For example, 'shampoo' has been traced thus in *Hobson-Jobson*, the Anglo-Indian dictionary:

> Shampoo, v., to knead and press the muscles with the view of relieving fatigue, & c.

The word has now long been familiarly used in England. The Hindi verb is *champi/champna*. The process is described, though not named, by Terry, in 1616:

> Taking thus their ease, they often call their Barbers, who tenderly gripe and smite their Armes and other parts of their bodies instead of exercise, to stirre the bloud. It is a pleasing wantonnesse, and much valued in these hot climes. (In Purchas, ii. 1475).

The process was familiar to the Romans under the Empire, where slaves employed in this way were styled tractator and tractatrix. (Perhaps the earliest reference to the practice is in Strabo (McCrindle, *Ancient India*, 72).) But with the ancients it seems to have been allied to vice, for which there is no ground that we know in the Indian custom.

In multilingual communities, such code switching and borrowing as well as code mixing is spontaneous and inevitable.

While code switching and code borrowing of languages help to break barriers between people, it is also true that, a lot in the way we use the language (idioms; comparisons; symbols etc) reflects our attitudes, our unconsciously imbibed prejudices. These tend to be perpetuated most significantly through language precisely because certain phrases/terms etc., through constant usage become colloquialisms and are such a routine part of our speech that one fails to observe the overtones.

For example, Ngugi wa Thiong'o, an African writer, observes that in his language the colour white is associated with death or widowhood (negatively), but when speaking in English, the common connection of 'white' is with purity, peace, etc. Thus the use of the word for 'white' in any language reflects cultural bias.

Language and Gender

Sexist Language

Just as we are unconscious of how racist our language often is, so also we are hardly aware of how sexist our everyday speech is; the fact that we have certain stereotyped

notions of women (and men) and that our attitudes are conveyed through our language. Some of the ways in which language turns sexist are:

1. The use of animal and food imagery where generally the image of women is far less positive than that of men whether it emphasizes negativity as in 'vicious as a bitch' or treats women like consumable items as in 'sugarpie', 'honey' etc.
2. The subordination of women in such instances as:
   a. the male form is taken as the base with a suffix attached to make it female; for example, lion/lioness, hero/heroine; actor/actress; poet/poetess, etc. These suffixes tend to diminish the significance of the women.
   b. The use of 'man' as a generic term for human kind; the constant references to 'his' and 'he' even when one includes the 'hers' and 'she' in the concerned context.

A politically correct writer would be aware of the inherent sexism in language and would either avoid it or alternatively, use such language appropriately to communicate a character's way of thinking or a cultural attitude.

Male versus Female Speech

As with the sections dealing with language and ethnicity or standard language and race, it is important to note that there is often a bias in distinguishing between male and female speech: usually male speech is the norm against which female speech is judged.

That women and men differ is an indisputable fact. That they differ in speech is what a writer needs to look at. Much research has gone into locating the linguistic differences between the two sexes; it is a vast area which can only be indicated briefly in this section. However, it will surely help the writer to maintain verisimilitude when writing dialogues or presenting verbal communication between the sexes.

In all-male conversations, men engage in floor-holding. Each man speaks in turn, while the other men remain silent. Apart from an occasional mutter to show that they are following and understanding. But women don't do this at all. Instead, while one woman is speaking, the others constantly chip in with supporting contributions, ranging from "That's right!" to completing the speaker's sentence for her. This difference, naturally, leads to confusion in mixed-sex conversations. While her male partner is speaking, a woman constantly chips in with supporting remarks. But the man, who is not used to this will very likely interpret these remarks as interruptions—which they are not—and become very annoyed. This is probably why so many men sincerely believe that women interrupt all the time—whereas, in fact, observation shows that, in mixed-sex conversations, it is men who do most of the interrupting. (Trask and Mayblin, 2000: 104–105).

Disordered Language

Sign languages: Are real languages like English, Hindi and French. A child can acquire any sign language as a first language with its rich vocabulary and grammar. Speakers and signers have basically one difference in their mode of communication; the latter do not use sound.

All the examples we have considered so far represent normal language use. But not all language use is normal. Most particularly, our language can become abnormal or disordered when we are suffering from an injury to the brain. This happens because certain areas of the brain are largely dedicated to the use of language, and damage to these areas therefore disrupts our language.

Disordered language resulting from brain damage is called **aphasia** (or **dysphasia**) and several different types are known. In the 1860s, the French surgeon

Paul Broca identified a particular disorder now called **Broca's aphasia**. A sufferer from this aphasia speaks painfully slowly and laboriously with very little in the way of grammar and his speech is some what slurred.

In the 1870s the Austrian neurologist Carl Wernicke identified a group of patients with a very different from of aphasia now called **Wernickes aphasia**. A sufferer speaks rapidly and fluently with normal rhythm and intonation but what he says makes no sense.

Not all linguistic deficits result from brain damage. Some of them appear to be caused by genetic abnormalities. A good example is the curious disability called **Specific Language Impairment (SLI)**. Sufferers from SLI are fairly normal in most respects, but they have a terrible time with grammatical words and endings. They can't learn them or produce them accurately, and often leave them out altogether or occasionally put them in where they don't belong.

ORALITY VERSUS WRITING:

- *Writing was invented only a little more than 5,000 years ago (at least there are no written records prior to this.*
- *Only a few dozen languages are frequently written, even today.*
- *Most of the languages have never been written at all.*
- *Languages are constantly changing so that sometimes it is difficult to decipher meanings whether in oral or written languages.*
- *Obviously we cannot SEE grammar, punctuation etc., in ORAL language; it depends upon the speaker's articulation.*
- *In writing, we cannot effectively HEAR such things as pronunciation etc., even if the writer describes/uses a certain kind of language.*

Another linguistic disability which results from a faulty gene is the **Williams syndrome.** Sufferers from this syndrome have some difficulty in finding words. It is not that they hesitate or stumble. In fact they typically speak in a breathless rush but that they often select the wrong words. So, for example, a Williams sufferer may say parrot when sparrow is intended or cake when cookie is meant. Moreover they not infrequently overgeneralize the rules they know so well and like very young children, say 'taked' instead of took or 'mouses' instead of mice. (Trask and Mayblin 2000)

ACTIVITY 10

1. Advertisements often convey sexist attitudes, through language as well as in visual terms. Look at any two popular advertisements and point out the sexism you observe in them.
2. Separate the following words into two categories: those with Greek roots and those with Latin roots. Refer to a dictionary.

Aqua	Phone	Video	Geo
Thermos	Pan	Homo	Art
Terminus	Tele	Corpus	Photos
Meter	Ode	Audio	

3. If a Tamilian, a Punjabi, an American, a Black American and an Australian were to converse with each other in English, what would be the categories of language variation you could expect from such a conversation?
4. What kind of language is aphasia, dysphasia, SLI and the Williams syndrome?
5. Is sign language a real language? How? Can you think of any film in recent times that has used sign language? Why was it used?
6. Make a list of at least 10 words in English that are used in India and reflect racist prejudices.
7. What are the main differences between male and female speech that the text has pointed out?

A NEOLOGISM. Produced by mixing 'chutney' [a word of Indian Origin] with the fication ending which is common to noun forms of many English verbs [e.g., pacification].

What is required for **chutnification?** Raw materials, obviously - fruit, vegetables, fish, vinegar, spices, |…| Cucumbers aubergines mint. But also: **eyes** **blue as** **ice,** which are undeceived by the superficial blandishments of fruit-which can see **corruption** beneath citrus-skin; fingers which, with **featheriest** touch, can probe the inconstant hearts of green tomatoes: and above all a nose capable of discerning the hidden languages of what – must – be – pickled, its **humours** and messages and emotions… at Braganza Pickles, I supervise the production of Mary's legendary recipes; but there are also my special blends, in which, thanks to the powers of my drained nasal passages, I am able to include memories, dream, ideas, […]. **believe don't believe** but it is true. Thirty jars stand upon a shelf, waiting to be unleashed upon the amnesiac nation (*Midnight's Children*, 460).

The DENOTATIVE meaning of this phrase would be the colour "blue". The CONNOTATIVE meanings, generated by the contexts as also the word "ice", would be "cold" "unemotional".

PUN

This is NONSTANDARD usage-creatively modifying the association of feathers and lightness. Thus 'lightest touch' becomes 'featherist touch'.

These two words are ARCHAISMS. Here they are not used in their modern senses, but in the older senses of "rottenness" and "bodily fluids which determine physical and mental qualities".

This usage has multiple aspects.

- *The phrase is a liberal translation of a common Hindi phrase, so some level of CODE-SWITCHING b/w languages taking place.*
- *Strong elements of an ORAL, INFORMAL manner of speech. The rules of written grammar are isolated, yet the meaning is effectively communicated.*

Playing with Words

Meanings of words are not inherent in the words themselves; rather the meanings lie with the people who use them. People respond to words on the basis of their individual experiences or on the basis of the shared, generalized meanings of the larger speech community. These two ways of looking at words and their meanings are related to (though not synonymous with) the connotation and denotation of words.

The average word is composed of three parts: the **sound**, **denotation** and **connotation**. It begins as a combination of tones and noises uttered by the lips, tongue and throat for which the written word is a **notation**. But unlike a musical tone or noise, it has a meaning attached to it. The basic part of this meaning is its denotation(s) i.e., the dictionary meaning(s) of the word. Beyond its denotations, a word may also have connotations. The connotations are what it suggests beyond what it expresses, or the overtones of meaning. These connotations are acquired by a word through various ways: by its past history and associations, by the way and the circumstances in which it has been used. For example the word 'home' could denote only a place where one lives but by connotation, it suggests security, love, comfort and family. It must be remembered that words may have a number of denotations, just as they have many connotations.

This multiplicity of meanings that words have is a rich resource for a creative writer especially a poet but it is a hindrance to a scientist who needs a precise language to convey information precisely. For a scientist, an ideal language would be one where there is a one-to-one correspondence between word and meaning i.e. every word would have only one meaning and for every meaning, there would be only one word. Since ordinary language cannot meet such expectations, the scientist invents a language that is stripped off all connotations and of all denotations save one. A statement in scientific language would perhaps read:

$$H_2O + SO_3 \rightarrow H_2SO_4$$

in which the symbols are free from ambiguity. The same H_2SO_4 which is sulphuric acid, conveys different meanings when used in literature where it has numerous connotations like fire, smoke and brimstone! (Akmaijan, Demers and Harnish 1984)

Not only do writers make use of the connotations of a word, they also indulge in **neologism** (in Greek, *neos* means new and *logos* means word) which consists of the coining of new words. Such new words enter the language all the time; writers generally coin these words for a particular purpose. For example, Tennyson's coinage of 'tonguester' to mean 'a talkative person'; or the word 'selfless' to mean 'unselfish'. Some of these words, when unforced and natural, become popular with time and pass into general literary use. Sometimes new discoveries and inventions also necessitate the introduction of new words such as 'aviation' or 'air conditioner' etc.

Writers also use **archaisms** (Greek *archaios* or ancient). These are words that were once current but are now out of vogue or even obsolete. Till recent times, archaisms were acceptable in the verse form but today, they are avoided unless used for the specific purpose of parody or historical reconstruction. The use of 'thee' and 'thou' or words like 'albeit', 'beholden', and 'belikely' are considered to be archaisms.

Again, the use of words that are particular to a certain dialect or are a part of provincial speech, i.e., **provincialism**, sometimes enter into writing. Such words are generally unintelligible to people living outside the areas within which they are in currency and so are best avoided. However, the creative writer can use provincialism to create local ambience and colour and be realistic. For example, the Americans use words like 'vamoose' (to run off) or 'skedaddle' (run away) which one does not hear in common parlance.

Grammar and Word Order

One of the most important properties of language is grammar. Grammar is a set of rules for combining words into sentences, for modifying the forms of the words for particular purposes and for interpreting the result. Every language has a grammar-indeed every language has quite a lot of grammar. There is no such thing as a language with little or no grammar. But the rules of grammar differ from language to language.

Take word order in English. The only normal order in sentences is subject-verb-object, or SVO as in 'Mike washed the car'.

But other languages may be different. Different examples of word order and location:

Irish is VSO and an Irish speaker says literally
Washed/Mike/the car.

Japanese is SOV and Japanese-speaker says
Mike/the car/washed.

Malagasy (in Madagascar) is VOS, and the result is
Washed/the car/mike.

Hixkaryana in Brazil, is OVS and so we get
The car/washed/mike.

In Hindi, the word order is SOV
Mike/did/car/washed

In these languages the English order would be just as wrong as the other orders are in English. (Trask and Mayblin, 2000)

Tense and Time

Or consider tense, the grammatical marking of time. In English, we have only a single past-tense form: I say 'I saw John' regardless of whether I saw him ten minutes ago or ten years ago. But some other languages make finer distinctions. In European Spanish you must say *Le he visto a Juan* if you saw John earlier today, but *Le vi a Juan* if you saw him before today. In the New Guinea language Yimas, there are four different past tense forms, all distinguishing different degrees of remoteness of the past. And in the African language Bamileke-Dschang, there are five. On the other hand, Chinese has no tense marking at all: there is nothing corresponding to the difference between see and saw.

Grammatical Differences

In English, if we want to refer to somebody or something we have already mentioned, we must choose among *he* for a male, *she* for a female and *it* for a sexless thing. In this case, English grammaticalizes sex. In Finnish, however, the word is *han* in every case. Finnish does not mark sex. Basque in northern Spain, does not mark sex either, but in Basque you must make a different choice: *hau*, if the person or thing is close to you, *hori*, if an intermediate distance from you, and *hura*, if far away from you. Basque grammaticalizes distance, but not sex.

In the North American language Kwakiutl, you must make yet another choice: you choose one form if you can see the person or thing you are talking about, but another form if you cannot. Kwakiutl grammaticalizes visibility. In standard English, the sentence *He's sick* can mean either 'He's sick at the moment' or 'He's chronically ill'. If we need to make the difference, we have to stick extra words into the sentence. However, in one variety of English, African-American English (AAE), spoken by many black people in the USA, the difference is grammaticalized. The rules of English grammar are not the same for all speakers. (Trask and Mayblin, 2000)

You might well ask, why does a Manual on Creative Writing for Beginners have to discuss language in such detail? In turn, the following questions could be posed by the writers: if you wish to set your novel/ poem/ play/ in say, an institution for the mentally challenged, what is the language you would put in the mouth of characters? Do you have any idea as to how you can even begin doing so? Imagination alone does not always suffice; one needs at least basic knowledge. This unit has aimed at just that : initiating the young writer into the different ways in which language is used and changes depending upon race/ gender/ culture/ community/ class/ country/ region/ individual habit/ abnormalities/ physical or mental impairment (the use of sign language for example)/ situation/ intention/ implication/ emotion, etc. Of course, such information will remain merely information unless suitably applied to writing. The teacher and student of this creative writing course are thus cautioned against shrugging this unit aside once it is 'over'; it would profit both immensely during the workshop sessions in the next unit, to keep these aspects of the art and craft of writing in mind.

ACTIVITY 11

1. (i) What is the difference between denotation and connotation?
   (ii) Which of the following words have the most 'romantic' connotations?
   a. horse; steed; equine quadruped
   b. China; Cathay
   Which of the following is the most emotionally connotative?
   c. mother; female parent; dam
   Which of the following have the more favorable connotations?
   d. average; mediocre

(Contd.)

e. secret agent, spy
f. adventure; adventuress

(Perrine, 1978, 585)

2. Point out the archaic words in the following excerpts:
   (i) Thou wast not born for death, immortal Bird!
   (ii) Little lamb, who made thee?
   Dost thou know who made thee?
   (iii) Behold her, single in the field
   Yon solitary Highland lass!

   Why are they called Archaic?
3. Give some example of grammatical differences between English and some other languages.
4. What is Neologism? Give some contemporary examples of neologism.
5. What kind of language does a scientist prefer and why?

Summary

- Tropes (devices involving meaning) and figures of speech (devices involving expression) are some of the tools that the creative writer uses to make communication more interesting; an idea more remarkable; transform a piece of writing; empower the writer.
- Figures of Speech based on similarity are metaphor, simile and homonym.
- Figures of speech based on association are metonymy, synecdoche, allusion and symbol.
- Figures of speech based on difference are antithesis, paradox and oxymoron.
- Figures of speech based on extension of ideas are personification (and pathetic fallacy) and hyperbole.
- Figures of speech based on obliqueness are irony, euphemism, ambiguity and pun.
- Figures of speech based on utterance are alliteration, assonance, consonance, onomatopoeia and homophones.
- Figures of speech based on word building are chiasmus, acronym and palindrome.
- Depending upon the occasion, language uses formal or informal speech.
- Standard language refers to a certain standard of correctness while non standard language is considered deviant due to its non conformity with the standard; these are only a reflection of social attitudes.
- Slang is a part of the usage of informal speech as are colloquialisms.
- Jargon is specialized vocabulary growing out of the specific needs of a particular profession or subject.
- Taboo language includes swear words and profanities and is avoided in polite circles; it is also language that is not used outside certain magical or religious contexts.
- Dialects are varieties of the same language spoken by different communities and groups; there are primarily regional, social and ethnic dialects.

- Individuals speak idiolects.
- Pidgin is created when people who share no common language come into contact with one another. When a pidgin begins to acquire native speakers, a Creole language is created.
- Code switching, borrowing and mixing are common in multilingual societies.
- Language reflects racist and sexist attitudes; differences between the genders; abnormalities (genetic and otherwise).
- Sign language is also a full-fledged language but without sound.
- Oral and written languages both change. Inherent differences exist between the two modes of language.
- Words have a literal meaning or denotation and a nuanced or suggested meaning or connotation.
- Neologisms, archaisms and provincialisms are all different forms of words.
- Grammatical differences exist between languages and even between the way different communities speak the same language.
- Application of this Information on the Art and Craft of Writing is the next step.

References

Akmaijan, Adrian, Richard A. Demers and Robert M. Harnish, *Linguistics: An Introduction to Language and Communication*, M.I.T. Press, USA, 1984

Baldick, Chris, *The Concise Oxford Dictionary of Literary Terms, OUP,* Oxford, 1990-91

Bose, Rai Radhika Nath and TS Sterling, *Elements of English Rhetoric and Prosody* Chuckervertty, Chatterjee & Co. Ltd, Calcutta, 1987

De Queiroz, Rachel 'Metonymy, or the Husband's Revenge'. *Other Fires: Short Fiction by Latin American Women* (ed.) Alberto Manguel. London: Picador, 1986.

Gibbs, Susie (compiled) *Poems to make your friends laugh,* OUP, Oxford, 2003

Gray, Martin, *A Dictionary of Literary Terms* York Press, England, 1992

Kolln, Martha, *Language and Composition A Handbook and Rhetoric,* Macmillan, USA. 1984

Perrine, Lawrence, *Literature Structure, Sound and Sense,* Harcourt Brace Jovanovich Inc; USA, 1978

Shovel, Martin, *Making Sense of Phrasal Verbs* Cassell Publishers Ltd, London, 1985

Trask, R.L and Bill Mayblin, *Introducing Linguistics,* Icon Books UK, Totem Books USA, 2000

Yule, Henry and AC Burnell, *Hobson-Jobson: The Anglo Indian Dictionary,* Wordsworth Editions Ltd., UK, 1996

3
Modes of Creative Writing

Writing to Communicate: The Writer and the Reader

Writing is an act of communication and while some of us may write for our own satisfaction, most of us write in order to be read. The reader is our addressee and mirror. Therefore, while planning our work we keep in mind the possible reactions of this auditor who will determine the success or failure of the literary artifacts we create.

If we agree that writing is a social act, then all writers write in order to share thoughts, ideas, feelings and experiences with others. The question 'why we write' can be answered in a variety of ways—for fame, money, or vanity. While all these may be a part of the whole truth, a basic motivation for all writers remains the need to reach out to others through an expression of one's inner thoughts, through the medium of language. As T. S. Eliot very appropriately remarked, 'You write because you feel the need to free yourself of something' and this adds a psychological motivation and aesthetic compulsion to the act of writing (IGNOU: DCE 1:6).

While all writing is creative, a difference can be seen in the kind of writing that informs and that which reveals or opens up the inner vistas of the mind and imagination. Depending on the content, the form is chosen, and the structure emerges from the manner in which the writer arranges the material. In addition to the structure, the other distinct signature of each writer is her/his style that can be explained as the 'handling of language that expresses the content in the best possible manner'.

For the aspiring writer, some essential preliminaries are (ibid: 5):

- Read extensively and with discrimination.
- Allow experience to mature.
- Write something individual and different–chart out your own course.
- Keep a diary of thoughts and experiences that you can refer to.
- Visualize your course of work clearly.
- Try and achieve maximum clarity, precision, and directness.
- Be your own best critic and be open to the criticism of others.

We talked about structure, form and style and the mastery of language. One of the important things to think about then is grammar. It would be constructive to see grammar as a mechanism, which enables us to convert semantics (what we mean) into utterances (what we say or write). This mechanism is part of a linguistic framework, which, far from being clearly defined, is a fuzzy, notional thing that derives from our innate ability as human beings to communicate. Superimposed on it are the accumulated influences of the real world and, for some people, half-remembered remnants of tuition in English grammar. Recently, there has also been a change in the way language is taught and perceived and the emphasis is on context and communication rather than accuracy and correctness. As a result of this, many writers, especially new entrants in the field, find themselves trapped in a kind of linguistic no-man's-land between the everything-is-permissible philosophy of modern language teaching on the one hand, and stone-clad prescripts of formal English grammar on the other. Adding to the writer's dilemmas is the fact of English itself having taken on a number of guises and forms of expression that share a lot in common and are yet distinct. However, if we accept the premise that grammar is a mechanism that enables us to express what we mean, it can be said to be 'good' or 'bad', 'right' or 'wrong', depending on whether or not it functions efficiently and enables us to express what we mean, and also whether this endeavour is as effective for the reader who is trying to decipher our linguistic codes. For, as E. B. White warns us, 'No writer improves his work until he discards the dulcet notion that the reader is feeble-minded; for writing is an act of faith, not a trick of grammar'. (Madden 2001: 475)

If your primary goal is to reach out to an audience of readers, then your work must be *readable*. In the words of Anthony Trollope, 'Of all the needs of book has, the chief is that it be readable'. Here are some of the ways in which you can make your writing accessible and enjoyable for a plethora of readers:

- Know your subject—to achieve clarity you must know, thoroughly and competently, what you are writing about. Until your mastery of the subject is complete, you will not be able to decide about form or structure and neither will you be able to write with conviction.
- Be interested in your subject—choose only those subjects that move you, for only if the writer writes with passionate conviction, will the reader be moved.
- Be clear—while the reader should be engaged in the unraveling of the mystery of what you are saying, don't make your writing so opaque that it is accessible only to an audience of one, yourself.
- Master the language you are using—it is only by manipulating the language skillfully that great and complex thoughts can be communicated effectively.
- Choose your words carefully—when readers encounter a word that they could not have foreseen, or which they could not have possibly thought of themselves, they get interested and pay attention. When the word is both unforeseen and effective, they are pleased.
- Engage the reader from beginning to end—if you let the reader's interest flag at any point, your writing will fall apart, the illusion will break and your reader will turn to something else. Let the reader feel that s/he is participating in an exciting adventure. This was also Joseph Conrad's chief credo as a writer and is one of the

primary reasons for his popularity across the world, 'My task which I am trying to achieve is, by the power of the written word, to make you hear, to make you feel it is above all, to make you see'. Andre Gide adds to Conrad's timeless words, when he says, 'To read a writer for me is not merely to get an idea of what he says, but to go off with him, and travel in his company' (IGNOU 1:15 and 3).

All this is easier said than done and no amount of advice or guidelines can make you a good writer. The key is to practise and persevere and also keep the reader in mind. As Linda Flower tells us in *Writing for an Audience*, 'any writer to be successful must establish a common ground between the reader and her/himself, one that lessens their differences in knowledge, attitudes and needs'. Although we can never be certain who might read what we write, it is nevertheless important for us to have a target audience in mind. All the decisions we make as writers, are influenced by that real or imagined reader. The goal of the writer is to create a momentary common ground between the reader and her/himself. You want the reader to share your knowledge and your attitude towards that knowledge. Even if the reader eventually disagrees, you want him or her to be able for the moment to '*see things as you see them*'. A good piece of writing closes the gap between you and the reader. The first step in closing that gap is to gauge the distance between the two of you. Sometimes obvious differences such as age or background will be important, but the critical differences for writers usually fall in to three areas: the reader's *knowledge* about the topic, his or her *attitude* towards it, and his or her personal or professional *needs and interests*. Effective writers do not simply express what they know, like a student madly filling up an examination answer book. Instead they use their knowledge: reorganizing, maybe even rethinking their ideas to meet the demands of an assignment or the needs of the reader (Flower 1994: 404-07).

A successful communicator thus makes full and proper use of all the grammar and lexical possibilities in the language so as to produce an attractive and effective result. If we think about writing as communication, a possible way to do so is to think of the process in six steps:

1. Idea.
2. Meaning (semantics).
3. Organization (grammar).
4. Fine Tuning (formulation of utterances).
5. Have I got it Right? (review and revision).
6. Eureka! (Text).

An accurate assessment of your intended audience will also help you to answer many of the formal and stylistic questions that arise in preparing a manuscript. Writers have complete freedom to choose their styles, but must try and aspire towards being direct and clear, organized and coherent, and forceful and convincing. Careful writers also avoid the use of language that is prejudicial to any class or category of people, and avoid statements that reflect or imply unsubstantiated generalizations about age, economic class, national origin, sexual orientation, political or religious beliefs, race or gender (Achtert 1985:1–2).

ACTIVITY 1

a. Why do you write? Discuss and write about all your reasons for writing?
b. How would you define 'good' grammar? Is it important, according to you, for the writer to master her/his language in order to write effectively?
c. Choose two works that you have read, one that you thoroughly enjoyed and one that you found completely unreadable. Try and analyse the reasons for the success of the first and the failure of the second.
d. Do you agree that you need to keep a reader in mind while writing? How are some of the ways in which you can display your concern for the reader in your writing?
e. Why is it important to avoid unsubstantiated generalizations while writing?

SECTION I

Writing Poetry

Ars Poetica*

A poem begins where prose ends—
at the edge of the word.
Every word that we speak
is composed of breath.
On this most intangible foundation
rests the way of poetry.
—R. Parthasarathy

(*The art of poetry (Latin). The title of a work on poetics by the Roman poet Horace (65–8 BC).

'A poem is an exploration rather than a disquisition.' By this, Robin Skelton means that a poem isn't a way of stating something you already know in a clear and precise manner. Instead, it is how a poet tries to figure things out—a way of trying to organize one's thoughts and feelings about a subject, to find a pattern in the chaos and come to some sort of resolution or conclusion. More mundanely, a poem is 'a metrical composition' or 'an elevated composition in verse' (*The Concise Oxford Dictionary*).

When we think of poetry, we think of lines and stanzas, rhythm and rhyme scheme, fancy language and beautiful words. Sometimes we think writing poetry is easy: it just flows out and every word is perfect and you should never edit or you'll lose the energy of the work. Other times we think we're just no good at it and we'll never be a poet and we should just stop trying.

Almost any poem can be improved by revising (some poems will need more revisions than others), and nearly everyone can become a good poet, if not a great one. The key to unlocking the mystery of poetry aside from learning the technical details, is finding the right things for to write about. These won't be the same as the right things for someone else.

Definitions of Poetry: What is a Poem?

When I tell you in class that we're going to be reading poetry, you all have a definite idea of what that means. And when you open up your anthology and read—

Success is counted sweetest
By those who ne'er succeed.
To comprehend a nectar
Requires sorest need.
—*Pain* by Emily Dickinson

—you easily recognize it as poetry. And we could pretty easily settle on a basic definition of poetry: poetry is imaginative language arranged in lines and set to a particular rhythm. That works at a basic level, but it has a few problems. First, not all poems are lined. There are things called 'prose poems' that are unlined poems. But those account for a very, very small percentage of poems. The bigger problem with this definition is that it doesn't account for all the many thing poetry can do. When a poet or critic defines poetry, he or she usually tries to capture that more elusive sense of what makes a poem special. Here are some definitions of poetry given by famous poets:

- '...the best words in the best order'—Samuel Taylor Coleridge.
- '...the spontaneous overflow of powerful feelings'—William Wordsworth.
- '...emotion put into measure'—Thomas Hardy.
- '...not the assertion that something is true, but the making of that truth more fully real to us'—T. S. Eliot.
- '...hundreds of things coming together at the right moment'—Elizabeth Bishop.
- '...life distilled'—Gwendolyn Brooks.

One thing you might notice about these definitions is that they're pretty vague. None of these definitions would explain in any detail how T. S. Eliot could come up with lines such as these:

Let us go then, you and I,
When the evening is spread out against the sky
Like a patient etherised upon a table.

ACTIVITY 2

Mention the word poetry and everyone has their own idea of what poetry is. Here are some common responses when readers/students are asked to respond to the word poetry: Poems rhyme; They're often about love; They can be funny, but have a serious side to them; They are full of lovely detailed descriptions; Poems are like photographs, a sort of snapshot of a moment; Poets write about—trees and fields and lambs and things, battles or deaths or disasters; Poets write about things that make them angry, or make them laugh or make them cry; A poem's got a sort of a rhythm, like a song in a way; and so on.

Look at the responses above and then think of all your favourite poems. Pick out about three or four of the responses that work for you.

(Ayers and Dayus 1999: 35)

One reason why poetry is so hard to define is that poems do so many things. In fact, poems can do anything that prose can do (and no one worries about defining prose). You can find poems on politics, religion, philosophy, and love. Poetry can even be advertising copy. Commercial jingles, after all, are a form of poetry.

The Four Functions of Language

One way to talk about what is happening in poetry is to look at the different functions of language or basic tasks of language:

- The Rhetorical Function: Language used to persuade someone of a particular point of view. Example: A politician's speech.
- The Definitive Function: Language used to define and describe the world. Example: A scientific report describing a new species of bird.
- The Informative Function: Language used to convey information. Example: An Encyclopedia.
- The Poetical Function: Language used for pleasure. Example: Poetry.

Most pieces of writing will contain a mixture of these four functions, but will emphasize one. For example, a politician giving a speech will mostly try to persuade you of his or her position. But as a part of that argument, the speaker may also have to inform people, define terms, and use language that sounds good. In his inaugural address, President John F. Kennedy said to the nation, 'Ask not what your country can do for you; ask what you can do for your country.' He was telling people they should work for their country, and not just expect to get stuff from it. That's not a popular message, but in part it was successful because Kennedy expressed it in memorable language. Poetry generally emphasizes the poetic function. Poems can, though, also persuade and define. When we analyze or interpret poems, we are usually looking at their rhetorical or definitive aspects (informative poems are rare), but don't lose sight of the fact that poems exist primarily to fulfill the poetic function: to please us (www.libarts.latech.edu).

ACTIVITY 3

What are the four functions of language? Give your own examples for each of them.

What to Write About and How to Start

As with any kind of writing, poets generally write about things that they feel strongly about. The first task in becoming a poet is to find out what affects you the most. What are the things that make you angry, that make you shiver, or cry, or grind your teeth so hard it hurts? Even if those topics seem trivial, if they cause a strong reaction in you, then you will be able to write honestly and strongly about them, and make them seem significant to your readers. Once you discover the things that affect you, you may need to push on one step farther. So think carefully about the things that disturb you, or fascinate you, or frighten you and see if you can figure out why you have that reaction. You may find that you then have the subject matter for a poem (or, more likely, many poems!).

By deciding to write poetry you have made a commitment to express your contemporary life and environment through the medium of language. Your content will be achieved through the words you employ, the constructs of language you use, and your application of the techniques of craft based on a knowledge of the elements of prosody. Your goal should be to make the medium and the content become one. To become a poet takes a combination of talent, sensitivity, pride and humility, knowledge and insight, and a fascination with the process of language as a living phenomenon (Riccio 1980: 3).

In writing your poems, you will call into play all levels of yourself—those readily available and some for which you will have to reach deep into yourself. You will rely on your thinking and your feeling; one without the other is addressing only half the process of creating a poem (Ibid: 15). The first thing to realize is that the real poet handles personal materials in such a way that it achieves universal quality that will include the reader in the experience. By all means, avail yourself of the treasures of your experience storehouse, but keep in mind your responsibility for refining, distilling and transforming that raw material into art, and the fact that your reader needs to empathize and participate in your poem. (Ibid: 18)

ACTIVITY 4

Write at least two lines on:

- Things that make you sad.
- Things that make you smile.
- Things that make you angry.

Emotions and Feelings are often used as synonyms, but have an important distinction you need to keep in mind: emotions—any one of the states designated as fear, anger, joy, surprise, disgust, hate, love, grief, etc.; feelings—appreciative recognition, a partly physical and partly mental response. A poem involves two people—the poet and the reader—and emotion is what connects them to each other. 'A good poem moves the reader' is a critical and artistic truism and it is emotion that gives atmosphere to the poem and feeling is what you, the poet, reaching out to your readers on a physical and emotional level, impart. The reader may be 'moved' for purely 'aesthetic reasons', that is, 'delighted' by your skill or craft; or, because the poem has touched a chord in her/him and evoked a response. While you are transmitting the poem's feelings in this way, to the auditors' intellect for interpretation the poem's structural and technical features are directing the meaning (Riccio 1980: 22). Rich and enticing as your own store of resources may be, you have the whole world around you from which you can cull ideas, if you let your imagination loose upon the environment—'appreciate subjectively, but appraise objectively'. That is to say—the poet while in the grip of an emotion is also in control of it; while possessed by the emotion, should also possess (have mastery) over it. All around you exist countless reasons for poems—people with whom you come in contact, read or hear about; events you witness; relationships you experience or observe; the phenomena of the natural environment—the list is endless. (Ibid: 24)

BOX 3.1

So at this point we can sum up the raw material that goes into the making of a poet as (Ibid: 26):

- commitment.
- an analytical appreciation of the self.
- a compulsive urge to express oneself in language.
- a critical assessment of the results of such expression.
- a knowledge of the state of poetry and an awareness of what its future directions may be.
- a respect for one's personal storehouse of feelings and experiences.
- a greedy reaching out to the outside world for more material to assimilate, digest and use.

Poetry and Prose

A recurrent question is the distinction between poetry and prose. A working definition with which to begin answering this vexing question could be: A poem is an integrated literary composition, tightly expressed, that is not restricted to discursive progression and logic but operates on a radiational level (Riccio 1980: 28). We saw above that words are used for ordinary speech, for discursive or logical thought and for literature. Discursive language makes statements of fact, is judged by standards of truth and falsehood, and is in prose. Literature makes no statements of fact, proceeds hypothetically and is judged by imaginative consistency. The best way then to distinguish literary from nonliterary writing is by looking at intention—what the writer hopes to do with what s/he has written. *If the writing is intended to describe and represent facts and be judged by its truth, it normally belongs to some nonliterary category; if it is to be judged by its imaginative consistency, it normally belongs to literature.* Some prose pieces are utilitarian, like a news story in the newspaper, a textbook, a biography and a book of spiritual guidance. Are these works of art, or are they artful uses of language? Are they primarily instruments for recording and conveying information or for moving people to action? They exist for the results they can produce. Other prose compositions exist for themselves, like novels, short stories and plays.

When we talk about prose, we do not mean the language of ordinary speech alone. 'Prose is ordinary speech on its best behaviour', it is the conventionalization of speech that is made by the educated or articulate person when s/he is trying to assimilate speech patterns to thought patterns. There are mainly two ways in which this can be done—by using a simple regularly recurring meter or by developing a sentence. When the former is used we have verse, and the latter makes prose. Prose then is an artful use of language, insofar as it is used consciously for effect, has a stylistic tradition and needs to be learned.

The main difference then between verse and prose is rhythm. Also, verse is able to absorb a much higher concentration of metaphorical and figurative speech than prose. (Preminger et al. 1974: 885-86) Poetry has form, shape, pattern, agreement as well as theme and subject. A common mistake made while defining poetry is to see it as having a distinct subject matter, a form and a mode of apprehension. This is not enough to help us as poets have used and continue to write on a huge variety of subjects and use a multitude of forms—new ones are invented every so often. By mode of apprehension we mean that the poet has looked at the external world in a particular way and transmuted this raw material into poetry. The problem with this is that it makes poetry a way of thinking, rather than a way of writing and poetry is after all 'a way of writing, a distinctive use of language' (Riccio 1980: 28).

Look at the examples below. The first two are written by the Indian English poet Agha Shahid Ali and on the same theme; about news he receives from his friends and family in Kashmir about the conditions there. Notice how the first is arranged and how it reads like a poem. In the case of the second, the letter, while the arrangement is more like prose, the rhythm of the lines indicates to us that it is poetry, a prose poem. Therefore, what you need to think about is, is it only the arrangement of words on the page or does a poem have a 'spoken rhythm' that makes it a different genre from the prose passage?

Postcard from Kashmir

Kashmir shrinks into my mailbox,
my home a neat four by six inches.
I always loved neatness. Now I hold
the half-inch Himalayas in my hand.

This is home. And this is the closest
I'll ever be to home. When I return,
the colors won't be so brilliant,
so ultramarine. My love
so overexposed.

And my memory will be a little
out of focus, in it
a giant negative, black
and white, still undeveloped.

Dear Shahid,

I am writing to you from your far-off country. Far even from
us who live here. Where you no longer are. Everyone carries his
address in his pocket so that at least his body will reach home.
Rumours break on their way to us from the city. But word still

reaches us from border towns: Men are forced to stand barefoot
in snow waters all night. The women are alone inside. Soldiers
smash radios and televisions. With bare hands they tear our
houses to pieces.

Another way we can try and get a grip on what poetry is is to see what it is not. Read the lines below and see ιow, although they look like poetry, something is missing:

Poetry is

A manifestation
Of the inner vistas
Of the human mind wherein it puts psychological
Crises on record and unwinds these through
Myth, Allegory, Metaphor, Image and Symbol.

How does one, in the final analysis, get to know this chameleon poetry at all? One way is to become familiar with the history, traditions, and development of this art. In art, nothing dies; it merely moves through change. Conventions, traditions, these offer temporary reference points—temporary because conventions and traditions also change with development and experimentation. Stylistic devices, persistent character types, forms, themes, pattern, manner and style of presentation of various subjects, recurring in poetry, develop into conventions. Adherence to a particular set of conventions over a period of time leads to the establishment of a tradition. In turn, traditions are influenced by further developments and experiments and through such cycles, the art of poetry continues to lead a healthy life (Riccio 1980: 28–29).

Shape, Form and Technique

There should be shape to all poems, whether determined by a traditional form, or by an organic form that results from a free play of ideas, or the design that evolves from working with open techniques. In addition to shape, the poem also has nature, an inner quality that is its essence. This combination of shape and nature gives the poem its appearance, 'that by which a thing is truly known'. Since a poem is a composition in which all the parts contribute to its total aesthetic effect and since the removal of any one part would destroy the poem, we are responsible for ensuring that the shape and nature of the poem combine in a synergistic whole. (Ibid: 27) Form in poetry may be defined as the manner in which a poem is composed as distinct from what the poem is about. Form could be the meter or verse that is used in the poem, the words that the poet chooses to express ideas, emotions, etc., the language and diction of the poem—in other words, the style of composition.

Poetry as an Auditory Art

Given all these theories, poetry is ultimately an art of sounds. The page on which the poem appears is the musical score for the reader, directions as to how the poem is to be sounded. Whether the form is fixed or free, the poem's structure guides the reader through its meaning and it is this we will now look at.

Experience and enjoyment of poetry starts with hearing it and when you look around you, you will see that your environment is full of verse—radio, TV, video and computer games, advertisements, greeting cards, films, etc. Poetry appeals to all our senses—the eye, tongue, ear, limbs, heart, bones and blood—but also to the mind. In its writing and performance it depends on the arrangement of sounds in space; it has its own choreography on the page and its rhythms, emphases and cadences on the airwaves. The heard and felt experience of poetry is the first step in the risky business of writing it (Bearne 2002: 109).

Prosody is the most general term in current use to refer to the elements and the structure involved in the rhythmic or dynamic aspects of speech and it is some elements of prosody that we will look at now.

Rhythm, Rhyme, and Meter

It is possible to write poetry without rhyme and meter, but impossible to do without rhythm. Whether you prefer the metrical designs of traditional forms or the freer rhythms of natural speech, making use of the rhythms of language is vital for crafting poetry.

Concerning the matching of sound and sense in the rhythm of poetry, Alexander Pope gives this advice to budding poets, in his *Essay on Criticism*

True ease in writing comes from art, not chance,
As those move easiest who have learned to dance.
'Tis not enough no harshness gives offence,
The sound must seem an echo to the sense.
Soft is the strain when Zephyr gently blows,
And the smooth stream in smoother numbers flows;
But when loud surges lash the sounding shore,
The hoarse, rough verse should like the torrent roar.

Rhythm in poetry includes stress or accent, quantity (the duration or length of a syllable) and pitch. Metrical stress is the emphasis or weight imposed in the line, dictated by the design of the meter. The (´) sign identifies the beats for long ones or stressed syllables and (˘) for short ones or unstressed syllables—in other words beat is measured in time, rather than by pitch and volume alone. Scansion is the analysis of the metrical rhythm of a line. When we scan a line of poetry in English, we count by syllable and stress to determine how many syllables there are and what kind of stress, and this helps us to measure the line in feet. A foot is a measurable, patterned unit of poetic rhythm (Preminger 1974: 285).

While rhythm and meter are related to each other, the difference is that rhythm is the natural beat as it exists in the words themselves and meter is the number of beats organized into a pattern (Riccio 1980: 138). Another word used for 'feet' is 'beat' and this poem by Samuel Taylor Coleridge is a great mnemonic to help you remember the most commonly used 'feet' that poets use to sing their songs. Each line of the poem not only defines each type of foot mentioned in it, but when scanned is also an example of the use of the particular foot in composition:

Metrical Feet – A Lesson for a Boy

Trochee trips from long to short;
From long to long in solemn sort.
Slow Spondee stalks, strong foot! yea ill-able.
Ever to come up with Dactyl's trisyllable.
Iambics march from short to long,
With a leap and a bound the swift Anapests throng.

BOX 3.2

The most commonly used feet in metrical composition are:

- The Iambic—a unstressed syllable followed by a stressed one, that reads as ˇ ´. This rhythm is called rising as it moves from the unstressed to the stressed.

  Ă séasòn dánk wíth místs aňd ráin

- The Anapest scanned by the sign ˇ ˇ ´ includes feet made up of two unstressed syllables followed by a stressed one and is also considered a rising rhythm.

  Ăs ă trée iň itš príme

- The Trochaic is composed of two syllables, the reverse of the iambic in order and is called a falling rhythm as it moves from the stressed ´ to the unstressed ˇ.

  Ṕipiňg dówn tȟe v́alley̌s ẃild

- The Dactyl is another example of falling rhythm as it reverses the syllable order of the anapest and is made up of a stressed syllable followed by two unstressed ones ´ ˇ ˇ

  Táke hěr ŭp téndĕr lŷ

- The Spondee shown as ´´ includes two stressed syllables and is normally found in words compounded of two one-syllable words

  Déw – clóth, dréam – dŕa pé rý

(Riccio 1980: 136–50)

ACTIVITY 5

Can you, with the help of the above, work out the rhyme and meter scheme of the popular nursery rhyme 'Jack and Jill'?

In *syllabic verse*, the measuring element is not quantity, stress or word accent, but the number of syllables in a line. Pattern plays an important part in this kind of poetry and the more complex the pattern unit, the more complex the rhythm. An interesting syllabic form of poetry is the *cinquain*—a syllabic five line poem in which the number of syllables per line is fixed: two syllables make up the first and fifth line, while the second, third and fourth have four, six and eight syllables respectively. This form was invented by Adelaide Crapsey (1878-1914) and her poem is an enduring example of the form's use:

Triad

These be
Three silent things
The falling snow...the hour
Before the dawn...the mouth of one
Just dead.
(Riccio 1980: 95)

BOX 3.3

If you have read *The Da Vinci Code* you know that one of the keys to unlocking the first clue left for the hero is the Fibonacci sequence. The sequence works like this: 1, 1, 2, 3, 5, 8... with each succeeding number being the sum of the previous two numbers. See if you too can write a Fibonacci poem with each succeeding line following the mathematical progression in its syllable arrangement like this one

So
You
No doubt
Will not find
It interesting
To talk to me about this stuff.

(*The Times of India*, 16 April, 2006: 16)

The syllable plays an important role in connection with the rhythms of poetry, as do the letters of the alphabet themselves as they create the syllables. Language is a living entity and has a variable and developing nature. Since poetry is an art intended to be heard, language as it is spoken plays a major part in the composition of poetry. Our professional interest in consonants and vowels, letters and their sounds, comes from the textures that they make possible in lines of poetry—smoothness, harshness, conflict, sibilance, harmony and dissonance.

> 'A syllable is something "held together" and can be defined as a group of letters taken together to form one sound, an uninterrupted unit of utterance, a complete word or part of a word.' You will notice as you speak that your voice mechanism adjusts itself to enunciate syllables rather than words and in voicing syllables you are therefore pronouncing combinations of letters. Keep this in mind while planning the sounds that will best support the sense of your poems. (Riccio 1980: 165)

As you take care to make sure that the syllables-formed-into-words echo the sense, see that the syllables are combined and sequenced in a way that is harmonious and do not jar and thump. The mood—theme and atmosphere—of the lines will determine the sound that should be heard, even by the inner ear, when the lines are read.

Just to give you an example of how sound translates into sense in a poem, depending on how you arrange the words, look at the two stanzas below, the first is melodious and pleasing in keeping with its theme, and the second, harsher and more jumpy in its sound and sense:

The Passionate Shepherd to his love

Come live with me and be my Love,
And we will all the pleasures prove
That hills and valleys, dale and field,
And all the craggy mountains yield.
—Christopher Marlowe

In my craft or sullen art

In my craft or sullen art
Exercised in the still night
When only the moon rages
And the lovers lie abed
With all their griefs in their arms
I labour by singing light
—Dylan Thomas

Diction is the selection and arrangement of words in a literary work. 'Poetic diction means the specifically poetic words and phrases which express the imaginative and impassioned nature of poetry' (Preminger 1974: 628). The diction you choose will be determined by the nature of the subject, the quality of the mood, the atmosphere and the current use of the language. Diction is, therefore, the vocabulary of the poem and the way this vocabulary is arranged into stanzas and word clusters will eventually constitute your style.

The first step for the poet is to be sensitive to the effect produced by words that are concrete or abstract, literal or figurative, common or technical, formal or colloquial, etc., and the degree to which they establish denotation and connotation in combination with other words. The tone of your poem will depend on your relationship to the material and your attitude towards your real or imagined audience. The tone of a speaker's voice may reveal information about his feelings, wishes, attitudes, beliefs, etc. … Thus attitudes determine tone and tone reflects attitudes. Since poetry is regarded as a specialization of language for the communication of attitudes, the determination of the exact shading of tone in a particular poem is very important.' (Preminger 1974: 856)

ACTIVITY 6

Tones can be challenging, reassuring, obsequious, condescending, formal, intimate, passionate, sly, persuasive, enticing, serious, solemn, comic, ironic, sardonic, sarcastic, witty, playful, etc. Look up the exact meaning of all these words in the dictionary and then think of situations or experiences that would best describe each of these feelings/reactions.

Images and Symbols

While writing poetry, your words, tone and diction are animated by Images and Symbols.

The *image* in poetry describes something in terms of concrete detail to form a word picture. *Imagery* is the term used to denote the totality of images appearing in the whole poem or a section of it. The most impressive quality of images is that they evoke mental pictures in the reader's mind so that the experience of reading the poem becomes a visual one along with the auditory. Imagery can also be mental—the focus is on what happens in the reader's mind; figures of speech—that use language in ways that are different from everyday speech; and symbolic—representative of something. Imagery can be interpreted in terms of whether it functions to vivify the subject, reveal the speaker's mood, externalize the speaker's thoughts, direct the reader's attitudes or guide his expectations. (Preminger 1974: 370)

Invention defines the quality of originality you can bring to bear on your choice of form and structure, diction and tone and the poetic/ linguistic devices you make use of. When we come to *symbol* we have come a full circle because a symbol like a word represents something else. The word Symbol derives from the Greek verb *symballein*, 'to put together'. It, therefore, denotes a joining or a combining whereby a material object is used to represent an immaterial idea/thought/experience. For example, the image of climbing a staircase/hill and the difficulty and effort involved, is used to represent the idea of raising oneself economically, spiritually or socially. While some symbols are universally understood, others are specific to the creative work itself and need to be decoded by the reader. Words normally represent agreed upon ideas or objects, but symbols are radiational (like the sun) and increase their significance through reappearance and communal acceptance. Traffic signs, flags, logos, doves, etc. are all universally understood symbols. However, in poetry, the symbol has a special significance as it allows the poet the freedom to exploit connotatative and denotative meanings in a wider sense for the purposes of intensification, tightness, heightening expression and so on. Quite often symbols help poets to express that which cannot be articulated directly and needs a more abstract means to bring out the meaning fully. (Riccio 1980: 202)

The form of a poem is easier to understand and detect than its contents, that is, ideas and their development, metaphor, mood, tonality, emotion, intensification, climax and resolution. The physical components rely on design and plan, and are revealed upon the analysis of the organization at a schematic level. The content elements are understood through interpretation of details, the development of imagery, diction, syntax, colour, atmosphere, etc. In traditional forms the poet has a diagram with which to work, in free verse the shape is generated by the material as it goes through the process of being designed into a poem. (Riccio 1980: 64)

Rhyme and Reason

The most familiar sound device in poetry is rhyme. Rhyme is commonly understood as the recurrence of duplicate or similar sounds at predictable intervals at the ends of lines. The rhyming unit is the syllable (Riccio 1980: 175–85). The meaning of the word is 'a metrical rhetorical device based on the sound-identities of words' (Preminger 1974: 705). The arrangement of final words in succeeding lines is called rhyme scheme. Besides calling attention to the words and syllables as musical sounds, rhymes mark the ends of rhythmic units represented by the lines. Rhymes also serve to meld the poem's lines into the pattern of the stanza and emphasize the melodic quality of the poem's diction. Now we will learn a little more about the kinds of rhyme that have been used by poets and will be a fund of ideas for you.

BOX 3.4

TYPES OF RHYMES

- Perfect, Pure, True or Complete Rhymes: the final syllables of two lines match in sound

  A poem should be palpable and mute
  As a globed fruit

- Masculine and Feminine Rhymes: When the final words that form the rhyme pair are one syllable each, the rhyme is masculine and when the rhyming words have two syllables or more, with the second syllable being unstressed, the rhyme is feminine. In these four lines, the rhyme is alternating with the first and third line using masculine rhyme and the second and the fourth using feminine rhyme:

  My true love hath my heart and I have his,
  By just exchange one for the other given.
  I hold his dear, and mine he cannot miss,
  There never was a better bargain driven.

- Internal Rhymes: When the rhyme occurs inside the lines

  And fate will wait to mate with night

- Initial Rhyme, also called head rhyme or alliteration: When the rhyme comes at the beginning of the words in the line

  She sells seashells on the seashore

Structural Elements

These are the physical parts of the structure of a poem and include meter and rhythm, lines, stanzas, rhyme and sound patterns. Here are some popular forms that are self-contained units in a poem, or sometimes the poem itself (See Riccio 1980: 63-75).

Couplet

A unit in poetry made up of two lines that usually rhyme and are composed in the same meter. If there is a natural pause at the end of the second line and the unit is complete, it is a closed couplet:

The Rape of the Lock

Unnumbered treasures ope at once, and here
The various offerings of the world appear;
From each she nicely culls with curious toil,
And decks the goddess with the glittering spoil.
This casket India's glowing gems unlocks,
And all Arabia breathes from yonder box.

—Alexander Pope

and an open couplet is one in which the second line is a run-on line and the sense and thought are completed in the succeeding couplet:

Endymion

A thing of beauty is a joy for ever:
Its loveliness increases; it will never
Pass into nothingness; but still will keep
A bower quiet for us, and a sleep...
Full sweet of dreams, and hearth
and being quiet breathing
—John Keats

The typical form of the couplet usually includes lines of five feet (pentameter) and is usually called a heroic couplet and the couplet that is cast in four-foot lines (tetrameter) is called the short couplet.

Tercet/Terza Rima

A stanza, that is, a group of lines related to an idea, metrics and forming a pattern, made up of three lines, either rhymed or unrhymed is a tercet or a triplet.

Ode to the West Wind

O wild West Wind, thou breath of autumn's being,
Thou, from whose unseen presence the leaves dead
Are driven, like ghosts from an enchanter fleeing,
Yellow, and black, and pale, and hectic red,
Pestilence-stricken multitudes: O thou,
Who chariotest to their dark wintry bed
—Percy Bysshe Shelley

Quatrain

This is the most popular organizing unit in English poetry and each stanza has four lines and the rhymes vary from none at all to two.

In Memoriam

I hold it true, whate'er befall,
I feel it when I sorrow most,
'Tis better to have loved and lost,
than never to have loved at all.
—Alfred, Lord Tennyson

Depending on the number of lines used in the stanza unit, other forms are the *Quintian*—a five-line stanza, *Sestet*—a six-line stanza, the *Septet* that uses seven lines, and the *Octave* that uses eight. The most common forms however remain couplets, tercets and quatrains.

Fixed Forms and Free Verse

From a basic introduction to stanza forms let us now look at some common forms in which poems are crafted. Poetic form is divided into two main categories: fixed forms, such as the sonnet and villanelle; and organic forms, which evolve from within poem itself. Within the former, we also have abundant examples of non-metric fixed forms that generally rely on a sculpted or 'picture' shape. The typographical arrangement is designed to reinforce the theme or sense. In *It Rains*, Apollinaire has arranged the lines in wavering verticals, and poems with the lines arranged in the shape of crosses, umbrellas and pears abound. See if you can find more such shaped or sculpted poems and then find out whether the shaping is in any way related to the dominant mood or the content of the poem, or is just a visual device.

George Herbert's *Easter Wings*, given below is wing shaped and the shape of the poem is in keeping with the theme—the desire of the devout and repentant believer to merge his soul with God's, with his belief giving him the wings to ascend to this blessed state.

Easter-Wings

LORD, who created man in wealth and store,
Though foolishly he lost the same,
Decaying more and more,
Till he became
Most poor:

With thee
O let me rise
As larks, harmoniously,
And sing this day thy victories:
Then shall the fall further the flight in me.

My tender age in sorrow did beginne:
And still with sickness and shame
Thou didst so punish sinne,
That I became
Most thinne.

With thee
Let me combine,
And feel this day thy victorie,
For, if I imp my wing on thine,
Affliction shall advance the flight in me.

—George Herbert

Sonnets

The sonnet is a poem of fourteen lines that expresses a single idea, thought or sentiment. The poem is normally divided into two parts—the octave (8 lines) and the sestet (6 lines); or into four sections of three quatrains and a couplet. The rhyme scheme varies, but is regular and the lines also carefully measured according to meter to give it a melodious rhythm. Another characteristic of the sonnet is the volta (turn), that is a shift in the direction of the poet's thought or emotion. The sonnet normally concludes by affirming the ideas explored in the course of its expression, or by completely turning the thought around to give the reader a surprise or a new insight. The sonnet is a simple form but makes great demands on the poet who needs to compress his/her ideas into the given form and this makes for a complex and intense expression of thought and feeling.

Sonnet 18

Shall I compare thee to a summer's day?
Thou art more lovely and more temperate:
Rough winds do shake the darling buds of May,
And summer's lease hath all too short a date:
Sometimes too hot the eye of Heaven shines,
And often is his gold complexion dimmed,
And every fair from fair sometimes declines,
By chance, or nature's changing course untrimmed:
But thy eternal summer shall not fade,
Nor lose possession of that fair thou ow'st,
Nor shall death brag thou wander'st in his shade,
When in eternal lines to time thou grow'st,
So long as men can breathe, or eyes can see,
So long lives this, and this gives life to thee.
—William Shakespeare

Villanelle

This is a poem in six stanzas, the first five of which are tercets and the final is a quatrain. The entire poem is constructed on two rhyme sounds and the stanzas are linked through repeat lines and the rhymes. The first line of the first stanza is repeated as the last line of the second and fourth stanzas; and the last line of the first stanza appears as the final line of the third and fifth stanzas; and both these lines, that is the first and last lines of the first stanza form the concluding couplet of the sixth stanza. The form is used to express a variety of ideas and emotions from the most serious and philosophical to the most light-hearted. The challenge lies not only in the form but also in intensifying the expression with every repetition so that the form and substance complement each other and the poem moves forward not in fits and starts but with a renewed power and evocation. The final stanza should draw the reader into the poem to share the poet's concerns and feelings (Riccio 1980: 105–08). While the best known example of the Villanelle is 'Do not Go Gentle into that Good Night' by Dylan Thomas, another well known practitioner of the form is Edwin Arlington Robinson, and here is his Villanelle:

The House on the Hill

They are all gone away,
The House is shut and still,
There is nothing more to say.

Through broken wall and gray
The winds blow bleak and shrill.
They are all gone away.

Nor is there one to-day
To speak them good or ill:
There is nothing more to say.

Why is it then we stray
Around the sunken sill?
They are all gone away,

And our poor fancy-play
For them is wasted skill:
There is nothing more to say.

There is ruin and decay
In the House on the Hill
They are all gone away,
There is nothing more to say.

ACTIVITY 7

Retaining the two rhyme sounds 'ay' and 'ill', see if you can rewrite this villanelle in a different mood, by changing the two refrain lines

Haiku This Japanese form is a short, self-contained seventeen syllable form that is composed of three lines with five, seven and five syllables respectively. The aim of the haiku is to express a delicate and nuanced insight through a concrete image. The poem evolves from a single image and the imagery is primarily drawn from nature with the time of the year (season) implied or stated. The last line of the haiku is vital since it is the insight line and reveals the intent or meaning of the whole poem. (Ibid: 98)

Now the Swinging Bridge
Is quietened with creepers
Like our tendrilled lives
—Basho

ACTIVITY 8

Now it is your turn to write a haiku. Try these exercises first:

(a) Fill in the 7 syllable line between these two 5 syllable lines to complete this haiku
Green elms in the woods
____
Standing tall and proud

(b) Now fill in the two 5 syllable lines above and below this 7 syllable line
____
The petals bend to the earth
____

Now write your own haiku. One of the things you could write about is your favourtie sport. Decide for what purpose you are writing and what is the mood you want to convey? Think of all the images and descriptive words, as well as figurative language you could use to convey the sounds, sights and smells.

Light Hearted Forms

Humour is also a vital ingredient of poetry and clerihews, limericks and epigrams, have been written to great poetic impact:

1. A **Clerihew** consists of two couplets of unequal length often with complex and sometimes ridiculous rhymes and presents a potted biography of a famous person or historical character. The humour consists in concentrating on the trivial, fantastic or ridiculous and presenting it with great solemnity as if it were characteristic, significant or essential. Examples from the poems of Edmund Clerihew Bentley who gave this form its name, are given below.

   The art of Biography
   Is different form Geography
   Geography is about maps,
   But Biography is about chaps.

   Sir Humphry Davy
   Detested gravy,
   He lived in the odium
   Of having invented sodium.

2. A **Limerick** is a verse form composed of five (or sometimes four) lines rhyming aabba, of which the first, second and fifth are trimeter and the third and fourth dimeter. Here is, for instance, an example by Edward Lear:

   There was an Old Man of Dee,
   who was sadly annoyed by a flea,
   when he said, 'I will scratch it',
   they gave him a hatchet,
   which grieved that Old Man of the Dee.

3. An **Epigram** is a form of writing that makes a satiric or complimentary observation with wit, extreme condensation and above all, brevity. Here are two examples of epigrams written by Samuel Taylor Coleridge.

   What is an epigram? A dwarfish whole;
   Its body brevity, and wit its soul.

   Sir, I admit your general rule,
   That every poet is a fool:
   But you yourself may serve to show it,
   That every fool is not a poet.

ACTIVITY 9

Find a clerihew, limerick and epigram, and bring them the class. Write a limerick starting with the line, 'Today is Monday...'

Free Verse

> This is poetry whose verse is not based on the recurrence of stress accent in a regular, measurable pattern, but rather on the irregular rhythmic cadence of significant phrases, image patterns, and the like. It is the refusal of English to conform to standard prosody that has given rise to free verse, but that does not mean that this form does not have any limitations or guiding principles. The crux of the question here is measure. In free verse the measure has been loosened to give more play to vocabulary and syntax—hence, to the mind in its excursions. The bracket of the customary foot has been expanded so that more syllables, words or phrases can be admitted into its confines. The new unit may be called the 'variable foot', a term and concept already accepted widely as a means of bringing the warring elements of freedom and discipline together. It rejects the standard of the conventionally fixed foot and suggests that measure varies with the idiom by which it is employed and the tonality of the individual poem. Thus, as in speech, the prosodic pattern is evaluated by criteria of effectiveness and expressiveness rather than mechanical syllable counts (Preminger 1974: 289).

If free verse is about the right of English to dance to a different rhythm, the opening stanza of this poem by Kamala Das is a wonderful example of freedom in verse and life (de Souza 1997: 10–11).

An Introduction

I don't know politics but I know the names
Of those in power, and can repeat them like
Days of the week, or names of months, beginning with
Nehru. I am Indian, very brown, born in
Malabar, I speak three languages, write in
Two, dream in one. Don't write in English, they said,
English is not your mother-tongue. Why not leave
Me alone, critics, friends, visiting cousins,
Every one of you? Why not let me speak in
Any language I like? The language I speak
Becomes mine, its distortions, its queerness
All mine, mine alone. It is half English, half
Indian, funny perhaps, but it is honest,
It is as human as I am human, don't
You see? It voices my joys, my longings, my
Hopes, and it is useful to me as cawing
Is to crows or roaring to the lions, it
Is human speech, the speech of the mind that is
Here and not there, a mind that sees and hears and
Is aware. Not the deaf, blind speech
Of trees in storm or of monsoon clouds or of rain or the
Incoherent murmurings of the blazing
Funeral pyre. I was child, and later they
Told me I grew, for I became tall, my limbs
Swelled and one or two places sprouted hair. When
I asked for love, not knowing what else to ask
For, he drew a youth of sixteen into the
Bedroom and closed the door. He did not beat me
But my sad woman-body felt so beaten.

Dominant Modes of Poetry—Lyrical, Narrative and Dramatic

Lyric

The *Lyrical Mode* refers to the nature of the language, tonality, mood and emotional expression in the poem. Lyric poetry is that which most prominently retains evidence of the origins of poetry in musical expression, singing, chanting and recitation to musical accompaniment. The musical element is, therefore, intrinsic to this mode of writing and becomes the focal point to the poet's expression. As Lascelles Abercrombie says, 'A poet does not compose in order to make of language delightful and exciting music; he composes a delightful and exciting music in language in order to make what he has to say peculiarly efficacious in our minds' (Preminger 1974: 462). That a lyric is primarily a poem written to be sung, is something we still agree with as we refer to the words of a song as its lyrics.

The forms and styles most often included in this category are songs, hymns and psalms, ballads, elegies, odes, sonnets, pastorals, idylls, epitaphs, reflections, and, poems on the subjects of religion, love, friendship, nature, patriotism, war, childhood, and other preoccupations of our daily lives. The principal quality of lyrical poetry is its melodic tonality working in accord with its rhythms. Below is an example of a conventional love poem by Elizabeth Barrett Browning:

Sonnets from the Portuguese *43*

How do I love thee? Let me count the ways.
I love thee to the depth and breadth and height
My soul can reach, when feeling out of sight
For the ends of Being and ideal Grace.
I love thee to the level of every day's
Most quiet need, by sun and candle-light.
I love thee freely, as men strive for right;
I love thee purely, as they turn from praise.
I love thee with the passion put to use
In my old griefs, and with my childhood's faith.
I love thee with a love I seemed to lose
With my lost saints – I love thee with the breath,
Smiles, tears, of all my life! – and, if God choose,
I shall but love thee better after death.

ACTIVITY 10

Poetry abounds with examples of love lyrics. Read as many as you can and find one that really appeals to you. Then try and find out what is it that you found appealing – the way the poet dealt with the subject matter, the words s/he used or something else, maybe the music of the words themselves.

Now compare a traditional love lyric with a contemporary one and try and see what has changed – the emotion, its expression, or both?

The most melodious form of the lyric is songs that originate from the time when poetry was actually sung and its inventory included songs of love, war, patriotism and peace. In songs, both sacred and secular, language is used in its simplest manifestations with reliance placed on emotional content to enhance the richness of the words even further, and the object is to let the sounds pour forth, directly and clearly. Poetry in English abounds with examples of lyrical songs that date back to the English Bible (King James version) and come right up to contemporary times.

One of the important forms of the lyric is the *elegy*, expressing themes of death, love and war, and often having a didactic purpose, that is, an attempt to teach the reader a moral or social lesson. A stanza from Thomas Gray's *Elegy Written in a Country Churchyard* will give you an idea of the form and its primary tone

Full many a gem of purest ray serene
The dark unfathomed caves of ocean bear;
Full many a flower is born to blush unseen,
And waste its sweetness on the desert air.

Odes

Ode comes from the Greek *aeidein*, to sing or chant. It is the most formal, complex and ceremonious of lyric forms. The ode is serious, elevated and paced in a deliberate and ponderous manner. The form is mostly used to express the poet's deepest personal feelings concerning an event or a person. The form originated in the songs of the chorus in Greek drama and has a three-fold division. The first stanza or section is the *strophe* (turn), the middle one the *antistrophe* (counter-turn) and the final stanza or section, the *epode* (after-song). The movement of the ode, like its stanza division is also three-fold and moves first in one direction, then in the opposite direction and the final stanza is one of repose or standing still. (Riccio 1980: 82). While this is the convention, many odes may not follow this scheme.

Ode on Melancholy

No, no, go not to Lethe, neither twist
Wolf's bane, tight-rooted, for its poisonous wine;
Nor suffer thy pale forehead to be kiss'd
By nightshade, ruby grapes of Proserpine;
Make not your rosary of yew-berries,
Nor let the beetle, nor the death-moth be
Your mournful Psyche, nor the downy owl
A partner in your sorrow's mysteries;
For shade to shade will come too drowsily,
And drown the wakeful anguish of the soul.

But when the melancholy fit shall fall
Sudden from heaven like a weeping cloud,
That fosters the droop-headed flowers all,
And hides the green hill in an April shroud;
Then glut thy sorrow on a morning rose,
Or on the rainbow of the salt sand-wave,
Or on the wealth of globed peonies;

Or if thy mistress some rich anger shows,
Emprison her soft hand, and let her rave,
And feed deep, deep upon her peerless eyes.

She dwells with Beauty – Beauty that must die;
And Joy, whose hand is ever at his lips
Bidding adieu; and aching Pleasure nigh,
Turning to poison while the bee-mouth sips;
Ay, in the very temple of delight
Veil'd Melancholy has her sovran shrine,
Though seen of none save him whose strenuous tongue
Can burst Joy's grape against his palate fine;
His soul shall taste the sadness of her might,
And be among her cloudy trophies hung.

—John Keats

Narrative Poetry

Narrative poetry is concerned primarily with telling a story in verse form and its two basic types are the *ballad* and the *epic*.

Ballads

An important form of the narrative is the ballad, which although it combines the lyrical, dramatic and narrative; also has a clearly defined pattern in which stanzas and lines are arranged in a regular, repetitive rhythm and the lines have a resounding interplay of rhyme. Ballads are normally set to music and can therefore be defined as 'a narrative poem that is lyrical in tonality, includes dramatic elements (character and dialogue) and reveals a situation already existing and follows it to its conclusion' (Riccio 1980: 79). Ballads focus on a single crucial episode or situation. The ballad usually begins at a point where the action is moving decisively towards its catastrophe and the focus is on the emotional impact of the climax. Folk ballads were originally passed on orally and developed into storytelling devices to describe events of general interest. You probably remember reading the much-anthologized *Lochinvar.* Read it again and see how the rhythm and the story move together.

Epics

Epics are long narratives, which deal with events that have importance in the life of an individual, community or a nation. You are familiar with the Indian epics the *Ramayana* and the *Mahabharata* and of course the famous Greek epics *Iliad* and *Odyssey*. Some of the defining criteria of epics are their seriousness of tone and excellence of expression; scope and inclusiveness; coherence of structure; and, a contemporary relevance combined with a universal appeal, that is, the poet speaks of a particular time and place but the ideas and emotions are for all time. Here are the opening lines from John Milton's *Paradise Lost*, a classic epic; followed by the opening canto (the equivalent of a stanza in a poem or a chapter in a novel) of Vikram Seth's *The Golden Gate*, an epic of today (from Paniker 2004: 167)

Book I

Of Man's first Disobedience, and the Fruit
Of that forbidden tree, whose mortal taste
Brought Death into the World, and all our woe,
With loss of Eden, till one greater Man
Restore us, and regain the blissful Seat,
Sing Heavenly Muse, …

— John Milton

I.1

To make a start more swift than weighty,
Hail Muse. Dear Reader, once upon
A time, say, circa 1980,
There lived a man. His name was John.
Successful in his field though only
Twenty-six, respected, lonely,
One evening as he walked across
Golden Gate Park, the ill-judged toss
Of a red frisbee almost brained him.
He thought, 'If I died, who'd be sad?
Who'd weep? Who'd gloat? Who would be glad?
Would anybody?' As it pained him,
He turned from his dispiriting theme
To ruminations less extreme.

— Vikram Seth

Narrative poetry continues to be a popular form as it evocatively expresses contemporary concerns as in this poem written by Wilfred Owen that expresses the horrors of war more vividly than newspaper reports or articles ever can.

Dulce et Decorum Est

Bent double, like old beggars under sacks,
Knock-kneed, coughing like hags, we cursed through sludge,
Till on the haunting flares we turned our backs
And towards our distant rest began to trudge.
Men marched asleep. Many had lost their boots
But limped on, blood-shod. All went lame; all blind;
Drunk with fatigue; deaf even to the hoots
Of tired, outstripped Five-Nines that dropped behind.

Gas! GAS! Quick, boys! — An ecstasy of fumbling,
Fitting the clumsy helmets just in time;
But someone still was yelling out and stumbling
And flound'ring like a man in fire or lime . . .
Dim, through the misty panes and thick green light,
As under a green sea, I saw him drowning.

In all my dreams, before my helpless sight,
He plunges at me, guttering, choking, drowning.

If in some smothering dreams you too could pace
Behind the wagon that we flung him in,
And watch the white eyes writhing in his face,
His hanging face, like a devil's sick of sin;
If you could hear, at every jolt, the blood
Come gargling from the froth-corrupted lungs,
Obscene as cancer, bitter as the cud
Of vile, incurable sores on innocent tongues, —
My friend, you would not tell with such high zest
To children ardent for some desperate glory,
The old lie: Dulce et decorum est
Pro patria mori.
—Wilfred Owen

Indian English poetry has abundant examples of narrative poetry that talks about the horrors and pathos of contemporary life. Whether it is Jayanta Mahapatra who talks in heart-rending verse about the poverty of Orissa or Keki N. Daruwalla who makes us feel for the suffering of the poor peasants of Uttar Pradesh who depend on the rain to survive; most contemporary poets seem to feel that the best use to which the vehicle of poetry can be put is to carry a message to readers about what the world outside is like. So poetry is not just about 'pretty images' and 'broken hearts' but is a powerful means of reflecting the reality of contemporary society.

Read this poem and see what a skilled poet like Jayanta Mahapatra can do with a newspaper headline

Victim Number 569, Leela, aged 5, daughter of Dayaram of Chola Kenchi, Bhopal. Died of gas poisoning on 3rd December 1984.

India Today
Cover Photograph, 31 December, 1984

Victim No 569

i

The eyes are deep and hard in Leela's sockets.
And the face looks peaceful in death.
That's what they say, the onlookers.
What would Leela have said
had she grown up to her father's age?

But her face,
it seems to grow best in death.
Her father Dayaram of Chola Kenchi
would never believe me, his half-waking mind
trying fruitlessly to drain the sea of his reality.
Soon he will burn Leela out of himself.
Soon her eyes will soften, turn glutinous and fume.
Perhaps something crueler
will happen even here along with the fish
rising gracefully from the river in wispy nets.

Poem No. 24, *Dispossessed Nests*, 41

Both Owen and Mahapatra use the narrative mode to talk about the death of innocence. Compare the two poems and see what the poet has done to evoke your response without making the poem too emotional or pathetic. Now choose a headline from the newspaper and write a stanza either describing the event or your reaction to it.

Dramatic Poetry

Dramatic poetry emphasizes the 'showing' rather than the 'telling' of experiences and presents its story in a dramatic form through dialogues, monologues, etc. The elements of time, place and the events described are made known by the poem itself. In the narrative poem, like the ones above, the poet speaks in her/his own person while setting the scene or explaining the event; in the dramatic, the group of characters created by the poet, including the persona in the poem, remain centre stage and the poet's intention is description without explicit judgement—that you as the reader need to work out for yourself.

The dramatic monologue is a poem consisting of the words of a single speaker who reveals the dramatic situation and his or her own character. Robert Browning is one of the finest original practitioners of this form and you should read some of his poems for models of dramatic poetry.

Rukmini Bhaya Nair puts the dramatic form to very good use in this poem to talk about the problem of identity.

Ordinary Things

Yesterday I stood on tiptoe like a goat
In search of high, tenderest leaves

The washing flapped in my face, a wind-
Blown tree in some strip of earth, somewhere

I turned to the sea, it lay at my feet
The Bay of Bengal, in a bucket, heaving

Now I had something rare, a catch
My clothes-line stretched across the sky

Six pegs dangled, coloured, tense and spare
Out-of-reach, they would not let me hang

My new sea-treasures by their branches
Their scabby protuberances meant for such

What goats do in such a happenstance
Feeding, frustrated, on a high promontory

Off a coastal strip, I do not know
Perhaps they turn their hairy butts

And walk away, but instead, I lifted
My unwary face, lashless, to the salty air

It was the sun that lay in wait
Rushed at me, a wild and hungry beast

Afterwards, I could not see, my eyes
Dripped, and the colour of my washing

Was neither white nor wholly soiled
Crushed bones or clothes, I did not care

The taste of fear remained with me
Goat stalked and caught defencelessly.

Hyoid Bone, 15–16

Another useful distinction that is made in poetry is that between *Classical* and *Romantic*. Classical poetry is that which displays balance and restraint, unity, proportion and purity of form; while romantic poetry relies for its effect on the subjective and personal expression of ideas. The latter kind of poetry is written when the poet sees her/himself at the center of a personal conflict or struggle and suffers because of an impersonal world. The poet who adopts the classical stance assumes a distance from her/his subject matter and attempts an objectivity and universality of expression. Romantic poetry exhibits lushness in contrast to the spare beauty of the classical.

Some of the finest and most evocative Indian English poetry is written in the classical style insofar as is very controlled in its expression and yet talks about thoughts and experiences that have made an impact on the mind and heart of the poet. Indian poetry in English is also classical in another sense—in its form and ideas it uses the traditions of the poet's mother tongue in a unique manner and the result is poetry that is individualistic and yet involves the reader in its universal concerns.

Here is a poem by R. Parthasarathy, whose theme is meta-poetic, that is about the writing of poetry itself. In a country where writers who chose English as their medium of creative expression, have had to fight a long battle to be accepted, Parthasarathy's concerns are of great interest to us. Please notice how he uses a series of tercets to create a poem about writing poetry in English, not by being derivative but using the rich reservoir of native traditions:

Homecoming

To live in Tamil Nadu is to be conscious
every day of impotence.
There is the language, for instance:

the bull that Nammalvar[1] took by the horns
is today an unrecognizable carcass,
quick with the fleas of Kodambakkam.[2]

There is little you can do about it
except to throw up your hands.
How long can foreign poets

provide the staple of your lines?
Turn inward. Scrape the bottom of your past.
Ransack the cupboard

for skeletons of your Brahmin childhood
(the nights with father droning
the Four Thousand[3] as sleep pinched

your thighs blue). You may then
perhaps strike out a line for yourself
from the iron of life's ordinariness.

—R. Parthasarathy, *Rough Passage*, 48

---

[1] Nammalvar (ca. 880–930) was a Tamil saint-poet.

[2] Kodambakkam, a suburb of Chennai, is the center of the Tamil film industry.

[3] The Four Thousand is a collection of hymns, including 1,102 hymns by Nammalvar, composed between the sixth and ninth centuries.

Ghazals in English are another example of the use of a classical form in a contemporary context. This poetic form has its origins in Persian, Arabic and Urdu and is made up of a series of couplets, each emotionally and thematically complete in itself. One couplet may be comic, another tragic, another romantic, another religious, and another political. The poem should have no enjambments between couplets and the ghazal as a whole has a complex *unity* built on association, memory and expectation. The opening couplet called the *matla* sets up the scheme of rhyme (*qafia*) and refrain (*radif*) by having it occur in both lines, the rhyme immediately preceding the refrain and then this scheme is repeated in the second line of each couplet. The themes are normally melancholic, amorous and philosophical. Another characteristic of the ghazal is the inclusion of the poet's name in the penultimate or last couplet (Ali: 2–4).

Here is a *ghazal* by another Indian English poet Keki N. Daruwalla

Partition Ghazal

This may pass muster and yet may not pass
This past we are talking about is not the past

This may pass muster and yet may not pass
The past is heavy on our shoulders, good it is the past

Tenses curve and coil through the murk of time –
The past erupts except that it is not the past

Beyond the linear and hence beyond the line
The magic lantern images of memory flash past

Gandhi's egg-shell head, round as a shrunken sun
Has it set for ever into a black-hole past

Not that Gandhi looked the only anchorite
Jinnah looked ascetic too – how the years passed

This should pass muster and yet may not pass
All tenses are tricky, especially the past

The lesson for you, wine-bibbling Kaikhusroo –
The past you talk of may not have been the past.

— Keki N. Daruwalla (Ali 2000: 48)

Notice how both the villanelle and the ghazal use the 'refrain' not only for emphasis, since the line that is echoed in the refrain is the central image/theme of the poem, but also to give the poem a rhythm that is song like in its harmony. Think of your favourite songs and see how many of them use a refrain to give the composition circularity (a repetitive recurrence) and rhythm.

Voices in the Poem

Every poem speaks through a voice or voices that the poet uses to communicate with the reader. Behind the voice is the 'persona' created by the poet and this could be the poet her/himself or a historical/fictional character created by the poet. The persona could also be symbolic, representative of a thought, idea or experience, represented through language and rhythm. The use of the persona helps the poet to depersonalize experience and make it universal so that readers across time and space can participate in the poem.

Here is the poem A *Morning Walk* by Nissim Ezekiel that brings together a lot of what we have been talking about. See how the effect of rhythm is achieved and the central image of the city around which all the minutiae of everyday existence become symbolic of the personal history of the poet and this in turn becomes a synecdoche for the history of the whole subcontinent. The tone combines irony and nostalgia with stunning effect and makes us see the poetic in the ordinary. The poem is written in a series of seven line stanzas (septets), with a variety of rhyme schemes. The poet uses the third person to achieve some distance from the feelings that the city has arouse in him and in the first stanza itself we are told that the poem will be about the relationship between the persona and the city in which he lives. As the persona climbs the hill, his thoughts become more introspective as he literally and metaphorically leaves the city and his daily concerns behind. The third stanza describes the city in vivid images, and the poet uses alternating rhyme and an abundance of adjectives to describe his view of the city. As the poetic persona returns to the city, nothing has changed but distance has given him some perspective and the final statement is one of belonging and acceptance, rather than alienation and rejection.

A Morning Walk

Driven from his bed by troubled sleep
In which he dreamt of being lost
Upon a hill too high for him
(A modest hill whose sides grew steep).
He stood where several highways crossed
And saw the city, cold and dim,
Where only human hands sell cheap.

It was an old, recurring dream,
That made him pause upon a height.
Alone, he waited for the sun,
And felt his blood a sluggish stream.
Why had it given him no light,
His native place he could not shun,
The marsh where things are what they seem.
Barbaric city, sick with slums,
Deprived of seasons, blessed with rains,
Its hawkers, beggars, iron-lunged,
Processions led by frantic drums,
A million purgatorial lanes,
And child-like masses many-tongued,
Whose wages are in words and crumbs.

He turned away. The morning breeze
Released no secrets to his ears
The more he stared the less he saw
Among the individual trees.
The middle of his journey nears
Is he among the men of straw
Who think they go which way they please?

Returning to his dream, he knew
That everything would be the same.
Constricting as his formal dress,
The pain of his fragmented view.
Too late and small his insights came,
And now his memories oppress.
His will is like the morning dew.

The garden on the hill is cool,
Its hedges cut to look like birds
Or mythic birds are still asleep.
His past is like a muddy pool
From which he cannot hope for words.
The city wakes, where fame is cheap,
And he belongs, an active fool.

—Nissim Ezekiel

ACTIVITY 11

In addition to the clues given above, to help you read the poem with insight, answer the following questions to try and unravel the mystery of technique, i.e., use of words, imagery, etc. (From Bearne 114–115).

- Look at the words chosen by Ezekiel:
  - Are they long/short vowel sounds?
  - What are the consonant sounds he has used?
  - What effects do these have?
- Look at the imagery:
  - What patterns can you find?
  - Do the images create a picture in your mind?
- Look at the way the poet has used
  - adjectives
  - verbs
  - What can you say about their effects?
- Look at the punctuation
  - What kinds?
  - Why?
- Look at the length of the
  - lines
  - stanzas
  - Does the arrangement of the lines contribute to the poem in any way?

Some Indian English Poets and their Works

Looking back at all that we have been talking about as far as the art, craft, techniques and types of poetry are concerned; we though that it would be interesting for you to know some more about some Indian English poets who are the corner stone of the edifice of Indian English poetry as they have set its standards and also given it a unique identity.

Henry Louis Vivian Derozio (1809–1831): Considered by the first major Indian English poet, his major works include *Fakeer of Jungheera: A Metrical Tale and other Poems* and *The Enchantress of the Cave*.

Toru Dutt (1856–1877) was one of the first Indian woman poets and novelists writing in English and French. Her most important books are *A Sheaf Gleaned in French Fields*, and *Ancient Ballads*

Nissim Ezekiel (1924–2005): The first major poet after Independence, Ezekiel continues to be a great influence and source of inspiration for Indian English poets till today. His collections include *A Time to Change, Sixty Poems, The Third, The Unfinished Man, The Exact Name, Hymns in Darkness*, and *Latter-day Psalms*.

Jayanta Mahapatra (b. 1928): This poet laureate of Orissa is a prolific writer on his home state and on the politics of India. His works include *A Rain of Rites, Relationship, Life Signs, Dispossessed Nests, Burden of Waves and Fruit, Temple* and *Bare Face*.

A. K. Ramanujan (b. 1929): This extraordinary poet and scholar has contributed significantly not only to the oeuvre of Indian English poetry but also to the study of ancient Tamil and Kannada poetry, that he has translated into English. His major collections of poems in English include *The Striders, Relations, Second Sight* and *The Black Hen*.

R. Parthasarathy (b. 1934): Inspired by the native poetic traditions of Tamil, Urdu and Pali, he is a poet whose single collection *Rough Passage* has done more for Indian English verse and the expression of its dynamics and dilemmas, than more prolific outpourings by other less skilled poets.

Kamala Das (b. 1934): Her bold and outspoken poems about freedom, both personal and poetic make her the first major female voice in post-Independence Indian English poetry. Her major collections include *Summer in Calcutta, The Old Playhouse and Other Poems* and *My Story*.

Keki N. Daruwalla (b. 1937): This policeman-poet has seen the underbelly of life from very close quarters and his experiences both professional and personal translate into vivid and gripping poetry. Some of his major collections include *The Keeper of the Dead, Landscapes, A Summer of Tigers, Winter Poems, Under Orion* and *Night River*.

Dom Moraes (b. 1938): He achieved fame early with his early collections *A Beginning, Poems, John Nobody* and *Beldam And Other Poems* which marked him out as a major talent on the poetic map of the subcontinent.

Agha Shahid Ali (1949 – 2001): This bard of Kashmir - its culture and music, and of Urud and Persian poetry has written some of the most evocative Indian English poetry drawing heavily on his familial and cultural inheritance. His major collections include *The Half-Inch Himalayas, The Country Without a Post Office* and *Rooms are Never Finished*.

Rukmini Bhaya Nair (b. 1959): This Professor of Languistics has a polyphonous literary style, and writes post-modern poetry that brings together her interests in linguistics, cognition, literature and cultural studies. She has written three collections of verse: *The Hyoid Bone* (1992), *Ayodhya Cantos* (1999) and *Yellow Hibiscus* (2004).

Finally, as students of creative writing, especially poetry, in English, we thought you would like to hear about the trials, tribulations and triumphs of writing poetry from a poet. We talked to the pre-eminent Indian English poet R. Parthasarathy and this is what he said.

A Conversation with a Creative Writer

R. Parthasarathy

When did you begin writing?

I began writing at fifteen with the encouragement of one of my teachers, Fr. Edward Corcoran of Don Bosco High School, Mumbai, who taught us English. He made us memorize hundreds of lines of poetry and recite them aloud in class. For many years I had clung to the green, clothbound Methuen anthology until we were separated in one of my many moves. Not long ago, on learning that Fr. Corcoran was ill, I wrote this poem.

An Irishman, tall, high cheekbones, rather
anemic (his trousers showed under his cassock)
romped in the field with the boys. It was he

who ten years ago taught me language,
not so much in class as in the penance study.
Together, we read *The Death of Socrates*.

The last I heard he was convalescing:
he has grown old in Yercaud. And the syllables
he taught a boy have grown to poems.

What forms of writing did you experiment with?

I wrote only verse. Fiction did not interest me. Like everyone else who begins to write at that age, what I wrote were no more than pastiches of the English poets, especially Keats and Shelley. Fortunately, those early exercises in versification do not survive. Throughout my adolescence, I had the good fortune to study with poets. The first was the Marathi poet Vinda Karandikar, whose course of lectures on "Pure Poetry" in graduate school in Mumbai introduced me to the French Symbolist poets such as Mallarmé, Rimbaud, and Valéry. Later, at the University of Leeds in England, the British poet Geoffrey Hill was my tutor. His example as a poet made a profound impression on me. It was in Leeds that I found my voice as a poet. But it was the novelist Raja Rao at the University of Texas at Austin who awakened me from my long sleep in the West. Evenings, after dinner (for I was living with him in 1982-83 in his apartment at 1808 Pearl Street), he would talk to me about our spiritual and philosophical traditions. I was then translating the Old Tamil epic, the *Cilappatikaram* and also editing his novel, *The Chessmaster and His Moves*. I had been his editor at Oxford University Press from 1971 to 1982. The essays in my as yet unpublished book, *The Forked Tongue: The Indian Writer and Tradition*, bear the imprint of those daily conversations in Austin. Over the years I have been translating classical Tamil and Sanskrit poetry. My later poetry taps into this inexhaustible reservoir.

What drew you towards poetry?

The idea of making objects with words. From then on, writing poetry became the most important thing in the world—being able to make poems out of that most intangible substance, one's breath. Poetry became an unusual way of seeing the usual things. Words helped to preserve objects and people from being forgotten. Though the English language has colored my imagination, my roots go deep into our Indian past, to Tamil and Sanskrit stanza poems. My poems speak to the redemptive power of language to help us bear our isolation in an indifferent world.

Would you say that certain forms lend themselves naturally to the expression of certain themes?

At the beginning of the twentieth century, traditional forms gave way to more open forms such as free verse. Spearheading this revolution in poetics were the two American poets, Ezra Pound and T. S. Eliot. It would not be correct to say that poets stopped writing in traditional forms. W. B. Yeats and Robert Frost are a case in point. For some of my short poems, I use the forms of the Tamil and Sanskrit stanza poems. In the end I don't think that there is a one-to-one correspondence between form and theme. Form evolves as the poet explores his theme. Form is a way of saying what has not been said before.

What tells you that you are ready to begin a poem?
Almost anything can trigger a poem. It might be an image, a phrase, an insistent rhythm, or some physical sensation. Poems have their beginnings in such uncertain materials, and the poet is constantly wrestling with them. There is thus an overwhelming need to translate experience into language to give it a more permanent form. The poem, 'At Ghalib's Tomb' (2001), was the result of wandering through the narrow lanes of Basti Nizamuddin in South Delhi one January afternoon in 2001 in search of the poet's *mazar.* It is not only a homage to a great poet but also a warning to ourselves not to turn our backs on the things that he had stood for, such as communal harmony. Here is the poem.

At Ghalib's Tomb

Wandering through dark tangled lanes, notice
how everything round here, not to mention
the dust under your feet, is touched by his breath.
Their faces scarred by graffiti, one by one
the havelis open their shuddering arms
only to be brushed aside by the passerby.
Will Time, that had once tightened its noose

around the poet's neck, keep its vaunted promise

not to disturb his peace? For how long
must Lal Qila, its florid pelt ruffled by the wind,
pace about the river before night

swoops down on it? "Today our verses,
Asad, are only an idle pastime.
What's the use of flaunting our talent, then?"

The lines, 'Today our verses,/ Asad, are only an idle pastime./ What's the use of flaunting our talent, then?' are my translation of the final couplet of Ghalib's (1797-1869) ghazal, 'Maze Jahan Ke Apni Nazar Men Khak Nahin:'

hamare sher hain ab sirf dil lagi ke Asad
khula kih fayda arz-e hunar men khak nahin.

Do you work to a schedule, a fully worked-out plan, and do you know where you are going when you start?
I don't write poems to a schedule. I compose orally, or at least as much of the poem as possible. Only then I put it down on paper and complete it. Once the lines are on the page, other lines follow on their own. I don't know how the poem is going to end. I keep working on the poem every day till I think it is finished.

What role does research/ background information play in your writing?
There is no research involved in writing poems of a personal nature. If the subject of a poem is historical, I research it thoroughly. I have recently completed a poem, 'The Arrest of the Last Mughal Emperor at Humayun's Tomb,' I wrote the first draft of the poem soon after watching the movie, *Bahadur Shah Zafar: The Last Mughal* (1986), with Ashok Kumar in the role of the emperor. To get my facts right, I began reading the standard histories of the Revolt of 1857 written by both Indian and English historians. In addition, I read contemporary accounts written by English

soldiers involved in the siege of Delhi as well as translations of works by Urdu writers who had witnessed the Revolt. The poem is a narrative of the momentous events that began on May 10, 1857 in Meerut and culminated in the fall of Delhi on September 20, 1857 and the arrest of the emperor, Bahadur Shah II (1775–1862), at Humayun's Tomb the following day by Captain W. S. R. Hodson (1821–58). Here is the poem.

The Arrest of the Last Mughal Emperor at Humayun's Tomb

They came as traders and stayed on as rulers,
grabbing a kingdom here, snapping up a city there.
No one dared to stand up to this juggernaut:
those who did were lashed to the mouths of cannons
and blown away. The last candle of Delhi
was put out by the snarling guns of Canning
and his proconsuls—Lawrence, Nicholson, and Hodson,
who mopped their brows with the tattered flag of the Jumna.
Gone was the color from the face of Red Fort;
the marble pavilions overlaid by barracks, gone.

Every street was desolate and desolate the city,
Shaken to its core by plunder and carnage.
Amid the smoldering ruins, the emperor fled
the palace, when Captain Hodson
with fifty of his sepoys caught up with him
at Humayun's Tomb. Flame-tree and laburnum groves
shaded the garden quartered by graceful canals.
The white marble dome tolled above the din
of the red sandstone, while all around
the dead slept undisturbed in their fretted vaults.

On that fateful September morning,
no cool breezes blew in from the river; no fountains
dreamed of Persia or windswept Samarqand.
To this mausoleum of the House of Temür
came the aged emperor with his young wife
like so many others had before him.
It was here that he was told: 'Your life would be spared
if you yielded yourself prisoner quietly,
but if any attempt was made at a rescue,
you would be shot down on the spot like a dog.'

It was here that His Exalted Majesty gave up his arms.
And with the emperor in tow, Captain Hodson
marched back to the palace gates to hand over
his royal prisoner to General Wilson, who said:
"Well, I'm glad you have got him, but I never
expected to see either him or you again!"
As for the decrepit emperor of Hindostan,
who could only breathe at the company Bahadur's
pleasure, he languished in prison
on an unkempt charpoy, awaiting trial,

crouched on his haunches, rolled in shabby
wraps and razais, a cambric skullcap on his head,
his spirit broken, murmuring verses
from the Quran. Was this the man who had
only four months earlier, 'hurled defiance
upon the race that held every throne in India
in the hollow of its palms?' 'In the end no one
was able to stop his fingers from moving:
'What rotten luck, Zafar! You couldn't get even
two yards of earth for a grave in your beloved's lane.' (2006)

The quotations in stanzas 3 and 4 are cited from W. S. R. Hodson's *Twelve Years of a Soldier's Life in India* (1860). The quotation in stanza 5 is cited from W. H. Russell's *My Diary in India*, vol. 2 (1860). The last two lines are my translation of the final couplet of Zafar's justly famous ghazal, *Lagata Nahin Hai Ji Mera Ujade Dayar Men*:

kitana hai badnasib Zafar dafn ke liye
do gaz zamin bhi na mili ku-e-yar men.

How many times do you revise your work, and are you ever fully satisfied?
I revise my work endlessly. I revise poems written ten or twenty years ago just as I revise poems written last year. The process of revision continues even after a poem has been published. I don't think that a poet is ever satisfied with his work. Every poem remains a 'work in progress.'

What is your experience with the publishing world?
The publisher's role is crucial in making the poet's work available to its potential readers. Not every publisher is interested in poetry. Fiction dominates the marketplace today. Increasingly, it is the university presses, rather than trade publishers, who publish poetry. As a literary editor with Oxford University Press, Chennai and Delhi in the seventies, I helped to initiate the 'New Poetry in India series', which included not only the works of such poets as Nissim Ezekiel and A. K. Ramanujan, but also an anthology, *Ten Twentieth-Century Indian Poets*, that I had edited. The anthology is still in print after thirty years. The fact that it is adopted as a textbook for required study in a course on Indian literature in English explains its long shelf life. The audience for poetry is, however, shrinking. College campuses keep both poets and their poems alive.

How do you deal with the responses of readers and critics?
Readers and critics have a right to read a poem in any way they like. There is no one way to read a poem. The poet's reading is not the only one. Misreadings are also attempts by readers to get a handle on the poem. Once written, the poem has an existence of its own independent of the poet. The poet should not, therefore, tell his readers how to read it.

Who is your ideal reader?
My ideal reader would be a *rasika*, a connoisseur, someone who has an inwardness with language, who has read widely in poetry in many languages and enjoys it, and who believes in the centrality of poetry to our understanding of the human condition.

What is your advice for aspiring poets?
Poetry, as I understand it, is a serious business. If you hope to be a poet, be prepared to give up a lot of things in life. Poetry is a hard and jealous taskmistress who demands total and unswerving dedication. There are no shortcuts. You have to learn the trade of putting words together, day after day, month after month, year after year, till 'words obey your call.' You should have a mind that is open to experience, any experience, a mind that is generous, compassionate, a mind that does

not stoop to anything low and dishonourable, a mind that constantly reflects on what it observes and experiences, a mind that is willing to look inside itself and explore it, however inconvenient or unpleasant it might be and learn from it. Poetry should become the oxygen you breathe daily for survival. Remember, all the poems that you will ever write are inside you, waiting to be written. So listen to yourself.

Saratoga Springs, New York
June 12, 2006

ACTIVITY 12

1. Discuss the following comment made by John Ciardi (Riccio, 213): "Above all else, poetry is performance … the unphrasable and undiminishable life of the poem lies in the way it performs itself through the difficulties it imposes on itself.
2. This is how the contemporary poet Maya Angelou describes her battle with words. Respond to her comments given below .

   I too have often hated words, despised them for their elusive nature. Loathed them for skittering around evading their responsibility to convey meaning. Conversely they have frequently infuriated me by being inert, heavy, ponderous—lying like stones on a page, unwilling to skip, impervious to my prodding.
3. Yeats wrote these lines, in the last century, about the angst of modern life. See if you can add same lines to the ones given below and make your poem speak about the present day:

   Things fall apart; the center cannot hold;
   Mere anarchy is loosed upon the world,
   The blood-dimmed tide is loosed, and everywhere

4. Take a look at this list of emotion/mood words—exhausted, confused, ecstatic, guilty, suspicious, angry, hysterical, frustrated, sad, confident, embarrassed, disgusted, frightened, ashamed, cautious, smug, depressed, overwhelmed, hopeful, lonely, jealous, bored, surprised, anxious, and shocked. Now see if you can find a way to express these abstract nouns through concrete images or ideas. For example,

   Pain is a rusty grey.
   It stinks of smoke and steam arising.
   It tastes of filthy, gritty salt.
   Pain screeches and yells like a steam train through a tunnel.
   It feels like a needle jabbing your heart.
   Pain lives in a hall of bewildering echoes.
   (Bearne 2002: 114)

5. Poetry or more specifically rhyme is used in a lot of advertising jingles. Here are two quatrains – both use the same form and both have rhythm. Read both and see if you would consider both of them as poetry, as we have tried to define it in this unit. Give reasons for your judgment.

   Murphy's beer, Murphy's beer,
   Brings you happiness and cheer;
   See it sparkle, see it foam,
   Take a case of Murphy's home.

(Contd.)

Tyger! Tyger! burning bright
In the forests of the night,
What immortal hand or eye
Could frame thy fearful symmetry?

6. Poems often have not only metaphorical riddles enclosed in them, but also literal ones. Here is one for you to figure out. Each line is one letter of the four-letter word that is the clue to understanding the sense of the poem:

My first is in life (not contained within heart)
My second's in whole but never in part.
My third's in forever, but also in vain.
My last's in ending, why not in pain?
Liz Lochhead

Writing Verse for Children

We will look now at some of the things to keep in mind when writing verse for children. One of the things we said earlier was that the poem basically has two people in it—you the poet, and the reader. While writing for children, we need to remember that they are our readers and so while the poems will use all the theories discussed above, they will be formed differently.

Stories and poems for children have a long history and lullabies were probably being sung to babies even before a lot of languages that exist today were even invented. In the early days, most children's literature would have been didactic—intended to teach the child about manners or morals, mathematics or the alphabet.

Here is a Cinquain—a five line poem where the number of words is fixed. The first line is a single word—a subject/noun, the second line has two adjectives that describe it, the third line has three verbs that relate to it, the fourth line has four abstract nouns that describe feelings, the fifth line has one word that is a synonym for it:

Triangles
Pointy Edges
Revolving, Rotating, Angling
Triangles are all Different
180°
(Teams Educational Resources)

In 1744 one of the earliest children's books A *Little Pretty Pocket Book* was published by John Newbery and had rhymes, stories, children's games and a free gift of a ball and a pincushion! It was an instant hit and as the gifts indicate, the publisher tried to combine work and pleasure, the serious and the comic. The earliest books for children had the moral embedded in lots of action and often horrific descriptions of witches and murderers. The earliest verse forms for children were of course Nursery Rhymes. As the name indicates these were simple rhymes composed for the nursery and sung to the children who memorized them. Most were sung to accompany games or at bedtime and had a simple vocabulary and rhyme for easy memorization.

Humpty Dumpty sat on a wall,
Humpty Dumpty had a great fall –
All the king's horses and all the king's men
Couldn't put Humpty Dumpty together again.

While very young readers were read to and mostly listened to nursery rhymes or lullabies, older children read stories and poems. Even though, not necessarily written for them, they had characters in them with whom they could identify, other young children, and also lots of action. After Newbery's book, the next poetry bestsellers for children were Robert Louis Stevenson's *A Child's Garden of Verses* published in 1885, Walter de la Mare's *Peacock Pie* (1913) and T. S. Eliot's *Old Possum's Book of Practical Cats* (1939). While the poems in these collections had stories, games, counting, lullabies and prayers, and riddles and tongue twisters; another kind of verse being written at the time was sentimental verses for and about children. What all these books had in common was the belief that childhood should be protected from all unpleasantness and there should always be 'a happily ever after' in verse and prose.

By the fourth decade of the twentieth century, a lot of this had changed and writers began exploring new themes and the fantasy quotient of the narrative was at its highest.

Themes and Types

Let us now look at some popular children's poems to see what appeals to young readers. Where do poems for children come from?
From Riddles and Spells; From Questions; From School And Maths And the Alphabet; From the Playground; From Sounds; From Happy Days; From Sad Days; From Nature; From Animals – in other words from anywhere and everywhere. The more vivid your imagination the more fun the poem will be. Just take the world as you know it and turn it upside down!

Topsy-Turvy Land

The people walk upon their heads
The sea is made of sand,
The children go to school by night,
In Topsy-Turvy Land.

The front-door step is at the back,
You're walking when you stand,
You wear your hat upon your feet,
In Topsy-Turvy Land.

And buses on the sea you'll meet,
While pleasure boats are planned
To travel up and down the streets
Of Topsy-Turvy Land.

You pay for what you never get,
I think it must be grand,

For when you go you're coming back,
In Topsy-Turvy Land.
—H. E. Wilkinson

Imagine yourself as something you are not – the further away from the living world the better—the child's world is anthropomorphic and if you can see yourself as a *Teabag*, a great poem is on its way.

Teabag

I'd like to be a teabag,
and stay at home all day
and talk to other teabags
in a teabag sort of way.

I'd love to be a teabag,
and lie in a little box
and never have to wash my face
or change my dirty socks.

I'd like to be a Tetley bag,
an Earl Grey one perhaps,
and doze all day and lie around
with Earl Grey kind of chaps.

I wouldn't have to do a thing,
no homework, jobs or chores -
just lie inside a comfy box
of teabags and their snores.

I wouldn't have to do exams,
I needn't tidy rooms,
or sweep the floor, or feed the cat
or wash up all the spoons.

I wouldn't have to do a thing –
A life of bliss you see...
except that once in all my life
I'd make a cup of tea.
—Peter Dixon

The world inhabited by children is a fairy tale one where the imagination has free play and the line between fantasy and reality is barely visible. See what Roald Dahl has done to this fairy tale, keeping his readers, the children of the twenty first century, in mind. Notice how he has used rhyme to great comic effect and the rhythm of the poem comes from the narrative that moves forward at a breathless pace.

Snow-White and the Seven Dwarfs

When little Snow-White's mother died,
The king, her father, up and cried,
"Oh, what a nuisance! What a life!
Now I must find another wife!"

(It's never easy for a king
To find himself that sort of thing.)
He wrote to every magazine
And said, "I'm looking for a Queen!"
At least ten thousand girls replied
And begged to be the royal bride.
The king said with a shifty smile,
'I'd like to give each one a trial.'

However in the end he chose
A lady called Miss Machalose,
Who brought along a curious toy
That seemed to give her endless joy –
This was a mirror framed in brass,
A MAGIC TALKING LOOKING GLASS.
Ask it something day or night,
It always got the answer right
For instance if you were to say,
'Oh Mirror, what's for lunch today?'
The thing would answer in a trice,
'Today it's scrambled eggs and rice.'
Now every day, week in week out,
The spoiled and stupid Queen would shout,
'Oh Mirror Mirror on the wall
Who is the fairest of them all?'
The Mirror answered every time,
'Oh Madam, you're the Queen sublime.
You are the only one to charm us
Queen, you're the cat's pyjamas.'
For ten whole years the silly Queen
Repeated this absurd routine.
Then suddenly, one awful day,
She heard the Magic Mirror say,
'From now on, Queen, you're Number Two,
Snow-White is prettier than you!'

The Queen went absolutely wild.
She yelled 'I'm going to scrag that child!
I'll cook her flaming goose! I'll skin 'er!
I'll have her rotten guts for dinner!'
She called the Huntsman to her study,
She shouted at him, 'Listen buddy!
You drag that filthy girl outside,
And see you take her for a ride!
Thereafter split her ribs apart
And bring me back her bleeding heart!'

The Huntsman dragged the lovely child
Deep deep into the forests wild.
Fearing the worst, poor Snow-White spake,
She cried, 'Oh please give me a break!'

The knife was poised, the arm was strong,
She cried again, 'I've done no wrong!'
The Huntsman's heart began to flutter,
It melted like a pound of butter.
He murmured, 'Okay, beat it, Kid.'
And you can bet your life she did.

Later, the Huntsman made a stop
Within the local butcher's shop,
And there he bought for safety's sake,
A bullock's heart and one nice steak.
'Oh Majesty! Oh Queen! He cried,
That rotten girl has just died!
And just to prove I didn't cheat,
I've brought along these bits of meat.'
The Queen cried out, 'Bravissimo!
I trust you killed her nice and slow.'
Then (this is the disgusting part)
The Queen sat down and ate the heart!
(I only hope she cooled it well.
Boiled heart can be as tough as hell.)

While all of this was going on,
Oh where, oh where, had Snow-White gone?
She'd found it easy, being pretty,
To hitch a ride into the city,
And there she'd got a job unpaid
As general cook and parlour-maid
With seven funny little men,
Each one not more than three foot ten.

Ex horse-race jockeys, all of them,
These Seven Dwarfs, though awfully nice,
Were guilty of one shocking vice –
They squandered all of their resources
At the race-track backing horses.
(When they hadn't backed a winner
None of them got any dinner.)
One evening, Snow-White said, 'Look here,
I think I've got a great idea,
Just leave it all to me okay?
And no more gambling till I say.'

That very night, at eventide,
Young Snow-White hitched another ride,
And then, when it was very late,
She slipped in through the Palace gate.
The King was in his counting house
Counting out his money.
The Queen was in the parlour
Eating bread and honey.

The footmen and the servants slept
So no one saw her as she crept
On tip-toe through the mighty hall
And grabbed THE MIRROR off the wall.

As soon as she had got it home
She told the senior Dwarf (or Gnome)
To ask it what he wished to know
'Go on!' she shouted. 'Have a go!'
He said, 'Oh Mirror, please don't joke!
Which horse will win tomorrow's race,
The Ascot Gold Cup Steeplechase?'
The Mirror whispered sweet and low,
'The horse's name is Mistletoe'
The Dwarfs went absolutely daft,
They kissed young Snow-White fore and aft,
They rushed away to raise some dough
With which to back old Mistletoe.

They pawned their watches, sold the car,
They borrowed money near and far,
(For much of it they had to thank
The manager of Barclays Bank.)
They went to Ascot and of course
For once they backed the winning horse
Thereafter, every single day,
The Mirror made the bookies pay
Each Dwarf and Snow-White got a share,
And each was soon a millionaire.
Which shows that gambling's not a sin
Provided that you always win.

ACTIVITY 13

Which is your favourite children's story? See if you can rewrite it as a poem, using any of the forms you have learned about.

The Ten Commandments of Crafting Verse for Young Readers

While it is interesting to know how and where children's verse started and the kinds of themes that have been popular, we are concerned here with the crafting of verse for children and will begin by looking at some dos and don'ts.

- Never preach to your reader—the first rule then is work with the theme and not the moral.
- Always write for yourself as well as your young reader—good children's verse appeals to all age groups.
- Don't be obsessed about vocabulary levels—children will read what interests and delights them—if they don't understand a word or two, so what?

- Remember a poem is a word puzzle—if you did not have fun putting it together, your readers won't enjoy solving it either.
- Think of your audience—what stage of development are they at? What are their concerns? What kinds of peer and parental/family pressure do they face?
- Think of the verse as a soundtrack. Use lots of alliteration, assonance, onomatopoeia, sibilance, consonance, delightful sound clusters and tongue-twisting syllables. Your readers should be able to taste the words on their tongues and delight in the noise of the words. Make sure you suit your rhythm and melody to the sense—alliteration speeds up the rhythm and makes the poem dance with joy, assonance slows down the rhythm and is better used for a more serious subject.
- Try a few traditional verse forms and see what you can do with them—while in adult verse we look for surprises—places where the meter breaks down, the pleasure of nursery rhymes and nonsense verse derives from its predictability—we may not know what the word means, but can guess which sound will follow.
- Think of the verse as an image track. Avoid abstract language and from your surroundings use as many concrete images as you can. Pay attention to the point of view and the eye of the camera and focus on what you can see with your naked eye and poet's vision.
- Try lexical ambiguity and oxymorons
- Think of rhythm as pulling the reader across the page—don't write long droning lines unless you are writing a lullaby.

Let us now look at what Sampurna Chatterji, a Bombay-based poet, short-fiction writer and translator, has to say.

The Problem with Writing Poetry

In January this year, I attended a seminar on 'Poetry for Young Audiences' organized by the Sahitya Akademi in association with the Max Mueller Bhavan and Loquations, a Bombay-based reading circle. As the discussion began on the participants' personal experiences of writing, reading or teaching poetry, a number of concerns gradually became apparent.

One, where was the poetry being written specifically for young people in English? As the students lamented, the poems being taught in the English class, be it at school or junior college level, ran the risk of seeming fossilized. The lack of context and the inability to relate to the poems in the syllabus seemed to be a common problem.

Two, how was poetry being taught? To understand a poem seemed to mean being able to paraphrase it. Where was the joy in the language, the pleasure of hearing poetry spoken out loud, and the resonance of communication?

Three, who was publishing new poetry written specifically for young audiences?

Clearly these and other vexing questions were a terrain fraught with pitfalls, some of which made me think of my own interactions with young people over poetry.

In July 2005, I was invited to conduct a session on images in poetry for a group of college students who were doing a film workshop and being taught the basics of editing and would make their own film, using archival material on Mumbai city. I had been asked to help them see that images are not the currency of the audio-visual medium alone, that poets use images in different complex ways. Use, seek, assimilate, construct, preserve, focus, frame. I decided to choose my words from a vocabulary that they might understand. We talked about images, silences and pauses. We talked of things difficult to capture through image-as-word, loss, transience, and exile. Poetry as tactile, breathing reality, tangential, symbolic, specific. And when I asked them why they thought no one reads poetry, they said, because it requires you to think. It takes time to understand, it's not easy. People are afraid. At the same time, we also talked about how infectious the joy of good poetry is.

At a workshop this May at the Prithvi, which I called 'A Poem in Five Acts', for thirteen to sixteen year-olds, I set out to make poetry a bit of all that it didn't seem to be— real, accessible, enjoyable and doable. Realizing also that the young poet is burdened with received notions of what poetry should be, my attempt was to make them arrive at other kinds of conclusions about the writing of poetry. The notion, for example, that poetry should be 'inspiring' or 'deep' or full of words like 'magnificent', 'extravagant', 'doomed' and 'divine'. Through a series of exercises and poems, I could see them relishing and realizing the fact that poems can be conversational, inhabit different personas and speak in different registers. Or the notion that poetry had to be rhymed, had to be written in neat little stanzas, and had to be a specific length. With all of these notions being challenged through the poems that we read, I could see it taking hold—the excitement of having the freedom to write a poem in 'one's own voice'. But not all at once. Very often, I could see at the writing stage how the tussle between 'sounding like a poet' and 'me, aged 20' muddied the clear and luminous line with clichés and borrowed phrases and images. Here was the age old tussle between poetry as something abstract and out of reach versus poetry as something direct, approachable and rooted.

Getting Down to Writing Poetry

No one can actually teach you to write poetry. You will learn best by reading and writing poems. But you have been introduced to techniques and types and also seen how careful your crafting has to be to achieve authenticity of expression.

Some Themes

Nature is a favourite theme with poets since it offers an abundant resource of ideas and images. If you are planning to write a 'nature poem', begin by going out and exploring it in its abundant variety. Some of the things that nature offers to us are: it stimulates our sensory perceptions, and symbolizes permanence and tranquility. Your poem with nature as its setting and theme should relate to human emotions, be expressed in simple language and have images that are taken from the world of nature. Since practically the beginning of literary criticism, nature has been seen as central to the art and craft of poetry since poetry is, in the words of Dryden, 'the image of nature'. In this context, nature includes rocks, streams and hills that men can admire, live among and fancifully rearrange, but also human nature that is universal in certain fundamental ways.

Social issues are also the subject matter of many poems whose interest is with the society and milieu in which they are located and from where they emanate. These poems normally adopt one of two stances – firstly, the universalizing of a topical occurrence;

secondly, the particularizing of a universal phenomenon. The subject matter of these poems is the environment we live in – social, political, economic, religious, etc.

Romantic Themes abound in poetry and such poems are characterized by a sense of wonder, mystery, subjectivity, emotional involvement, infinity and freedom. Romantic poems normally talk about nature, love, memories of the past, etc. A 'poetic' description of this kind of poetry can be found in this section of T. S. Eliot's *Preludes*

I am moved by fancies that are curled
Around these images, and cling:
To the notion of some infinitely gentle
Infinitely suffering thing.

> A language is a system of verbal signs by means of which humans can communicate with one another, one of its outstanding features is that these signs have content, refer to the world of experience, and stand for things. Ordinarily this is the feature of greatest use, and everyday language functions in the main as a way of transaction: to pass something on from one person to the next. Its content is what matters. We must now think of language in poetry as having somehow escaped the servitude under which language toils in everyday life. It is as though language had long nourished an ambition to be, itself, the subject of the transaction rather than the means, as though somehow this were the goal which the inherent logic of its nature made desirable, despite the fact that by far the greatest proportion of language, however, is measured, continues without any appearance of strain to function referentially, as indicated above. Poetry is language that asserts itself. … Poetry is refractory, opaque, durable. Using materials from the verbal traffic of everyday life, poetry manages to secure for them exemption from the common fate of language. It is not even defeated by our lack of complete understanding … it prevents this easy transaction by perpetually withholding some indefinable remainder of its meaning, forcing us to come back to the language again and again. …Having placed ourselves within the charmed circle, we can share in the feeling of achievement, even though we are in some sense the victims. For language is a human achievement, and poetry is language triumphant (Wheeler, 30-31).

Our proposal is that you don't worry too much about 'correct' and 'wrong' definitions or methods, but give yourselves plenty of opportunities to discover for yourself what kind of poems you like and what you don't and also take time to work out why. We also think you need to begin with models to work from and say what you want to say in whatever form you choose. (Bearne 2002: 108)

Let's Write a Poem

Step 1: Start with an idea, an object, an experience, a person, a memory, a phrase, an image or even a word. What sort of poem will it be? Long or short? Lyric, Narrative or Dramatic? Sonnet, Haiku, Syllabic? An experimental gamble? Who are your readers? Sometimes the answers to these and other initial questions will not be visible at the beginning. You will find yourself working with and on the material before recognizing what shape the poem is going to take. Keep yourself open, intellectually and emotionally.

Step 2: Get your raw material into some kind of temporary organization so that you can grapple with it. You've responded to the initial impulse, prompted by what seeded the poem in you. Now you have to struggle to achieve a rough shape and sketchy sequence, even if these change completely later.

Step 3: Write down your tentative lines and find words to express what you want to say and decide how you want to say it.

- How would you like to open – directly, by indicating clearly what is to follow; obliquely, so that the reader is shocked/surprised later; dramatically, so that attention is drawn to your poem right at the outset; with an image that can be expanded or changed later; or, casually and conversationally, so that you have the freedom to move in whatever direction the poem takes you?
- What kind of lines will you write in – long or short or a combination of both?
- How will you develop your theme – through metaphors and other figures of speech, through language, or in some other way?
- How will your poem end?

Step 4: Read the poem to yourself. Does it have substance? Does it have a shape that looks authentic enough? Is there some kind of unity? Does it make sense? Does it seem to move logically to its ending? You now have a full-fledged first draft.

Step 5: Revise by yourself and discuss the poem in your group and then revise again. Keep doing this till it 'sounds' right.

Remember, a poem is many things at the same time: an expression of emotion, a felt experience, a performance and a created illusion. How can these ineffable things be communicated? Feeling, by itself, does not make a poem. A poem cannot be written without it of course, but depth of emotion alone does not make a poem. Neither do craft and skill. You have already come equipped with feeling and sensitivity and the skills you have acquired help you incorporate these into your poem. The tension in your poem will come from the conflicts of your created situation, event, whatever else you've decided as your vehicle. The dynamics will evolve from your progression, pacing, pattern development and intensification. Tone and mood come from your word meanings, styles of diction, assonance and dissonance. But finally, what counts is the effect of the poem as a whole. (Riccio 1980: 209–225) The art of poetry does not come from skillfully putting words together to give information or express emotion. The art evolves from a skilled arrangement of language to realize its greatest power, to use words in a manner and combination that have never been done before and yet seem so 'right'.

Happy Writing!

WORKSHOP 1: Practice

Given below are the opening stanzas of two poems. Complete the poems, using the same form as far as possible.

Love Poem

When I was one-and-twenty
I heard an old man say:
Give crowns and pounds and guineas
But not your heart away.

Now I am.......................

A Life

At three he was sober

At six he was drunk, a robber
In a fantasy train

He went on ....

WORKSHOP 2: Share and Learn

Read out the poem you composed in Workshop 1 to the other members of your tutorial group who should respond with questions, comments, etc.

WORKSHOP 3: Create

Using one of the words given below, think of a possible poem Keep the points given as Step 3 of 'Getting Down to Writing Poetry', in mind, and discuss your idea with your group. Compose a poem for your portfolio.

DEW CHOCOLATE CRIMSON PHOTOGRAPH LOVE SWIM SILENCE

While you are reading through your draft, there are many things to think about.

Here are some questions that may help you.

Language

- Do you repeat some words too often?
- Is any of the phrasing awkward?
- Are there too many overused adjectives—nice, lovely, beautiful, etc.?
- Are you using clichés (unoriginal phrases) that could be changed?
- Are you using metaphors or similes? Are there too many?
- Do your rhymes work well? Are you using words just for the sake of rhyme?

Image

- Are you painting a full picture for your reader?
- Are your descriptions too vague and unclear?

Structure

- Do you have a good beginning, middle and end?
- Does the opening grab your attention and make you want to go on?
- Have you got the best possible opening line or stanza?

Rhythm

- Do the words, phrases and lines flow?
- How well does it read out loud?
- Is the rhythm working well overall?
- Do you keep the same rhythm throughout?

General

- Are your lines the right length?
- Should the poem be in a different form?
- Is the poem too complicated?
- Is the title right?
- Is the poem original in any way?
- Is there anything in the poem you don't need?
- Does the poem do what you want it to do?
- Will the poem make sense to the reader?
- How will the reader respond to this?
- What are the strengths and weaknesses of the poem?

The Next Step

- How can it be improved?
- What needs to be done next?

If you have gone through this checklist and you are not sure what needs to be done next, leave your poem for a while and come back to it later.

(Bearne 2002: 118)

SECTION II: FICTION

Fiction

We have all enjoyed stories about human beings who we will never meet in real life; about places that are not on the map; about animals who talk; about fairies and demons. Fiction (from the Latin fictio, 'a shaping, a counterfeiting') is a name for stories not entirely factual but at least partially shaped, made up, imagined (Kennedy 1991).

However, fiction cannot be merely defined as a story that is not 'true'. The relationship of fiction with real life events is not a straightforward one. It is not as though fiction has nothing to do with reality. People often exclaim after reading a good novel: 'It is so life-like' or they might complain after reading a bad story, 'It doesn't work; it is not believable.'

Fiction needs to relate to real life but not necessarily through 'facts'.

> In fiction the 'facts' may or may not be true and a story is none the worse for their being entirely imaginary. We expect from fiction a sense of how people act, not an authentic chronicle of how, at some past time, a few people acted (Ibid).

As fiction is more about insight into life and events than about facts, works of fantasy are also classified under it. We read fiction both for pleasure and instruction but the kind of instruction fiction imparts is different from that provided by books of history or sociology.

Non-Fiction

There is a view that story telling is as old as human communication. We relate to each other through stories: stories about what happened to us and our loved ones this morning or years ago, what we hope and wish for, what we dread. Some people are better at making stories than others. Some stories—although interesting and enjoyable—may indeed be factual.

In recent times 'creative non-fiction' has emerged as a separate category of creative writing. As the nomenclature suggests it deals with real life events narrated imaginatively. Frank McCourt's memoir *Angela's Ashes* (1996) is an excellent example of what is meant by creative non-fiction. Frank McCourt was brought up in the slums of Limerick, Ireland.

> Frank's mother, Angela, has no money to feed the children since Frank's father Malachy, rarely works, and when he does he drinks his wages. Yet Malachy does nurture in Frank an appetite for the one thing he can provide: a story.
>
> Perhaps it is a story that accounts for Frank's survival. Wearing shoes repaired with tires, begging a pig's head for Christmas dinner, and searching the pubs for his father, Frank endures poverty, near-starvation and the casual cruelty of relatives and neighbours—yet lives to tell his tale with eloquence, exuberance and remarkable forgiveness (Blurb of Simon & Schuster edition).
>
> McCourt writes in *Angela's Ashes:*
> When I look back on my childhood I wonder how I managed to survive at all. It was, of course, a miserable childhood: the happy childhood is hardly worth your while. Worse than the ordinary miserable childhood is the miserable Irish childhood, and worse yet is the miserable Irish Catholic childhood.

Truman Capote, the famous American writer is credited with having invented the genre of creative non-fiction with his chilling non-fiction novel *In Cold Blood* (1965).

> If all Truman Capote did was invent a new genre—journalism written with the language and structure of literature—this 'nonfiction novel' about the brutal slaying of the Clutter family by two would-be robbers would be remembered as a trail-blazing experiment that has influenced countless writers. But Capote achieved more than that. He wrote a true masterpiece of creative nonfiction. The images of this tale continue to resonate in our minds: 16-year-old Nancy Clutter teaching a friend how to bake a cherry pie, Dick Hickock's black '49 Chevrolet sedan, Perry Smith's Gibson guitar and his dreams of gold in a tropical paradise—the blood on the walls and the final 'thud-snap' of the rope-broken necks.[1]

Non-fiction is defined by its fidelity to facts; it may occasionally touch the borders of journalism. Fiction, on the other hand, is a looser category that embraces both facts and fiction. Many autobiographical novels that are based on 'facts'—like D. H. Lawrence's *Sons and Lovers*—are classified under 'fiction'.

[1] Editorial review of *In Cold Blood* from Amazon.com http://www.amazon.com

ACTIVITY 14

1. Describe the relationship between fact and fiction on the basis of a novel you have read.
2. Define creative non-fiction. With examples from a creative non-fiction text that you have read describe the criteria that distinguish it from fiction.

Fiction and the 20th Century

Stories used to have a beginning, middle, and an end. Often there would be a 'moral' to them. Generally they had characters the reader could empathize with; and plots that were discernible. But that was earlier. Today, fiction is vast and complex: some stories still look like this but a lot of fiction poses a challenge to the reader's intellect. The stories of the progress of fiction worldwide are too many to be narrated here. But we can try to pick up some relevant episodes from its long and multitudinous history in English.

In the realm of English fiction in the eighteenth century we hear of two kinds of writing: romance (stories about the 'ideal') and realism (stories about life as it is). Romance—which was the older form and included both prose and verse narratives—sought to please the reader with 'tales of horror and adventure'; with stories of 'far far away and 'once upon a time' and later on with 'tales of love'. It dealt with heroes and villains. Realism was concerned with 'social or historical change'. So realistic fiction attempts to picture society as it is and human beings as they are.

Gradually realism came to be thought of as 'High' art and reading and writing of romance came to be considered 'Low'. We will discuss this distinction further in the present day categorization of fiction as 'Literary' and 'Popular'. By the nineteenth century realism was established as the mode associated with the novel.

In the twentieth century the two world wars, emergence of new nations, scientific and technological advancement, and radical experimentation in the arts brought about radical changes in the English novel. With modernist experimentations, between 1900–1940, the territory of fiction expanded considerably. Of course the process of change had started even earlier. Challenges had begun coming in to the hegemony of realism by the end of the nineteenth century. One of them was 'impressionism'. The term impressionism is associated more with painting. It may be explained as, 'A style in painting developed in France in the late nineteenth century that uses colour to show the effects of light on things and to suggest atmosphere rather than showing exact details.'

Impressionistic literature can basically be defined as when an author centers his story/attention on the character's mental life such as the character's impressions, feelings, sensations and emotions, rather than trying to interpret them. Realistic fiction would describe the appearance and thought process of the characters with great authority. Such details were left out or left to the imagination of the reader in impressionistic fiction. Thus, suggesting rather than telling was the order of the day as far as literary impressionism is concerned.

Celebrated novelists of this period are supposed to have been influenced by impressionistic painters. Joseph Conrad's novels *Heart of Darkness* and *Lord Jim* written in the early twentieth century show the influence of the painter Turner. Cezanne, another impressionist painter influenced Ernest Hemingway the author of *A Farewell to Arms* and *For Whom the Bell Tolls*.

Modernist literature also owes a lot to developments in psychology. Sigmund Freud changed the way people think about the human mind. Freud brought in the concept of the unconscious mind and established the fact that the individual is not always in complete control of his or her thoughts and desires. Modernist fiction expressed internal conflict of individuals. A good example is "stream of consciousness" writing where one thought or word would lead to the next. In Virginia Woolf's *Mrs Dalloway* and James Joyce's *Portrait of the Artist as a Young Man* the subjectivity of the individual is being tapped without any consideration to the beginning, middle, or end of the story.

After 1941 and especially after World War II in 1945 the individual becomes redundant in 'Post-modern Fiction'. Internal conflict began to be avoided in favor of a more complex consciousness. The tortured, isolated anti-heroes of the modernists make way in post-modern writing for the self-consciously deconstructed and self-reflexive narrators of novels by Vladimir Nabokov, John Fowles, John Barth, Julian Barnes or Salman Rushdie. In Salman Rushdie's *Midnight's Children* the protagonist is by no means like any human being we know. He is at best a collection of fragments.

The Importance of History

If we were to pick up a 19th century realistic novel like Jane Austen's *Pride and Prejudice* and contrast it with a contemporary post-modernist novel like Toni Morrison's *Beloved* we will see a difference not only in the concerns of the story but also a marked evolution in the way it is told. We would have to work much harder to 'understand' the latter and it is entirely possible that we may find the reading of it far more rewarding. Are we saying that Austen is irrelevant to a student who is trying to write in the present time?

Socio-political factors determine the way we tell stories and Morrison's world is necessarily more complex than Austen's. But Jane Austen has definitely not become irrelevant as is evident from her presence not only in English Literature syllabi but also in popular cinema. In fact both romances of the eighteenth century and realistic novels of the nineteenth are extremely popular even today. For instance, Indian writers of realistic fiction (like Vikram Seth) have acknowledged the influence of nineteenth century masters on their work.

When we teach ourselves how to write fiction it would be helpful to keep the history of fiction down to the present time in our minds and read as much as we can from both contemporary and earlier works. We may get our inspiration from any period and our writing will only be enriched if we know what has been attempted before.

We give below (Box 3.6) a list[2]—by no means exhaustive—of the possible types of novels that have been written.

---

[2] Adapted and modified from *A Little Bit About Novels* by Renée Goodvin <http://literaryexplorer.blondelibrarian.net/novel.html>

BOX 3.5: TYPES OF NOVELS

Realistic Novel
A fictional attempt to give the effect of reality. A realistic novel can be characterized by its complex characters with mixed motives that are rooted in social class and operate according to a highly developed social structure. The characters in a realistic novel interact with other characters and undergo plausible and everyday experiences. For example, Jane Austen's *Pride and Prejudice* deals with the manners and morals of 19th Century landed gentry.

Prose Romance
This is a novel that is often set in the historical past with a plot that emphasizes adventure and an atmosphere that is removed from reality. The characters in a prose romance are sharply drawn as villains or heroes, masters or victims, while the protagonist is solitary and isolated from society. For example, Charlotte Bronte's classic romance novel *Jane Eyre.* The story is that of a governess, Jane Eyre. Despite her plainness, she captures the heart of her enigmatic employer, Edward Rochester, but soon discovers he has a secret that could jeopardize any hope of happiness between them.

Novel of Incident
In a novel of incident the narrative focuses on what the protagonist will do next and how the story will turn out. Agatha Christie's *Murder on the Orient Express,* where the detective Hercule Poirot investigates the mysterious murder of a passenger, is typical of the genre.

Novel of Character
A novel of character focuses on the protagonist's motives for what he/she does and how he/she will turn out. For example, Henry James's *Portrait of a Lady* is the story of a spirited young American woman, Isabel Archer, who 'affronts her destiny' and finds it overwhelming.

Epistolary Novel
This first person narrative progresses in the form of letters, journals, or diaries. For example, Jean Webster's *Daddy Long Legs* where a young orphan being sponsored by a mysterious benefactor, writes letters to him, telling him about her life.

Picaresque Novel
A picaresque novel relates the adventures of an eccentric or disreputable hero in episodic form. For example, Daniel Defoe's *The Fortunes and Misfortunes of the famous Moll Flanders* in which Moll Flanders is a successful thief.

Historical Novel
A historical novel is a novel set in a period earlier than that of the writing. For example, Paul Scott's *Jewel in the Crown* published in 1966, is set in Pre-Independence India, and evokes the atmosphere of the Raj.

Regional Novel
A regional novel is a novel that is set against the background of a particular area. For example, Thomas Hardy's *Return of the Native* is set mainly in the semi-imaginary county of Wessex, which is based on the English county of Essex.

Non-fictional Novel
This type of novel depicts living people and recent events fictionalized in the form of a story. For example, Truman Capote's *In Cold Blood*

(Contd.)

Bildungsroman
German term that indicates a novel of growth. This fictional biography is concerned with the development of the protagonist's mind, spirit, and character from childhood to adulthood. For example, Charles Dickens's eponymous novel *David Copperfield.*

Roman à thèse
French term that refers to a social novel that has an argument, social, or political message. For example, in Victor Hugo's *Les Miserables* the two central themes are the moral redemption of its main character, Jean Valjean, an ex-convict, and the moral redemption of a nation (France) through revolution.

Roman à clef
French term for a novel with a key; imaginary events with real people disguised as fictional characters. Eg. Shashi Tharoor's *Great Indian Novel* is a re-interpretation of the *Mahabharata* framed in India's struggle for independence, and the political aftermath of colonization, where well-known contemporary personages make their appearances under altered names

Roman-fleuve
French term for a narrative that has a common theme or range of characters that stretch across a number of novels. For example, P.G. Wodehouse's Jeeves series.

Graphic Novel
A graphic novel is a long-form work in the comics style, usually with a lengthy and complex storyline, and often aimed at mature audiences. This is a recent form, a little over 25 years old. It is becoming popular in India, and Sarnath Bannerjee's *Corridor* is credited with being the first Indian graphic novel.

ACTIVITY 15

1. Consult an encyclopaedia and write a paragraph on Impressionistic Art
2. Make a list of ten modernist and post modernist novels giving their years of publication.
3. Find a definition of 'realism' from a literary encyclopaedia and make a list of five Indian novels written between 1947–2006 that fit the bill.

Literary and Popular Fiction

The discussion above about literary impressionism, modernism and post modernism and most of the examples cited pertain basically to what publishers would call literary fiction, Romance on the other hand would be classified under popular fiction. The publishing industry worldwide makes a distinction between literary fiction and popular or commercial fiction.

The modern literary story and novel may be abstract and difficult to figure out; but popular fiction works differently. Ann Maxwell and Elizabeth Lowell observe:

> In popular fiction the only critics who really matter are the readers who pay money to buy books of their own choice. Reviews are irrelevant to sales. Readers of popular fiction judge an author by his or her ability to make the common language uncommonly meaningful, and to make an often-told tale freshly exciting. The amount of

> effort a reader puts into this fiction is minimal. That after all, is the whole point: to entertain readers rather than to exercise them.

The writers complain in the same article,

> Through the years I've discovered that most publishers talk highly of literary fiction and make money on popular fiction; yet asking them to describe the difference between literary and popular fiction is like asking when white becomes gray becomes black.

Publishers may be forgiven for not being able to articulate it, as the difference between literary and popular would run into many tomes of theory. We too will not spend too much time in trying to distinguish between what are basically fluid categories. Popular and literary overlap and intermix. A popular text may well elbow its way into the literary category (Jules Verne's work is a classic example); a literary text may be a bestseller (Toni Morrison's *Beloved*). Yet the distinction is worth making, if only to remind us that there can be no fixed rules for fiction.

Popular literature needs to sell. When publishers package texts as popular they have the market in mind. The following have a vibrant market:

> Popular romance: Love stories. Like Mills and Boon.
>
> Chicklit: Emerged as a distinct genre in the 1990s with the publication of Helen Fielding's *Bridget Jones's Diary.* About young women in metropolitan settings. Airy and irreverent in tone.
>
> Science fiction: Usually futuristic; called Sci-fi. Inspired by science and technological advancements. Like Arthw Clarke's novels.
>
> Writing for children: Like the Harry Potter series.
>
> Thrillers: Novels with action heroes. Like the James Bond series.
>
> Detective Fiction: Crime stories with detectives who solve the mystery; sometimes called 'whodunits'. Like Agatha Christie's novels.

The sales of such books—even without the help of positive critical reviews—are astronomical. *Gone with the Wind* published in 1936 is a good example. This mother of all modern romances, often derided for its 'unremarkable' prose by the literary establishment, had sold 28 million copies by 1993.

Some critics call popular fiction *formula fiction* or *genre fiction* although writers and publishers hotly deny that there can be a formula to popular fiction. In our view, formula is indeed central to popular fiction, as is the related concept of the target readership. For example Romance (Formula: boy meets girl; there are problems; problems are resolved through 'true love') is targeted for women. In the U.S.A you don't have to go to a bookstore to buy romances; the superstore from where housewives pick up grocery would stock romances. In our country the market for popular fiction in English is still untapped. However, a new book by Shobha De is likely to be sold with magazines like the Cosmopolitan at traffic lights unlike books by Salman Rushdie or Amitav Ghosh that would be packaged far more gravely.

We must not make the mistake of underestimating the importance of popular fiction. The sheer number of readers popular fiction attracts makes it a significant marker of culture. Also to new writers it is heartening to know that there is a place for all kinds of writing. The student would have to discover his\her potential. The student may go on to write highly abstract stories, realistic stories or detective stories, sci-fi, crime fiction or romance. There is also a chance that the student might write something in-between: a literary detective story, for instance. Hard work and insights into characterization, plot, milieu, setting, etc., would be required for all kinds of writing.

ACTIVITY 16

1. Try to find Indian examples of popular romance, detective fiction, spy thriller, science fiction, and children's fiction.
2. Read and discuss a work of popular fiction.

The Short Story and the Novel

There are many types of fiction. We have all heard of the novel and the short story; the former being long, the latter short. The difference between the two forms has been theorised and we will deal with it later. Various sources identify other intermediate and extreme types, based on length:

- Epic: A work of 200,000 words or more.
- Novel: A work of 60,000 words or more.
- Novella: A work of at least 17,500 words but under 60,000 words.
- Novelette: A work of at least 7,500 words but under 17,500 words.
- Short story: A work of at least 2,000 words but under 7,500 words. (1,000 words minimum by some definitions).
- Flash fiction: A work of less than 2,000 words. (1,000 by some definitions).

Some may complain that differentiating between forms like novella and novelette or flash fiction and short story would be to indulge in making distinctions without difference; and that the epic is a misnomer where bestsellers like *The World According to Garp* (John Irving) are meant. But the classification is useful for new writers who are trying to decide the ideal length of their fictions or for those who are looking for publishing avenues.

The difference between short stories and novels is not only about the number of words. The stylish works of Chekhov, Joyce, Hemingway, Faulkner, etc. have given a distinct identity to the short story. The short story today is a sophisticated literary form that according to Tobias Wolff invites passion and reverence from the reader. Moreover, Wolff observes:

> But beyond passion, beyond reverence there is a certain tone we use in discussing short stories that we do not use about novels. It is a tone close to that of shared confidence, even occasionally confession, as if the moments we recall from certain stories arise from our own experience….. And that may be the particular power of the short story-the way it imitates memory. (*On Writing Short Stories* Ed Tom Bailey.)

V. S. Pritchett as quoted by Francine Prose in her article 'What Makes a Short Story?' in the same book gives an elegant and incisive formulation:

> The novel tends to tell us everything whereas the short story tells us only one thing, and that intensely....It is, as some have said, a 'glimpse through', resembling a painting or even a song which we can take in at once, yet bring the recesses and contours of larger experience to the mind.

The analogy with painting is a good one and we can stay with it. Just as we take in a painting all together with our eyes, similarly the mind takes in a short story all together in one sitting. Although novels too have been compared to paintings (*The Portrait of the Artist as a Young Man* by James Joyce and Henry James's *Portrait of a Lady*); the analogy for obvious reasons works much better for the short story.

Using a term impressionism common to painting and literature Suzanne C. Ferguson in her article 'Defining the Short Story', goes into the similarities and differences between the short story and the novel. Ferguson observes that although the main formal characteristics of the modern novel and the modern short story are the same, the modern short story is even more heavily influenced by turn of the century impressionism than the novel. The most dramatic innovation is in the plot where the traditional beginning, middle and end is rejected by short story writers in favour of 'suggestion'.

Thus, if we complain that the modern novel is abstract, than the short story will be even more so. The readers have to exercise their intellect and make use of past experience of reading fiction to understand contemporary stories.

The readers cannot rely any more on a narrator who will tell them everything and also underline the message of the story. The modern short story will usually limit itself to a single points of view; tell only some things and not necessarily in order, keep back others, leaving the reader to figure out the message if any.

Figuring out a modern novel can be a lot of work too. But again because of the size the kind of challenge and excitement that the novel poses to the reader is likely to be qualitatively different from that of the short story. 'In the modern novel we move from epiphany to epiphany, or in Woolf's image, along a series of small revelations, "matches struck unexpectedly in the dark". In the short story, we frequently see only one such privileged moment which takes the place of the traditional "turning point", the climax of the plot' (Ferguson 1988).

The 'single effect' that the story wreaks is inevitable because of its shortness. In the space of less than 7,500 words the writer would have to be very discerning about what to include.

> Unlike most novels, great short stories make us marvel at their integrity, their economy. If we went at them with our blue pencils, we might find we had nothing to do. We would discover there was nothing that the story could afford to lose without the whole delicate structure collapsing like a souffle or meringue. And yet we are left with a feeling of completeness, a conviction that we know exactly as much as we need to know, that all our questions have been answered—even if we are unable to formulate what exactly those questions and answers are (Prose Ibid).

Thus, far from being an unfinished novel the short story is a complete whole; it is highly polished; it makes an intense and immediate connection with the reader. In the present time the short story is celebrated as an evolved art form that makes intellectual demands on the reader. It does not give away its secrets (its 'meaning' or 'message') immediately. It has to be read like a poem and the meaning teased out through the complex interplay of form and content.

According to the writer Vilas Sarang the short story form has always occupied a pre-eminent place in Indian literature. We reproduce below a section from his essay 'notes of a working writer.'

BOX 3.6: THE LONG AND THE SHORT*

It's curious in English, the short story as a form is scarcely taken note of, is seen as marginal. In the Indian languages, on the other hand, short fiction is taken seriously, on par with the novel. Many prominent Indian have produced the main body of their work in the *Katha* form.

This has to do mainly with the economics of writing. In England or America, a writer can hope to survive (and even become wealthy) by writing. But only novels bring in profits: short story collections, like those of poetry, seldom do. In the Indian languages, writers can rarely survive by writing alone. Whether it is novels or short stories, the economics are largely the same, which is to say, negligible.

The mode of literary production and the career graph of a writer are different in the West. Observing the credit page in my 1990 collection, *Fair tree of the void*, a British friend noted with some surprise that the stories were written over a period of fifteen years. For the professional writer in the West this would be woefully low output. Yet, if you compare it with the work of a poet, it wouldn't seen so aberrant. These hundred pages of poetry is substantial work for a lifetime. So it may be with the fiction artist.

The trouble is, we don't quite think ok fiction as art. Literature used to be counted among the arts: but the novel, from the beginning, has retained an ambivalent character. The novel is part literature and part sociology (which is why it is the favoured form for Marxist critics). The novel is commonly a combination of social chronicle and biography. Usually, large chunks of the life history of the central character (s) are narrated over several hundred pages. As a literary form, the USP of the novel is information; information about social mores, chiefly, but also about different regions and countries, about various professions, and various fields of knowledge, such as history. There used to be a theory of literature as the sugar-coated pill. Today what the sugar-coated pill makes swallow able is not morality, but information. Lucien Goldman, a Marxist critic, puts it bluntly; in capitalist society 'art' is merely an inferior, form of knowledge;

No doubt, the novel is multi-purpose, which is the reason for its survival in an age where information has gone high-tech and the modes of dissemination are numerous and extraordinarily competitive. One purpose that the novel serves is what Freud told us about a long time ago: daydream (Only the cinema can beat the novel here.)

But the mainstay of the novel is still information. This is pretty accurately reflected in the gauging of public taste: there is a best-seller list of fiction (meaning the novel) and that of non-fiction. The two are on par; in fact interchangeable. The two categories fulfill the same need: information. An obvious connecting link is biography, which is acknowledged to be major component of fiction. Biography – especially autobiography – is also a prime subdivision of non-fiction. Non-fiction provides information without the addition of fictional

(Contd.)

*Vilas Sarang, 'Notes of a Working Writer', *The Women in Cages* (Delhi: Penguin Books, 2006) pp. 277–83.

embroidery. But in popular perception, there is little difference between the two. A reviewer in *Time* magazine (13 September 2004) speaks of the novel becoming a 'Trojan horse of non-fiction'. This reviewer remarks that Amitav Ghosh, the Indian English novelist, is a purveyor of facts about some academic discipline, with the facts being suitably 'sugar-coated in fiction'. The *Time* reviewer was perhaps unaware that he was using a concept that has its origin in Horace and Lucretius, with only a little change in the terms of reference.

So if you see a lot of tourists inspecting churches for hidden clues to the life of Christ, don't be too sure it is under influence of some non-fiction work; it might be a novel.

The strength of the novel is length. (The law of diminishing return begins to apply the more length stretches; but novelists believe there are other factors which counterbalance it.) To achieve length, the novel has to carry a lot of excess baggage, which, anyway, is built into the from as biography and concentration—the—'critical pressure'—that most art forms strive for. (Edvard Munch' 'the Scream' is a classic example of critical pressure. So are many lyrics.) The short story is more proactive and fastidious on this front: information, yes, but the most cunningly chose. The short story writer can legitimately aspire to write the 'perfect story'. No novelist hopes to write the 'perfect novel'

But aesthetic appeal is not—or should not—be the supreme goal of the short story. The short stories of Kafka do not seem to care much for aesthetic perfection. Nor do those of the early Hemingway, or of Borg's. What these writers focus upon is not beauty of form, but a kind of Knowledge. (Not the inferior from of knowledge' which Goldman speaks of.) Great short story writers offer us a singular vision. The short story gives us knowledge, but not knowledge as information. The short story at its best goes beyond sociology, or biography, or information of any kind. Twisting the words of Aristotle around, we might say that most novels are closer to history than to philosophy. The short story, on the other hand, is apt to become obsessed with pursuing a vision, frequently treating the business of (hi)story telling with scant regard, at times almost playfully. However, if fiction is to be taken as an art from, it cannot be straightforward philosophy, or history; it must transcend these spheres of human understanding.

A lot of Indian writers have published accomplished short stories: R.K. Narayan, Salman Rushdie, Rohinton Mistry, Vikram Chandra, Githa Hariharan, Amit Chaudhari, Jhumpa Lahiri, Manju Kapur, to name only a few.

Some novels by contemporary Indian novelists are:

- Amit Chaudhari – *A New World*
- Amitav Ghosh – *The Shadow Lines, The Hungry Tide*
- Arundhati Roy – *The God of Small Things*
- Githa Hariharan – *The Thousand Faces of Night, When Dreams Travel*
- Jhumpa Lahiri – *The Namesake*
- Manju Kapur – *Difficult Daughters, Home*
- Rohinton Mistry – *Such a Long Jouirney, A Fine Balance*
- Salman Rushdie – *Midnight's Children, Shame, The Moor's Last Sigh*
- Shashi Tharoor – *The Great Indian Novel*
- Vikram Chandra – *Red Earth and Pouring Rain*
- Vikram Seth – *Golden Gate, A Suitable Boy, An Equal Music*

ACTIVITY 17

1. Make a list of 5 novellas.
2. Discuss the difference between the short story and the novel.

The story 'Sweet Rice' is from the collection *The Blue Direction and Other Stories* (Delhi: Penguin India 1999) by Aamer Hussein[3] originally published as *This Other Salt* by Saqi Books. Commenting on the collection Amit Chaudhuri observes:

> To paraphrase Wallace Stevens, it is equal to living in a tragic time to live in a tragic land; and this is the sense one gets from Aamer Hussein's stories, on whose fringes lie countries of the mind, Pakistan, India, Indonesia, England. These nations' political histories are drawn subtly into the psychic drama of the narrator's own story of regret, childhood, love, loss, displacement and wonder. The narrator gropes his way through dark and light; but the stories themselves are wonderfully controlled written in a tactile and musical prose, and with a very individual sense of beauty.[4]

We will try and read 'Sweet Rice' in terms of its characters, plot, point of view and setting to get an insight into craft. We hope that through this exercise the students will learn to ask similar questions of everything they read. Reading creatively is an essential exercise for all writers.

Sweet Rice

For Yasmien Abbasi,
who suggested a final, vital ingredient

A few weeks after her fortieth birthday (unremembered, unsung), Shireen underwent a brief crisis and then received an unexpected gift. This is how it happened:

Jamil, her husband – one of those dedicated bankers who spent his life between his office, his associates, his business trips and his bed – announced to her one Sunday from the shallows of early morning sleep that he had important people visiting from abroad and other to whom he desperately owed a seasonal invitation. In short, she had to cater for more than a dozen guests at less than a week's notice. The dinner, Shireen grumbled silently as she lowered herself deeper into the depths of Capricornian gloom, was to be next Saturday; and she knew she would have to excel herself, for even her best was never good enough for Jamil's Libran discernment.

[3] Aamer Hussein was born in Karachi, Pakistan, in 1955 and moved to London in 1970. A graduate of SOAS, he has been writing and publishing fiction, reviews and criticism since the mid-eighties. His first collection of stories, *Mirror to the Sun*, was published in 1993, followed by *This Other Salt* (1999), *Turquoise* (2002) and *Cactus Town: Selected Stories* (2003). At present Aamer Hussein is Course Director of the MA in the National and International Literatures in English at the Institute of English Studies, School of Advanced Studies, University of London. He is also a former convenor of the Undergraduate Creative Writing course at the University of Southampton. He lives in London. (http://www.english.soton.ac.uk/hussein.htm)

[4] Note on Aamer Hussein's new stories, 19.3.1998, http://www.salidaa.org.uk/salidaa/site/

And so it had always been. In this impossibly difficult city of London where even a powerfully-situated husband did not guarantee a work permit or a job for a doctor with a third world (read by the British as third class) degree and experience, her medical expertise – so many years, and so much of her widowed mother's savings spent on it – had been displaced to an ongoing culinary struggle to keep her husband tied to her table, with sundry colleagues (for deals meant more to him than domesticity) in tow.

Such was life, Take Timur – now seven, and growing away from his mother – to school; do the shopping at Safeway and Marks and Spencers on Edgware Road; go the Marylebone library for some Han Suyin books in which other Asian lands far from her own were reflected in a doctor's eyes; come home and desultorily clean up. (She'd dispensed with the idea of an au pair a while ago, for she needed something besides shopping to fill up the time that reminded her of the globe of her days which was filling up with sand, taking her further and further away from any chance of regaining her fine hospital job in Karachi. Or, indeed, of adding to her qualifications the required British degrees; Jamil had always found some excuse, saying Timur was too little and medical training here expensive, and then he didn't know how long this English stay, sojourn for her and idyll for him, was going to last. If Shireen asked him for what she called a time-table – 'How long will we be here, when will we go back? My job isn't going to wait forever, you know' – he'd respond, 'Don't be silly, you have to understand the New Economics; professionals like us don't have front doors in one place any more.' She didn't know whether to be insulted at his negation of her profession, or flattered by his inclusion of her in his. And now a Malaysian woman, who'd soon become more a friend than a cleaner, came in once a week to do what Jamil called the heavy jobs.

Then she'd cook for Jamil and his guests as well, for this, too, she insisted upon. But lately he'd suggested they order food from one of the fancy Pakistani lady caterers who were now proliferating in London, because once she'd said in irritation that she hadn't been brought up to cook for armies when he sprung a dinner for six on her. And now he thought her home cooking wasn't quite fancy enough for his guests though he thrived on it himself. But she wasn't going to subscribe to his theory of two weights and two measures – more than good enough for him but not for outsiders – and refused even to consider food from elsewhere. This, he claimed in contradiction to his earlier protests about her elitist disdain for polite feminine values, was due to what he called her elemsee upbringing…And once she'd seen a poster for an orchestra called LMC and wondered aloud why an orchestra would name itself Lower Middle Class until her friend Yasmien with whom she was walking down High Street Kensington shoved her in the ribs and said 'No, silly, that's a typically Pakistani term, LMC stands for the London Musician's Collective' … one did still laugh with one's friends sometimes. Usually, though, when Jamil wasn't here. And that was more and more often. Then she'd follow her daily routine with the addition of a visit or a walk with one of her two close friends, and come home and still persist in cooking, against modern dietary prescriptions, the dishes she loved like spinach with meat or potatoes, oil-rich courgettes and aubergines, rich buttery breads and dry, fragrant pea-speckled rice tinted yellow. Since that was the role she'd been allotted by life's scene-shifters, she'd be a housewife with all the perfectionism of her medical training. But all too often she couldn't eat alone, and her friends were occupied with their matrimonial tasks, so she'd freeze the food for some day when it rained or snowed. Then, in her favourite armchair, late into the night, she's read and recreate the stories of Han Suyin's life among the women of China and Malaya.

Now, this party. This time most of the expected guests would be associates or prospective clients from Asia-Pacific and the Americas. Monday today; Jamil had gone off to Brussels earlier this morning, flying from the City Airport which he found most convenient for flights to Europe (but all too often it was to the Asia-Pacific region he went, for that, he said, was where the economy was booming, and other Asians, too, should make sure of their slice of the cake.) Though Shireen dreaded his guests, with their wives who looked suspiciously at the clothes she'd had sent to her from Pakistan and snooped around her fixtures and fittings, she was determined to prepare something really special, and outdo those society hostesses whose homes he dragged her to every sixth week or so when he was here. She'd already run through her repertoire of homely fare; after all, as a medical student and then a practitioner, she'd hardly had time to acqire the skills of her family's women; some passive knowledge, some pragmatic tips and some inherited skills had so far sufficed. But now, with the frustrated and frustrating perfectionism that constantly chilled her bones, she wanted to cross the final boundary and cook one of the feasts she'd heard her grandmother describe with such chop-licking ecstasy.

Sweet rice. A delicacy remembered from the day she'd kept all her Ramzan fasts for the first time. Not the insipid sweet yellow stuff speckled with shaved nuts, but something lush and golden orange, laden with succulent pieces of chicken and ripe with the subtle and suggestive perfume of fruit. Grandmother had made it for her and named it – or so, in her eight year old's arrogance, she'd imagined – after her. Shireen pulao. Sweet rice.

Shireen's father was from Multan, but her mother's parents - as they'd loved to remind her - had come from some town in what were now the United Provinces in Northern India. They'd settled in Lahore many years before Partition, but retained the gentle gestures, the sweet tongues and the richly aromatic cooking of another era, another land. After 1947 the landholdings that had given them a small revenue and some claim to feudal graces had vanished; and unlike many others, they'd never applied for recompense, which would have been a futile endeavour, as those who complained of properties lost were so many and there just didn't seem to be enough to go around. Her grandfather had lived all his life on his physician's earnings, and her father, too, was a doctor; simple people, who'd fallen in a world that continued to respect material manifestations of heritage, but hardly elemsee as Jamil put it. That term, she thought in catty moods, suited him better; and what was worse, his family had the mentality of shopkeepers with new money. But that was the way things were these days in Pakistan…

Enough reminiscing for now, she thought as she turned the corner from Seymour Place into York Street, which led her home. (Above her, the inverted grey tin bowl of sky.) Grandmother was no longer there, and Mother had probably long since forgotten a recipe of such absurdly luxurious pretensions. Now where could she find it? Hardly any chance of recovering it from the exercise books filled up with recipes her mother had copied out in her arthritic hand, or Shireen had painstakingly translated or transcribed – her Urdu, so fluent when she was younger, had grown almost rusty from years of disuse. (Medical textbooks in Urdu? Don't make me laugh. They're written in untranslatable gibberish.) Then there were the volumes of Madhur Jaffrey cookbooks that Jamil had brought for her, probably as a burdensome hint – they'd been placed by her on a corridor shelf, proudly forgotten; thought friends had told her the recipes within them were authentic, timesaving and good, the vanity of a good daughter, rich in the dowry of a thousand recipes tested and proved, forbade her from turning to them. Once upstairs, in the comfortable sitting room of her flat, feet tucked up beneath her in a favourite pudgy armchair, she swallowed her lumpy, irksome pride; a pile of discarded notebooks beside her, she inspected Jaffrey's tomes as if in search of some obscure remedy in a respected encyclopaedia. But to no avail. What would she do? Her goat-like determination refused to allow her to give up.

Sweet rice. It would have been a gesture so grand, so uncharacteristically flamboyant, a celebration of her home, and above all a defiant signature (named after her, the sweet rice, the indulgent grandmother had deceitfully said, the indulged child had gullibly believed)... What have I ever signed with a flourish, Shireen said to herself, do I even remember my signature? And this son of mine is his father's child, an English child, who prefers dubiously prepared hamburgers and chips fried in the greasy remains of God knows what forbidden animal to his mother's wholesome cooking, give him a fresh, sweet lassi and he asks for an artificially flavoured yoghurt...

Then a picture teased her visual memory. She went to the hall cupboard – in use this season, as their coats and winter things were stored there – and retrieved a chest in which some ancient objects of sentimental value (don't look back and above all don't smell or sniff, it only takes you to places surrendered) were stored. She knelt there on the carpet, rummaging, foraging. A red scarf. Two saris. And the bundle of books. They tumbled out – Perveen Shakir's first two volumes of verse, the single working woman's inspiration of her twenties. Those novels of A. R. Khatun that had delighted her between the ages of twelve and fifteen. ('Chaste, pragmatic romances', as a Frontier Post columnist, Shahnaz Aijazuddin – who'd recently written about the creative apathy of Western-educated Pakistani women, too – had described them, in a fulsome tone that amazed her because, as a teenager, she'd finally, regretfully relegated them to a corner, submitting to the senior schoolchild's unwritten law of westernization which decreed that anything local or ethnic, except the odd piece of mystic music, was suspect, unworthy, elemsee, while English was chic and desirable). Then, some romances of Islam and of colonialism and the '57 uprising by Abdul Halim Sharar, whom the Urdu scholars of today considered as dated as Rider Haggard. Here, now. The classic book of recipes she'd been searching for. She'd taken the bundle of books from her grandmother's cupboard when the old lady died, aged eighty three; a sentimental gesture, followed by the contradictory, even furtive, action of hiding them, once she'd carted them to London, under piles of gauzy unusable garments behind her husband's sports gear and her son's array of sundry school things. A moth-eaten, mildewed book. The Urdu script was old-fashionedly pure and clear, faint now with time but still legible. On the frontispiece, under the title, the year of publication – 1911. *Naimatkhana*, the book was called... the traditional larder. She had never, when she took it away, imagined she'd have use for it in these labour-saving days and even the names, weights and terms in it, as she browsed, were archaic. But after a false and disappointing start, since it wasn't included in the book's list of contents, and she couldn't locate a familiar heading, the recipe appeared. On page 89. Orange rice, the author had called it. Chicken or lamb, rice, clarified butter, onions, coriander, garlic, salt, cumin, black pepper, cloves, cardamom and sugar. And then, for the remembered fragrance (heady, like playing the circle game with your favourite boy cousin in the sun), she had to turn to recipe no. 249, on page 192. A sauce of orange peel, almonds, pistachios, cardamoms, water and – for the final, special, touch – crystallized rock sugar. All ingredients so easy to find nowadays, in this city with no cuisine of its own to boast of; which had, in its usual, grudging and offhand way, taken to guzzling the delicacies of its erstwhile empire and was even developing an increasingly discerning palate for them. Little Asias of restaurants and eating places had taken over the city – the revenge of the spice islands, as she and Yasmien jokingly said when they chose places to shop and eat. The rock sugar, perhaps, would be difficult to locate – but Drummond Street, for a sturdy walker like her (she walked for hours in post-autumnal, leaf-bare Regents Park some-times) was only a short walk away, though she hated its dinginess and its stalely spicy smells. And if not, then Harrods or Fortnums would be sure to stock it… In the end, she'd have gone even beyond the remembered delight to create something new, something lavish and wonderful, a festive concoction that bore her name…

Later, though. For now she had found a companion. (Jamil always said, when he saw the increasing pile, in her usually orderly surroundings, of medical digests and newspapers, imported Heralds, Shes, and Frontier Posts, free handouts, Big Issues, and mail order catalogues she saved because there was always something she wanted to read again, that Shireen would even find something to devour with her eyes on the back of a cereal pack, an airline ticket or a postage stamp. It was a joke she was sure he'd picked up from one of the American men's magazines that were his only leisure reading, or from an in-flight journal, this tasteless description of the kind of passionate, indefatigable reader she was). The book would keep her engrossed, amused, transported, for hours.

When she reached the last of the recipes (Homesickness sometimes is closer than anything to happiness), she still had half an hour before she left to pick up Timur, who she'd remembered had football practice after classes today, from his school near Marble Arch. She discovered an index of recipes at the end of the book; no point now regretting that she hadn't located it earlier, for half the fun of finding the recipe for sweet rice had been the search for it. Beyond the index was a list of books published by the same house. She realized that they were all by the author of this book, whom she'd imagined as a semi-literate bourgeoise, a turn-of-the-century housewife. Her ignorance astonished her – this woman, Muhammadi Begum, had been the editor of the first influential Urdu journal for women, which her husband had founded in Lahore in 1898. She had written at least a dozen books in the span of just ten years. Some were guides to housekeeping and good manners, but the titles of others, and the short, pithy blurbs below, made Shireen long for a grand library. A book for children: a young girl seeks a magic fountain, tree and bird to free her brothers, who have turned to stone, from captivity. (Will Jamil, too, free his limbs one day, from their pervasive torpor?) A tale for adolescents: a poor but highly learned young girl works day and night, setting up a school for girls, using her intelligence and wits to pay for her brothers' education and her mother's recovery from mental illness. (And here I complain, listless.) Two novels for adults: one about the evils of forcing an educated young woman – interested in the study of medicine and the art of herbalism – to marry her incompetent, dissipated cousin, and driving her to despair and death. (And what have I done? Jamil was not my cousin, but I didn't love him, and settled for a marriage of convenience because my work didn't give me time and I was afraid and over thirty.) A biography: of a role-model, an impoverished widow who'd become the principal of a vernacular girls's school in colonial Lahore, well over a century ago.

Muhammadi Begum. Who was she then, this master cook who'd stirred the ingredients of romance and realism into platters of parables that had nurtured generations of women, secluded or newly emergent from the confines of four walls and veils, adding a special prescription for those women who, almost a century later, were doctors and lawyers and opposition leaders and even prime ministers? Dead – so the prefaces, written by her stepdaughter and stepdaughter-in-law told Shireen – in 1908 at the age of thirty (and I am already forty, and still alive, and have abandoned my years of useful training and service to languish and moan in a luxurious central London flat), finding time to leave behind this keepsake of herself, this cookery book, the only work for which she was remembered, by a multitude of women who continued to share her bounty (and sharing bread is the closest form of love), taken from this naimatkhana she left behind her.

Naimatkhana. Simply translated, a larder or storehouse. Literally, a house or chamber of bounty. And it was from this chamber of bounty of blessings that Shireen would draw sustenance. She would share what she had, give unstintingly, take what was offered, laid out, out on the dastarkhan, the fresh white banqueting cloth of life. All the way to Timur's school, she pondered, she brooded Yes, the dish that bore her own name, that she would prepare; but she'd do much more. She'd go to the India office library and excavate, reclaim whichever of Muhammadi Begum's writings she could find; she'd spend her remaining fallow years in this foreign country recreating a forgotten time from her own past, giving back to this amazing woman – of whom no photograph existed since, as a traditional Muslim woman, she had never forsaken her purdah – her purloined history.

On her way home, holding Timur's unwilling hand in the bus (like his father, her son didn't like to walk), Shireen paid little attention to the child's customary pampered nonsense. Streams of history flowed in her head. Like Shireen's own father, Muhammadi Begum's husband Mumtaz Ali had encouraged her endeavours – a radical religious scholar, Mumtaz Ali was a fighter for the right of women to choose their own destinies, to emerge into the light of education and the dignity of unveiling , to marry and to divorce whom they chose, to walk and work in the world as men's equals. Recognizing her superior talent, he had set up a press for his youthful bride, published her books, and kept them and her memory alive for many, many years after her death… (and will Jamil think of me when I go? Or has living abroad pushed him back into some realm of the colonized, the spineless, who fear the vocal freedom of their equals and partners, as the ruler fears the mocking songs of his subjects? Does this city allow freedom only to those that fill its treasuries with borrowed or stolen pounds? And who will support me if I spend years researching the life of a woman whose potent writings are probably interred, by a trick of history and idle conservation, in the mildewed and mite-infested coffers of empire?

Shireen had decided. When she'd finally settled Timur in front of one of his interminable Mario games – a special favour, on a weekday – she picked up the phone and dialed Yasmien's number. Yasmien's machine switched itself on. Resignedly, Shireen said: 'Call me when you can, it's nothing important… Well, actually, I wondered if you and your husband are free on Saturday, for dinner…'

'My husband's not here, 'Yasmien's voice interrupted her, 'and I'm free all week. Sorry about the machine. I was avoiding Tehmina, you know how long she goes on…'

'Listen, I'm thinking of compiling a recipe book. You know, based on those recipes from our grandmothers' time? I'm thinking of calling it 'Sweet Rice'.

Half an hour later (or maybe two hours, for she hadn't looked at her watch when she called Yasmien, and they'd traversed a century and more in their conversation) she had a collaborator, a fellow conspirator. Yasmien knew of someone who knew a publisher in Pakistan, who may be interested in assisting Shireen in her project of writing about her new heroine's life. With the fashionable status of Asian food in Britain, they'd have no major problem in finding an outlet here for 'Sweet Rice'. The fancy Pakistani lady caterers, once they'd wept their kohl in streams down their faces, would throng to the spectacular launch, and afterwards claim that the recipes they'd copy had originated in their mothers' kitchens. And Yasmien had suggested a subtitle, and a vital ingredient for their Bountiful Feast: there'd be lots of bright illustrations, and between the recipes, to refresh the palate like cool sweet water, they'd serve whatever stories they could uncover of the life of Muhammadi Begum, and as condiments they could recount their own experiences of living and cooking at home and in alien lands.

ACTIVITY 18

1. What is the apparent reason for Shireen's decision to make sweet rice? What is the other more hidden and compelling reason suggested in the story?
2. The careful reading of the recipe book *Naimatkhana* provides a moment of illumination for Shireen. What does Shireen see when 'a match is struck unexpectedly in the dark' for her in her London flat?
3. Identify the passages that suggest
   a. Jamil's socio-economic status.
   b. Jamil's male-centred point of view.
   c. Limitations of Jamil's world.

Character

Characters are things of the past; insists the contemporary French novelist Alain Robbe-Grillet. Can one write a story without characters? A character is presumably an 'imagined person' who inhabits a story (exceptions could have rabbits or inanimate objects like the wind as inhabitants). Readers demand consistency from fictional characters and look for reasons in their behaviour.

E.M. Forster suggested two ways of building characters: a writer may sculpt a *round* character or sketch a *flat* character. The former is made up of many personality traits and tends to be complex and both more life-like and believable, while the latter consists of only a few personality traits and tends to be simple and less believable. Flat characters tend to remain the same throughout the story; round characters usually develop or change. In 'Sweet Rice', Shireen is a round character; whereas Timur may be described as a flat character.

Experimental writers may deliberately use only flat characters. Usually, fiction has both round and flat characters. Major characters are round and minor characters flat as more space is required for round characters. Characters may at times be symbolic (of greed or of a figure like Christ; for example in John Updike's stories certain characters are Christ figures making redemption possible); sometimes representative (for example Jamil may be seen to represent the successful subcontinental banker in 'Sweet Rice') and at other times historical or biographical (modeled on real people; for example Muhammadi Begum in 'Sweet Rice' is a historical character).

In the twentieth century some fiction writers challenged characterization as practiced in the nineteenth century. 'You mustn't look in my novel for the old stable ego of character,' wrote the modernist writer D.H. Lawrence to a friend about *The Rainbow*; and in that novel and other novels Lawrence demonstrated his view of individuals as bits of one Life Force, spurred to act by incomprehensible passions—'the dark gods' in them. James Joyce wrote *Finnegan's Wake*, allegedly a novel without characters. The protagonist in Franz Kafka's *The Castle* has no markers—no home, no family, no definite appearance—not even a name, just the initial K.

These exceptions only prove the rule that characterization is central to writing fiction. If a writer wants to join the ranks of the novelists mentioned above s\he too will have to internalise the art of characterization in order to reverse it.

Writers need to avoid certain pitfalls in characterization. All of us live in cultures that have certain stereotypes. All Bengalis according to North Indian stereotyping love fish and football. If a stereotype creeps unawares into fiction, it would pull the fiction down making it lifeless. However, if a writer is aware of the stereotype and exploits it s/he would be able to infuse life and excitement into the work. Stereotype production is based on:

- Simplification
- Exaggeration or distortion
- Generalization
- Presentation of cultural attributes as being 'natural'

Stereotype sometimes results in stock characters. A stock character is a fictional character that relies heavily on cultural *types* or *stereotypes* for its personality, manner of speech, and other characteristics. Stock characters are instantly recognizable to members of a given culture (Wikipedia). The small-town girl and the socialite are some examples of stock characters in Indian television serials. *Gone with the Wind* is peopled with stock characters: the loyal black Mammy and the wild, rapacious free nigger. In 'Sweet Rice' from Shireen's description of them we know immediately what the society hostesses who are coming for dinner would be like. A *stock character is likely to be flat and not very life-like.*

ACTIVITY 19

1. What do you understand by the term 'Character'? Discuss your favourite fictional character.
2. Shireen is the only round character in the story 'Sweet Rice '. How does she develop and change? List the characterisitics that make her life-like.
3. In spite of being sketched very economically Yasmein is a memorable character. What role, in your opinion, does she play in the story?
4. What kind of character is Jamil? You may use more than one heading. List his characteristics to support your answers.
5. How does Hussein use\exploit the following:
   a. The stereotype of a Pakistani child brought up in England.
   b. The stereotype of exotic Pakistani women and food.
   c. The historical character of Muhammadi Begum.
   d. Shireen's family history.

Plot

According to Aristotle's *Poetics* plot is 'the arrangement of incidents'. Aristotle also argues that art succeeds when the beginning, middle and end of an action are clearly and persuasively motivated.

A lot has happened since Aristotle. We already know that many elements of the traditional plot have been deleted or transformed in the contemporary story: an image or an unrelated event may substitute the events of the plot (metaphoric plot); beginning or middle or end may be dropped (elliptical plot). 'Sweet Rice', for instance, has a metaphoric plot. It has two strands running through it: the story of the relationship between Shireen and Jamil and the story of Muhammadi Begum. The two strands are knit together. It may seem that no resolution has been posited for Shireen and Jamil's story. On close reading it would be clear that the climax—Shireen's discovery of the recipe book *Naimatkhana*—doesn't merely usher in the second story but actually paves the way for the protagonist to resolve the impasse (conflict or problem) of the first story: Shireen decides to empower herself with the history of her admirable ancestress by writing the recipe book Sweet Rice.

Some modernist or post-modernist fiction writers would be impatient with the very concept of plot preferring to drift along with the consciousness of their characters.

So we will limit our definition of plot to 'the series of events which form the story of a novel, play, film\movie, etc.' (*Oxford Advanced Learner's Dictionary*).

The following have been suggested as elements of plot:

1. Initial situation—the beginning. It is the first incident that makes the story move.
2. Conflict or Problem—goal which the main character of the story has to achieve.
3. Complication—obstacles which the main character has to overcome.
4. Climax—highest point of interest of the story.
5. Suspense—point of tension. It arouses the interest of the readers.
6. Denouement or Resolution—what happens to the character after overcoming all obstacles/failing to achieve the desired result and reaching/not reaching his goal.
7. Conclusion—the end of the story.

However, one the other element may be dropped, transformed, or substituted in the story.

Aspiring writers often ask the question, 'Where should I start? Do I need a plot?' A plot occurs 'when a character encounters circumstances which threaten their rhythm of living: a loss, a meeting, a sudden break of routine' (Mills 1996). Events in 'Sweet Rice' take place when Shireen, the main character, decides to go against her husband's advice of calling in a Pakistani caterer and resolves to prepare a dish that bears her own 'defiant signature'. This way of looking at a plot assumes that characters precede the plot.

Plot is sometimes explained as 'the pencil outline that guides the painter's brush.' It is assumed here that writers begin writing fiction with a plot. According to this view 'Sweet Rice' came about when Aamer Hussein thought of writing about the empowerment of a Pakistani woman who has had to relinquish her medical practice due to the demands of her family.

We do not whether plot precedes characters and perhaps we don't need to. A creative writing course cannot and should not prescribe what a writer should start with although in the workshops we will suggest some ideas that might help. Some writers feel more confident working with an outline; others like to begin with a face, an expression or an incident. In all cases the story should take over very quickly—and various ingredients of the fiction i.e. character, plot, setting, point of view—begin to work together in harmony.

How, at which point and if at all, emplotment is to take place is a decision every writer needs to make independently for every work.

ACTIVITY 20

1. **What do you understand by the term 'plot'?**
2. If we take the initial situation in 'Sweet Rice' as Jamil's announcement of a dinner party on Saturday, what would constitute the subsequent elements: conflict, complication, climax, suspense, denouement, and conclusion?
3. Discuss Shireen and Jamil's story in terms of beginning, middle, and end. Would you say the events follow logically one from the other or are there gaps that the reader is supposed to fill in?
4. Describe Muhammadi Begum's story. What relevance does it have for Shireen?
5. Rewrite the last four paragraphs of the story giving it another ending. Begin changing the story from the line, 'Shireen has decided…'

Point of View (Modes of Narration)

A very important question we need to ask when we are reading or writing a story is, *Who is the narrator*? It is rare in modern fiction for a writer to step out from behind the computer and tell the story. We must not confuse the narrator with the author.

The Narrator is the entity within a story that tells the story to the reader. It is one of three entities responsible for story-telling of any kind. The others are the author and the reader (or audience). The author and the reader both inhabit the real world. It is the author's function to create the alternate world, people, and events within the story. It is the reader's function to understand and interpret the story. The Narrator exists within the world of the story (and only there) and presents it in a way the reader can comprehend it.

Stories may be narrated in the first person 'I' but usually the 'I' is a major or minor character in the story, and not the author. For example, Truman Capote's *Breakfast at Tiffany*'s where an unnamed character tells the story of Holly Golightly, who he used to know some fifteen years ago. Stories may also be narrated in the third person. In this case the narrator would be one of the following:

1. All-knowing or omniscient. For example Jane Austen's novels where characters are described with 'irony'.
2. Seeing into one major character. For example 'Sweet Rice'.
3. Seeing into one minor character. For example *Madame Bovary* when she is described from the perspective of Charles Bovary who she later marries.
4. Objective (not seeing into any characters). For example mystery novels or stories are sometimes written in this way where the narrator observes, eavesdrop and reports.

As we know from our earlier discussion limitation of point of view is an important feature of the modern short story and novel. The omniscient narrator is an exception rather than the rule these days.

In 'Sweet Rice' we see that the point of view remains fixed and the narrator follows the thought process of only the protagonist, 'Shireen'. S\he does not tell us about what is going on in Jamil or Timur's head but gives enough information about them to enable us to come to our own conclusions. The narrator is neither Shireen nor Aamer Hussein; s\he is a fictional construct that inhabits only 'Sweet Rice'.

Limitation of point of view works well in Sweet Rice. We see Jamil the banker through his wife's eyes and hear his borrowed ideas and words through her consciousness. 'Hamburger and chips and artificially flavoured yoghurt' have also claimed Timur the son we are told. Shireen's point of view forces us to reinterpret Jamil's idyll : the age of the booming new economy. It also makes us see Muhammadi Begum who spent her short life in purdah in a new light.

ACTIVITY 21

1. Describe a short story\novel that you have read that has an omniscient narrator.
2. How would the story 'Sweet Rice' change if the narrator were to be omniscient and also express Jamil's point of view?
3. Rewrite the first page of the story in the first person from Yasmein's point of view. Remember, Yasmein is a close friend of Shireen. She is more aware of the difference between Pakistani English and London English. She is also the one who suggests the vital ingredient for 'Sweet Rice': asking Shireen to include in her proposed book the historical and present day culinary experiences of women at home and abroad.

Setting (Milieu)

Setting in literature is the time, place (locale), and sometimes the weather in the story. Setting is not merely the backdrop to the action; in effective stories it plays a symbolic or even an active role. Writers take great care to choose the appropriate setting for their stories. The hour, the day, the year and the century have to be kept in mind whether one is writing a historical piece or a contemporary one. The passage of time in fiction also has to be monitored: effective stories can be written about an hour, a day, a year or several centuries.

Similarly, writers research or explore the place they are writing about. Some writers who focus on a particular geographical area repeatedly are called Regional Writers. Thomas Hardy is one example. William Faulkner who set all his work in his native Mississippi is another good example. Through their writings they make the place come alive to the readers. At times the weather – snow, storm, wind, or the heat – are also important constituents of fiction.

Some writers depict characters as products of heredity and environment and even as helpless puppets in the hands of these factors. Such fiction is classified under Naturalism or fiction of grim realism. Theodore Dreiser and Thomas Hardy are examples of writers of naturalistic novels.

There are also writers who deliberately eschew setting in order to give a fable-like effect to the story. In Somerset Maugham's 'The Appointment in Samarra' details of the marketplace in Baghdad are avoided to focus on 'death' that is the main point of the story.

'Sweet Rice' is set in London. The texture of Shireen's life unfolds in her daily routine of dropping and picking up Timur, shopping at Safeway and Marks and Spencers, and cleaning and cooking in her York Street flat. Her misreading of a poster for an orchestra called LMC suggests an emotional distance from her surroundings. London also embodies the erstwhile empire. Her reality, Shireen feels, is interred in the India Office Library as a relic of colonialism. She resolves to look for it in the history of Muhammadi Begum. Thus, the India Office is much more than a mere place-name in the story.

ACTIVITY 22

1. What role does 'setting' play in a short story?
2. What is the duration of the events in 'Sweet Rice'?
3. Identify portions where Shireen personifies London attributing motivation and agency to the city.
4. Do you think the same story could have been set in Lahore or Karachi? Give reasons for your answer.
5. Rewrite the fourth paragraph of the story setting it in another foreign city. Begin changing it from the line, 'Such was life.' You will need to find out the names of streets, the mode of public transport, names of public buildings etc. of your chosen location.

A Conversation with a Creative Writer

Anuradha Marwah

Anuradha Marwah, one of the authors of this book, has published three novels: *The Higher Education of Geetika Mehendiratta* published by Disha Books, Delhi in 1992, *Idol Love* published by Ravi Dayal Publisher in 1999 and *Dirty Picture* published by Indialog in 2007.We reproduce below her replies to our questionnaire:

When did you begin writing and which forms did you experiment with?

I can't remember a time when I was not writing. As a child I used to fill notebooks and diaries with poems. I graduated to writing fiction at 26 when I realized I was not a poet. I have tried my hand at short stories, drama and screenplay as well; but my primary form is the novel.

What drew you towards the novel?

The realization that I was not writing poetry seriously enough. It came too easily. I suppose my poems were facile. Whatever one writes should be from the gut. The novel form provided the scope to me to use all of myself.

Would you say that certain forms lend themselves to the expression of certain themes?

Definitely. Form should go hand in hand with content. For me poetry is primarily aesthetic; it needs a light touch even if there is protest. I used poetry in Idol Love but I couldn't have written the novel as a poem. For one, I needed a lot more space. The dystopic sensibility of the narrator of that novel could find full expression only in a combination of descriptions, ruminations and dialogue.

Drama too is different from prose fiction. I am reminded of what John Fowles said comparing films and novels: 'the novel is much better adapted to moral and psychological discrimination.' Later on, predictably, he was disappointed with the film version of

The French Liutenant's Woman. Being a novelist he obviously privileges the novel. The visual form would emphasize other aspects. Theme can never be separated completely from the form.

What tells you that you are ready to begin a new novel?

When I can no longer bring myself to work on the old one. I realize a chapter (in my life) is over and the next must begin.

Do you work with a schedule or a fully worked out plan? Do you always know where you are going?

I usually start with character. I saw Geetika clearly in my mind when I began my first novel. My third novel *Dirty Picture* has a strong plot but that too began with the image of young girl. No, I did not know, when I began, where these women intended to go. They let me know by and by.

What role does research\background information play in your writing?

I like to write about places I know. Ajmer, the place I was born, is important to me. All my work is set or at least partially set in Ajmer. The small town is more than a theme for me; it is a synecdoche. Its limitations are that of human existence.

But I obsessively research other kinds of information: the school syllabus for a character; the job profile; the restaurant he or she went to; sometimes the historical period like the mid-nineteenth century in Delhi for *Idol Love*; or contemporary stuff like High Court judgement and police records for *Dirty Picture*. I invariably interview ten to fifteen people for a novel.

How many times do you revise your work and are you ever fully satisfied?

I am more of a re-writer than a writer. Each novel goes through several revisions—till I am sick of it.

What is your experience of the publishing world?

My first two novels got published easily. I had much more trouble with the third and not only because it has a controversial subject. I feel that Indian publishing is expanding at a delirious pace and like most other areas it is getting commercialized and hype-driven. A reaffirmation of certain old-world values like respect for merit and scrupulous editing—the kind we associate with the late Ravi Dayal—would in order.

How do you deal with responses of readers and critics?

By dividing them into two categories: what I can use and what I can't. Responses are usually a mixture of grain and chaff. The writer has to be discerning about what to take.

Who is your ideal reader?

I can't see him\her. But s\he doesn't put the book down till the last page.

What is your advice for aspiring writers?

Rewrite till you drop. This is where creative writing courses can play a significant role. New writers are usually resistant to revising their work. We need to keep in mind that writing is craft.

Writing Fiction for Children

In India we associate Children's literature in English with the name Ruskin Bond. We reproduce below a profile of the author:

BOX 3.7: BOND WITH THE BEST

ZIYA US SALAM

He wrote his first book at 17 and hasn't stopped writing since then. Meet Ruskin Bond.

WHEN in school, Ruskin Bond wrote a short novel about his teachers. 'I was rather frank in my comments. Some teachers came to know of it. The novel was torn up and thrown into the dustbin,' recalls the man who penned his first novel *The Room On the Roof* when he was 17. Before he passed teenage he had penned *Vagrants in the Valley* too. 'It took me a couple of years to get the first novel published. I had my share of rejections,' he recalls, sitting in New Delhi on the eve of the release of *Rusty Runs Away*, brought out by Penguin India.

'I have written stories like "Rusty's Alter Ego". They never appeared in a sequence. The Penguin people took all the Rusty stories, put them all together and gave them continuity. Now it reads like a three-volume novel,' says Ruskin thanking the publishers for getting into children's literature in a big way. 'Bigger publishers are getting into it. People are beginning to buy children's books. In the past children's literature did not get much recognition. You could not even get a book review. It is still not very viable financially but it is getting better. But I have scratched my living off writing. I cannot complain personally. My books have remained in print all these years. They may not be bestsellers but they have been steady sellers. I always had self-confidence that in course of time I will get recognition. I worked hard, wrote for two-three hours a day besides other work.'

Though a successful author, Ruskin did not want to be that when he entered teenage. 'I wanted to be a football goalkeeper!' A couple of years into senior school and there was no looking back on a possible career in the world of letters. 'I started scribbling for the school magazine. I was a fairly good all-round student, played games, was in-charge of library. When I was young I took myself seriously. It was only in my 30s that I started writing for children though I did not always think of the readers,' recalls the much-acclaimed author of *Delhi Is Not Far* and *Night Train at Deoli*. In the 1950s he wrote for The Hindu. 'I used to write for Sport and Pastime,' he says rather wistfully, adding, 'When you are young you look for admiration. As you get older the desire for applause recedes. You become less egoistic.'

Ruskin Bond, who has given children's literature a rare dignity otherwise reserved for those winning international acclaim, feels that literature for children is still very much an urban phenomenon. 'Literature is often aimed at children going to paying schools. They come from homes where parents can afford books. However, books are available only in urban India. In small towns only textbooks are available. There are no well-stocked bookshops. Small town India is neglected. The National Book Trust fills in to some extent. They do a lot of translation. Every title is translated into 12 major languages. That helps but a lot more needs to be done. But with some good publishers coming through it might get better.'

He recalls, 'some 20 or 30 years ago it was unthinkable that frontline publishing houses will come into children's literature. Till 1980s only academic books were published, it was hard to get a publisher for fiction. It was easier to find publishers for children's literature in London though my books were basically meant for Indian readers.'

Based in Mussoorie, the author of 100 short stories and novels, besides 30 children's book, he is now 'a little bit more desk-bound. Making a living is easier now due to accumulated works. I am writing short essays on meditation and looking for a chance to present the works of old authors in anthology form.'

He has a message for budding writers: 'Make sure you can write first. Don't give up easily, be persistent.' So, kids, be the best to Bond with the best

(<http://www.hindu.com/>).[6]

What is Children's Literature

We instinctively know that writing for children is different from writing for adults. However, the distinction is often blurred where the finished product is concerned.

Mark Haddon's *The Curious Incident of the Dog in the Night-time* is the story of fifteen year old Christopher who has a photographic memory and who is a Science and Maths Prodigy. However, Christopher has an emotional disability; he can't understand human beings. His parents are separated and he is living with his father who has told him that his mother is dead. When Christopher discovers his neighbour's dog lying dead on the lawn, he decides to track down the killer and write a murder mystery about it.

This book went on to win the prestigious Whitbread Award (2003) in the novel category. Whitbread Award has five categories: novel, first novel, children's book, biography, and poetry. *The Curious Incident of the Dog in the Night-time* had been simultaneously published in two imprints: one for adults; the other for children. The text is identical in both editions. The book has sketches and maps allegedly made by Christopher; it also contains Maths problems. It looks like a book children (or Young Adults) would enjoy. However, it was not nominated for the Whitbread Children's section at all and went on to win the award in the novel category.

Who decides whether a book is for children? Publishers, Award Committees, Guardians and Parents or Children themselves?

The curious incident of Mark Haddon's novel goes to substantiate the point we have already discussed earlier: there can be no water-tight compartments between the literary and the popular (or genre) fiction. The boundary between Children's literature and literature for adults is porous. *Huckleberry Finn* and *To Kill a Mockingbird* are further examples of books that have been enjoyed by both adults and children for years.

This unfortunately might not be of much help to a writer who wants to write for children. It is interesting that Mark Haddon himself felt that he wrote his novel *The Curious Incident* a little differently from his previous novels intended for children:

> When I was writing for children, I was writing genre fiction. It was like making a good chair. However beautiful it looked, it needed four legs of the same length, it had to be the right height, and it had to be comfortable...with *The Curious Incident* I was trying to do something different... (Haddon, Observer 11 April 2 004 from Paul Mills)

Haddon goes on to say that young adults enjoyed this book as it had a carefully shaped plot but his primary intention was not to address it to them. The analogy of the chair that has to 'work' is a good one for fiction intended for children. Children's fiction must work for children.

Writers usually want concrete points: how does a story for children differ from a story for adults regarding characterization, plot, point of view, and setting? We will try and provide some answers. When you are writing for children the factors that are different compared to writing for adults are:

1. Being conscious of the age group of the reader and so changing your vocabulary accordingly.
2. Being careful that the subject matches the maturity of the child.
3. Doing research especially for information books, historical fiction and science fiction. Kids are fascinated by facts.

4. The vital importance of plots in fiction. Children are impatient readers and will not wait for you to get into the action.
5. The need to think visually and the importance of descriptions—images, taste, smell, sound.
6. The importance of format. Various kinds of books – novels/stories/picture books/comic strips/non-fiction/quizzes/games & puzzles may be used.
7. The need to work with illustrators, designers, photographers. Writing for children offers many opportunities for collaborative work.

Let us look at the following story to discuss exactly how a children's story works.

The Sword of Dara Shukoh

Subhadra Sen Gupta

DILLI. Akram and his companion Majid were riding through Faiz Bazar when the two men attacked them. It was early on a sunny winter morning, the best time to go riding, before the streets filled up with people. As always the boys had galloped around the open fields beyond Dilli Gate and now going home, they were trotting through the sleepy streets of Dilli when from a shadowy side lane two horsemen came charging straight at them. "Look out!" Majid yelled as they quickly wheeled their horses trying to avoid a collision. But before they knew it, the two riders were right on top of them, their faces masked by the ends of their turbans.

"Robbers!" Akram said, startled. "Here?"

The boys carried no arms. The taller man reached forward to grasp Akram's rein, a dagger gleaming in his hand. "Get down," he sneered.

The other man held Majid by the arm. "Be still and you won't get hurt," he said menacingly.

"I have no money," Akram said quietly.

"Get down," the man repeated. "We want you, not your money."

Majid looked around desperately. They were before the closed gates of a haveli and hearing the noise the watchman had peered out. Down the road Majid spotted some bhishtis carrying skins of water walking towards them. With sudden speed he dug his elbow into the masked man's stomach making him bend in surprise and began yelling, "Bachao! Help! Robbers!" As the watchman and bhishtis ran towards them, with sudden desperation the two men tried to pull a struggling Akram out of his saddle and onto the tall man's horse. The watchman arrived and hit at the arms of the masked man with his stick. The dagger dropped to the ground with a clatter. One of the bhishtis raised his skin bag and sprayed their faces with icy water.

Realising they were outnumbered the two men let go of Akram and turned to flee. In all the confusion the cloth had slipped from their faces and the boys got a good look but they had never seen the men before. Kicking and punching at the boys and their rescuers the two men backed off, then wheeling their horses they galloped away.

"Let's follow them!" Akram shouted at Majid, about to ride after them in pursuit.

Majid stopped him. "No," he said, " They are too strong for us. Let's go home."

Thanking the men who had helped them, the boys began riding at a smart trot towards their haveli in Dariba. They had just gone past the closed shops of the Khas Bazaar opposite the red sandstone walls of the fort when, behind a tree, Akram spotted two riders. "They are waiting for us. Majid! Ride!"

They dug their heels into their horses' flanks, tightened the reins and yelled at the animals, urging them on. The two followed. Turning sharply, they galloped through the broad Chandni Chowk. As they turned into Dariba, Akam looked back. The men were getting closer but, thankfully, home was near too. They sighed in relief when they saw that the gates of the haveli were open.

Seeing them rushing in, the people in the haveli ran towards them anxiously. The two men halted sharply at the gate. Their faces were masked again. Before Akram or Majid could get anyone to follow them, the men had galloped away.

As the boys slid off their panting horses Majid looked at Akram and said, "Why were they trying to kidnap you?"

Akram, his face pale and tense, looked at the drops of blood on his hand where the man's dagger had scratched the skin and shook his head, "I don't know. I really don't know."

The boys walked to the Nawab's baithak. Akram was the son of Nawab Amanullah Haider. Majid and he had grown up together and were very close friends. Majid's father Basheer Khan was the Nawab's manager and he was also famous for his expertise with horses. That was how the boys could ride so well.

Everyone had collected in the baithak to hear of their morning's adventure. Nawabsaab heard them through and said, "Now describe the men to me. Did you see their faces?"

"We saw their faces, Abba huzoor," Akram said, " but we did not know them."

"They wore good clothers, "Majid added, "velvet jackets and silk turbans, and the taller man wore two big rings."

"What about their horses?" Basheer Khan asked his son.

"Very good Arabs, Abba," Majid replied, "like our best horses–with expensive saddles, too.

Nawab Amanullah and Basheer Khan looked at each other, puzzled.

"You are sure they were trying to kidnap you, Akram?"

"Yes," Akram said quietly. "They tried to pull me onto their horse and they said they didn't want my money."

"But why? If they are rich men why should they kidnap anyone? If they are after a ransom, there are richer Nawabs then me. I have no enemies as far as I know." Nawabsaab was truly puzzled. " Why kidnap my son?" No one had an answer.

For the next few weeks the boys went everywhere under guard. The both found it a big bore. But as the weeks passed and nothing happened they were allowed to go out alone again but only to crowded places. "You know, no one really believes any more that those men were trying to kidnap me." Akram said one day as they were walking towards Chandni Chowk. "They think I imagined it, that the men were just ordinary robbers."

"I believe you. I heard them."

They reached the corner of Chandni Chowk, facing the Lahori Gate of the Lal Qila. The emperor was going to come out of the fort in procession and they had come to watch it. As they settled down to wait, Majid said, "It should be a good show, the procession of our new badshah."

"Remember the last processions we saw, when the old badshah Aurangzeb was going to pray at the Jama Masjid at Id?"

Majid nodded. Now Aurangzeb was dead and as they watched, the royal procession of the new Mughal emperor Bahadur Shah come slowly wending out of the red stone fort. First came the horses ridden by the chobdars–soldiers each carrying a mace of silver. Then swaying majestically come the richly caparisoned elephants. "Just look at that!" Akram pointed out. "They've even decorated the elephant's trunk with gold."

Then the bhale-bardars, foot soldiers carrying spears came marching. The royal insignia of the sun made of solid gold was fitted on poles of silver and carried atop elephants. The nakara players followed playing loudly on kettle drums. More drummers, shehnai players and soldiers rode by on horses. The gunners, gola-andaz, and the dhalet, shield bearers, marched past.

Bahadur Shah came riding on the largest elephant, magnificently decorated with jewellery, velvet and silk. The emperor's howdah was splendidly made of enameled gold. Everyone watching the procession salaamed as the emperor passed by. Akram was studying how the mahout sat on the emperor's elephant, when Majid clutched his arm.

"Akram," Majid was whispering into his ear, "turn slowly and look at the man standing by that tree on your left. He's wearing a green dress."

Casually, as if admiring the camels going past, Akram turned to look. Under the tree, his face raised watching the procession stood the tall man who had held the dagger at his throat at Faiz Bazar. Akram felt his heart thump. "What do we do?"

"He hasn't seen us. Let's wait and see what he does next."

Going deeper into the crowd, standing half-hidden behind some tall men, they kept a steady eye on the man in green. As the last row of horses was going past, the man turned and began walking away. The boys followed at a distance. Through the crowds, past the shops, the man walked quickly into Chandni Chowk. He had no idea he was being followed. He turned into a gali and entered a food stall. As the boys watched hidden from a corner they saw the man sit down and order food. "Let's get help." said Akram. "We can't catch him alone." They ran home.

"We found him! We found him!" they yelled as they ran inside the haveli.

"Come on! Follow us."

Basheer Khan and his assistants were in the stables checking out the horses. As they all hurried out of the house one of the assistants turned to Basheer Khan, "Who are we going to catch?"

"The kidnapper, you fool!" Basheer muttered irritably. "Who else?"

As they reached the corner of the gali, Majid waved them to a stop. "He was inside a food stall on the left. A tall man in a green silk jacket and fur cap."

"You two wait here," Basheer Khan said. "If he sees you he'll try to run. Let us go in and surround him first and then you follow." They watched Basheer and the two assistants enter the food stall, look around and then go and sit down on both sides of the tall man. The man looked up, irritated, from chewing on a chicken bone and said, "Why don't you people sit somewhere else?"

"We want to sit next to you," Basheer said politely.

"Why?" The man looked nervous.

By then Majid and Akram had come to stand next to Basheer, who waved at them and said, "These boys want to meet you again. Remember them?"

The tall man's swarthy face paled. There were beads of sweat on his forehead. Basheer held his arm and said, "If you don't want to get hurt come with us quietly. We are five and you are alone. Only a fool would try to escape."

As the man got up, one of Basheer's men reached inside the man's jacket pocket and pulled out some money. "Just paying your bill," he said grinning. Surrounded by them the man walked to the haveli.

Nawab Amanullah Haider looked up from his hookah as Basheer and his men dragged the man into the baithak. "This is one of the men who attacked the boys, huzoor," Basheer said. "The boys saw him at the procession."

Nawabsaab looked closely at the man. He wore an expensive quilted silk jacket, woolen pajamas and shoes made of embroidered leather. His fur cap had a jewel in front. He wore rings and earrings.

"You do not look like a poor man," Nawabsaab said quietly.

"I am not," the man said.

"Who are you then?"

The man remained silent.

"You look like a horseman and a soldier. Isn't it beneath you at attack two unarmed boys?"

Still the man would not reply.

Nawabsaab took a drag at his hookah and then said, "So far I have been asking you politely. And I don't mind waiting for an answer. If you don't answer now I'll just wait until you do." He looked at Basheer Khan. "Take him to the cellar and no food or water." Basheer Khan nodded.

The man looked at their faces. "You are correct, huzoor. I'm a soldier from Agra."

"Who do you work for?"

"A mansabdar in Agra."

"His name, please.

The soldier looked uncertain and then after a moment's hesitation said reluctantly, "Nawab Saifuddin Haider."

"What!" Nawabsaab sat up in astonishment. "Saifuddin Haider of Agra? But he's my cousin!"

"Ji," the soldier nodded.

For a moment the room was silent in surprise. Nawabsaab was the first to speak, "You mean that my own cousin wants to kidnap my son? You lie!"

"No, huzoor. We were not to harm him. Just hold him in a safe place until; you gave the ransom.

Nawabsaab was sitting cross-legged on his takht, holding his heat in disbelief, "I can't imagine Saifuddin doing such a thing. If he needed money he could have asked for it."

"He was ashamed to. They were very heavy gambling debts. He is a proud man."

"But he was going to demand money as a ransom," Basheer said angrily. "You think that was a better thing to do?"

"We were not going to demand money. Nawabsaab had to give us his collection of miniature paintings to free his son."

"My miniature collection?" Nawabsaab asked surprised. "But why? It's nothing very precious."

"I don't know, huzoor. He would not tell us why he wanted it. And you are right. I do not like kidnapping boys. That is why I have left the employ of Nawab Saifuddin."

"I didn't know Saifuddin was a lover of paintings," Nawabsaab said thoughtfully. And then he suddenly sat up, "Wait a minute. Basheer, remember that merchant from Agra who came to see me some months back?"

"Ji, He wanted to buy something from you."

"Yes. The miniatures. He offered me a lot of money for them."

The soldier nodded, "Ji. Nawab Saifuddin sent the man but when you refused, he made me and another soldier travel to Dilli to kidnap your son." The man looked disgusted, "His debts have made him mad."

"The only way to find out the reason for Saifuddin's actions," Nawabsaab said, "is through the paintings. The answer must lie in them." Then he waved at the soldier, "And let this man go. I think he's telling the truth."

The soldier bowed low, " I beg a thousand pardons of you and your son. And I promise I will never make such a mistake again. I'm staying at a sarai at Ballimaran. If you ever need any help please call me. And I beg pardon again." He bowed to the nawab and to Akram and left the room.

Majid looked pleadingly at the nawab, "Huzoor, can we see the paintings now?"

Nawabsaab laughed. "I don't think you'll be able to solve the mystery, Majid. They are paintings like all others. I'm very fond of them because my grandfather gave them to me but they are nothing particularly special."

"Then what do we do?"

"We find a painter," Basheer Khan suggested. "We could get a miniature painter to study them. We are no experts. It's possible that these paintings are very rare and can be sold for a fortune."

"Akram, Majid,' said Nawabsaab, "tomorrow you two will find out the best painter in Dilli and bring him to me. I want my collection assessed."

Next morning the boys had to walk a lot going from shop to shop near the fountain in Chandni Chowk where they sold paintings until they got the address of the best painter in the city. Then they trudged past the Fatehpuri Masjid to his house. The main door was open. They entered the courtyard and peered into a room. Inside, the painter sat with his assistants working. They sat in a row on the floor with small wooden tables before them. There were pots of paint and bunches of brushes beside each man, who sat bent over a sheet of paper painting the small delicately coloured miniatures. The painter looked up as Akram and Majid salaamed and entered. He listened to the boy's request and laughed, "But why do you need me to see the paintings? Any shopkeeper who sells miniatures can do the assessing for you. They know better than I about prices."

"Perhaps it's not the price that is important," Majid said.

The painter looked puzzled, "What are you looking for?"

"We don't know," Akram said apologetically, "but it was important enough to make someone try to kidnap me and ask for the paintings as ransom."

The painter sat up in surprise, dropping his brush into the bowl of water with a 'plop'. He got up, slipped on his shoes, wrapped a shawl around him, put on his fez cap and said, "Let's go. Paintings worth a ransom! They must be very rare."

At the haveli, the ardali and his assistants brought out the bundles of miniatures wrapped in layers of muslin cloth. He laid them out on the baithaktakht. There were paintings of kings at court, queens in the harem garden, birds and flowers, men riding horses and elephants.

Slowly, the painter studied every painting. Finally he looked up with a frown, "I don't understand. These are good paintings but neither very old not very rare. I wouldn't recommend selling them. You won't get much."

"I thought so," Nawabsaab nodded. "Could you suggest why else anyone would want them?"

"Is there any history behind these paintings?" the painter asked. "Sometimes information is hidden in paintings instead of being written down. You know, like a puzzle."

"Do any of them look like puzzles to you?"

"I'm not sure," the painter said thoughtfully. "But somehow this painting is technically inferior to the others." He laid one painting before them.

In the painting a man in the dress of a nobleman sat on a prancing horse. In his hand he held a beautiful curved sword with jewels set in the handle. In the background there was a haveli with gardens around it and a gate with carved lions on both corners. "Can you make out what it could mean?" the painter asked.

"The best person to answer the question would be my mother," Nawabssab said. "She was present when these miniatures were painted." He turned to the ardali, "Send word inside that we are requesting Ammi Sahiba to come to the baithak."

On one side of the baithak the chik curtains were let down and after a while behind the curtain Nawabsaab's mother Begum Shaukat Jaan came and sat down with her maids. "Let me see the painting," Begum Sahiba said. "Oh! Dara Shukoh's sword. It was painted before the sword was lost."

"We had Dara Shukoh's sword?" Nawabsaab looked startled.

"Yes. Shahjahan was still the emperor then. Your grandfather was a good friend of the emperor's eldest son, the Prince Dara Shukoh. Then the battle for the throne began between the four sons of Shahjahan. Your grandfather naturally helped prince Dara but he lost to prince Aurangzeb."

"And Aurangzed became the emperor and executed Prince Dara," Nawabsaab broke in.

"Yes. That good prince was paraded through Chandni Chowk in chains and then killed. By then your grandfather was also seriously ill from the wounds that he had got in the battle. In all the confusion the sword that Prince Dara had given your grandfather was lost. And with Aurangzeb on the throne we did not look for it."

"That's why Emperor Aurangzeb never liked our family."

"Yes. He spared your grandfather because he was gravely ill. But he never really forgave us."

"It was beautiful," Begum Sahiba said simply. "The hilt was in the shape of a curved head of an eagle. The eyes were two large rubies and the rest was set with emeralds and pearls on gold."

"And cousin Saifuddin thinks this painting tells us where the sword is hidden."

"He's mistaken. If he hid it anywhere your grandfather never told anyone. After he died your father looked everywhere for it. Believe me, Dara Shukoh's sword is lost forever," said the Begum with a sigh and they heard her leave the room.

Late into the night Akram and Majid sat with the miniature. "Do you think the man is Prince Dara himself." Majid wondered.

"It could be my great grandfather too."

"Where do you think that miniature was painted? That's quite a grand haveli there."

"Which haveli?" Basheer Khan had entered the room and peered over their shoulders. Suddenly he bent closer, his sharpened. "Wait a minute. Are those lions on the gatepost?"

"You know the haveli, Abba?" Majid asked.

"I think so. You can't forget those lions. The local people use to call it the Sherwalli Kothi."

"Where?" Akram asked, excited.

"On the outskirts of Agra, on the road to Fatehpur Sikri. When I was young I worked at a haveli near this one. It was the ruins of a nawab's garden house. Only a few walls remain. But those lions still stand on the gateposts."

"Could the sword be there?"

"What if it is?" Majid said. "What can we do?"

"Go to Agra, naturally," Akram grinned. "Old Sherwalli Kothi here we come!"

AGRA. Majid and Akram had never been there before. And here they were with Basheer Khan standing before the stunningly beautiful Taj Mahal, its pure marble glittering in the noon sun. They had arrived in Agra that morning and Basheer had decided that they would go in search of the sword the next morning. Even though the boys were dying of impatience they knew he was correct. The horses were tired and needed to be rested. Also it was possible that Saifuddin's men were watching them. So for a day they were going to act like ordinary visitors to Agra, going sightseeing. To put Saifuddin off the scent Basheer had not even brought any of his men with him. They planned to ride out before dawn next morning. Till then the boys had to wait.

That night, they were going back to the sarai after dining in the bazaar. The streets were empty because of the winter cold. The roads were in shadows, at spots dimly lit from the light of shops or bonfires on the corners, where shadowy figures sat huddled around the burning logs. A light mist drifted in the air. Majid had dropped back to go and buy some paan. As he turned to follow the others, a man wrapped in a shawl stepped out of a dark corner and began walking next to him. "I'm a friend," the face hidden in the shawl whispered. "Tell your father I will come to meet him tonight with some news of Saifuddin Haider." Silently the figure melted into the gloom.

The three of them waited in the sarai room. It was past midnight . Basheer Khan sat with an open sword beside him, worried. "I made a mistake. I should have brought some men with me. We need soldiers here. Agra is, after all, Saifuddin Haider's city."

"What about us?" Akram interrupted, "Do you think we can't fight?" and he pointed to the daggers he and Majid were carrying. Basheer Khan smiled.

There was a soft knock on the door and they all stilled to listen. Majid opened the door a few inches to peer out and saw only the man in the shawl standing outside. He slipped inside and quickly closed the door behind him. As he removed the shawl they saw in surprise that he was an old white-haired man. He salaamed and said, "I am an old khansamah of the Haider family, huzoor."

"What do you want?"

"Nothing. I have eaten the salt of the Haider family for forty years.I do not like what is happening. I have come to warn you.

"Warn us? What about?"

"Saifuddin Haider knows you are in Agra. He has men watching your house in Dilli and they have been following you since you entered the city. I do not know what he wants from you but it cannot be anything good. I beg of you to leave the city. Your lives may be in danger. Nawab Saifuddin is not a man you should make an enemy."

Basheer looked thoughtfully at the old khansamah and said, "I thank you for your help. You have taken a great risk to come and warn us. And I agree we should not stay on in Agra without the protection of our soldiers. Do not worry. Tomorrow we leave."

The old man bowed, " Give my respectful adaab to Nawabsaab. He is a good man. And tell him that whatever it is, it's not worth risking the life of his son." And wrapping the shawl around his head to hide his face, the old man left.

"Are you serious about going back, Abba?" Majid asked.

"Yes," Basheer said shortly.

"Your mean, without even trying to find the sword?" Akram put in.

"Right. Now go to bed. We start for Dilli tomorrow morning." He smiled consolingly, "If Nawabsaab is serious about searching for the sword we can come back later with more men. It's too dangerous to search for it now." Basheer got under his quilt and went to sleep.

Majid and Akram sat staring at each other in disappointment as Basheer began to snore. Then they crept out of the room and stood shivering in the verandah. "I don't want to go back without the sword," Akram said.

"Neither do I," Majid added. "There is one chance tomorrow if we can get away before Abba wakes up. He said it's a couple of hours ride to the kothi. If we can start early we'll be back by noon."

"Right. If we can find the kothi by ourselves…"

"And if we don't we'll come back same day anyway. Abba said so."

It was still dark when they woke up. Basheer still slept deeply. Creeping about they got ready and tiptoed out of the room.

"Taken the daggers?" Akram whispered. Majid nodded without speaking.

In the stable the stablehand was huddled before a dead fire and woke up to the sound of hooves as they were taking out the horses.

"Oye! Where are you two going?" he said, struggling out of his quilt, "It's still dark."

"We're going for an early morning ride before we leave for Dilli," Akram said firmly.

"You're mad. Going out in this cold." The man yawned as he helped them saddle the horses. "Where are you going?"

"The road to Fatehpur Sikri. How do we go?"

"Straight down this lane and then turn left. It's the direct road."

They swung onto horses and rode out of Agra as the sky was lightening towards dawn. The road was empty. In some foodstalls shadowy men were lighting chulas, the smoke rising lazily in the air. The chill air froze their cheeks as the horses' hooves echoed down the road. They had ridden for about an hour when they saw another foodshop.

"Majid said, "I,' m hungry. Let's stop here."

"A hot bowl of milk and some kachoris would be nice," Akram agreed, as they tethered their horses to a tree behind the shop, so that they could not be seen from the road. Majid was soon warming his hands around the milk bowl and looked up curiously when he heard the sound of horse's hooves coming down the road from Agra. They had not met any rider so far. He and Akram looked worriedly at each other. Could they be Saifuddin's men? Hidden behind the shop door, they peered out.

Down the road three horsemen came, their turbans and capes flowing behind them in the breeze. They were bent low over their horses, riding at a furious pace. As they galloped past the shop towards Fatehpur Sikri, Majid said, "They look as if they are following someone."

"Us?"

The shopkeeper put some hot kachoris and pickle before them and said, "Where are you boys going? It's early–pretty cold for a ride."

"We were planning to see Fatehpur Sikri."

"Oh! Then why not take the shorter road?" He pointed to a rough country lane curving away behind his shop. "It'll take you to Sikri much faster."

"That's a good idea," Akram said politely.

As they were getting onto their horses the man said, "Go straight for about ten minutes. You'll reach a crossing. On the left is a broken down haveli with two lions on its gates. Turn past it and you'll see the walls of Sikri before you."

"A haveli with lions on its gates!" Majid exclaimed with a laugh of triumph as they wheeled their horses towards the lane, "Thank you, janab!"

SHERWALLI KOTHI. The broken gates of Sherwalli Kothi loomed before them as they sprang down from their horses. One of the lions had toppled over and lay in shattered fragments in the courtyard. The other was tilting dangerously.

Just to be careful, Majid and Akram walked their horses to the back of the haveli and tied them behind a hedge so that they were hidden from the road.

They entered the courtyard and looked around. The ruins of Sherwalli Kothi stood between overgrown bushes, creepers and collapsed rubble from broken walls. Pigeons cooed on the stills of the gaping windows of what must have been the baithak. They wandered inside, to the inner courtyard. The dark back rooms were full of bats. Akram, flapping away a pigeon, said, " How do we look for the sword? It could be anywhere among the rubble."

"Think," Majid said. "If that miniature told us where the sword was hidden, it should also tell us where it is kept inside the haveli." And he closed his eyes trying to remember the miniature. "There was the gate, the haveli, the horseman, the lions, pigeons flying in the sky, a fountain, a… the fountain?" He looked enquiringly at Akram.

They raced to the inner courtyard where the cracked, dry marble fountain stood. They walked around it slowly searching for any hiding place large enough to hide a sword. Then they scrambled in on top of the base to where the ornamental spout must have once sprayed water. Akram felt around the base and shook his head, "It looks solid to me."

"What about the spout? Remember in the fountain at home you can open it for cleaning."

They grabbed the spout and twisted. It squeaked and moved a bit. "This can be unscrewed," Akram said, struggling to twist the jammed spout. He gave a big heave and with a crack the spout turned, broke and came away in his hands. In the marble base of the fountain, there was a deep hole. Akram reached inside and in a moment pulled out a long thin object in a velvet case. Carefully they opened it. Inside there was a leather scabbard and from it Majid pulled out Dara Shukoh's bejeweled sword.

He held it up and the unmarked steel glittered in the morning sum. They looked closely at the hilt. It was more beautiful than the picture. The ruby eyes of the carved eagle glowed back at them. It was so beautiful they couldn't say a word for a while. "I think we should go back now," Akram said finally, "or your father will come in search of us."

"Or Saifuddin's men."

"Who cares!" Akram grinned. "We have the sword." Akram slid the sc to his belt. "Just a minute boys," said a deep voice behind them. They wh to find three men blocking their way. 'Oh no!, Majid thought despera riders we saw on the road!'

"What do you want?" Akram tried to look surprised and angry.

"Give me the sword," said the man who had spoken earlier. A big fleshy man with a large moustache; wearing jeweled rings, brooches and a furlined cape.

Akram kept a hand tightly clutched to his side, holding the sword, as the boys drew closer. "Who are you?" he asked.

"I am your uncle, dear nephew." The man gave a sneering smile. "Saifuddin Haider. Now give me the sword. It's mine."

"How did you find us?" Majid asked.

Saifuddin laughed, "Your foodshopwalla friend told us. When we saw that the road to Sikri was empty we rode back and checked at all the shops on the way. Now give…"

Just then Majid looked behind the three men and said with a relieved smile, "Abba!"

The men turned to see who was behind them and finding no one, realized that Majid had tricked them. But by then the boys had sprinted through the courtyard into the backrooms of the haveli.

"Catch them!" they heard Saifuddin shout to the sound of pounding feet.

The boys vaulted through a broken window to the back garden. With the bats and pigeons flapping all around in panic, Majid looked back to see Saifuddin's men getting closer, with the fat Saifuddin panting behind them. They crashed. through bushes, jumped over broken walls, dodging trees. 'We have to get to the horses,' Akram thought. He picked up a pebble and sent it whizzing towards one man who ducked, stumbled and fell. By then the boys had reached the horses and quickly untied them. As Akram scrambled onto the horse's back the man reached out to clutch at his leg but Akram managed to kick free.

As they galloped round the haveli to reach the road Akram looked back to see Saifuddin and his men running back through the garden to reach their horses tethered to the haveli gatepost.

They bent low over their speeding horses. The chill winter air whipped at them and the horses' breath came out in smoky puffs. As they turned into the main Sikri road they heard the thunder of horses' hooves behind them. Saifuddin was chasing them again. The five horses raced down the road. 'If he catches us now,' Majid thought worriedly, 'he'll surely hurt us.'

"Look!" Akram yelled. A group of riders was coming towards them down the road.

"It's Abba!" Majid laughed in triumph.

In a moment they were with Basheer Khan. Surrounded by friendly faces, they turned back to Saifuddin and his men had halted at seeing the men around the boys. Defeated, they turned their horses and rode away.

The boys looked at the other riders in surprise. They were all Basheer Khan's men. "How did you get here?" Akram asked.

"Your father is here in Agra," Basheer said smiling, as they rode back to the *sarai*. "They caught the man who had been watching our house in Dilli. So Nawabsaab felt that we would need some protection in Agra."

At the *sarai* Nawab Amanullah Haider was waiting anxiously. The boys sprang down their horses and Akram pulled the scabbard out of his belt. Carefully Majid took the sword out and laid it in Nawabsaab's hands. "Your sword I believe, Nawab huzoor," he said, smiling.

"No," Nawabsaab said quietly. "This sword belongs to the people who found it. It belongs to you and Akram. What do you plan to do with it?"

"I know!" Akram gave a wide grin. "We'll call the miniature painter and both of us will be painted riding on a horse and holding Dara Shukoh's sword. Just like in the painting."

Majid held the sword up, a hand on his hip, struck a warrior-like pose and said, "Hey! Akram! How do I look?"

"Like a bad painting.!" said Basheer Khan.

The Sword of Dara Shukoh, first published in *Target* in 1988, is a delightful story and has been a favourite with children for many years. It is a historical story set in a period when young boys rode about on horses and bhishtis carried water in skins in the streets of old Delhi. The author does not fight shy of writing about family rivalry and revealing the low-down behaviour adults are capable of sinking to.

If we were to enumerate the reasons for its success we would come up with the following characteristics:

1. **Has children as protagonists:** Children like to know about children. Of course there are exceptions to the rule. But in this story—as in a lot of children's literature—a process of identification is at once set in motion on the part of the young reader when the protagonists are children. Akram and Majid also express an important part of a child's life: friendship with other children.
2. **Plot-oriented with more dialogue and events but fewer ruminations:** This might be an important distinction between children's literature and literature for adults. Most children's stories have a strong plot. 'The Sword of Dara Shukoh' is a story of adventure and mystery. There is initial suspense as to why attempts are being made to kidnap the children; followed by the mystery of the sword, which is finally unravelled by the children after a series of adventurous events.
3. **Written in simple language:** Children's literature needs to be accessible to children. Simple and direct narration is the best. The writer has fewer opportunities to make stylistic deviations. However, some children's literature successfully uses neologisms and other devices. 'The Sword of Dara Shukoh' is written simply; as though the writer were actually narrating the story to a group of agog children.
4. **Educational:** Children hate to be preached to. In this story we find the protagonists going against the orders of the guardian and in fact getting into a lot of trouble. It is hardly a story with a moral. However, what the story does successfully is introduce the reader to historical personages. Some children might be interested enough to find out more about Aurangzeb and Dara Shukoh. Its connection with history, might account for the continuing appeal of this story.
5. **Happy ending, in which good triumphs over evil:** Can Children's literature express shades of grey? When stories deal with difficult subjects then shades of grey are inevitable and we have already hinted that the writer should not be pusillanimous about selecting appropriate subjects for children. Everything that affects their world could become an appropriate subject for children's literature. How-

ever, children's literature should not be 'literature of despair'. The 'Sword of Dara Shukoh' deals with betrayal and greed but it also affirms goodness. To the extent that the valuable sword becomes the property of the children who found it.

A Conversation with a Creative Writer

Subhadra Sen Gupta

Jaideep Krishnan, our Research Associate, met the writer of *The Sword of Dara Shukoh,* Subhadra Sen Gupta, and asked her a few questions. We reproduce below some of things she said:

Is action the difference between writing for adults and for children?

Yes. Children are impatient readers; you have to move into action very quickly. Plot is absolutely important. You have to talk to them straight, not speak down to them. Do not ever give advice—they hate it.

What kids like is a lot of detail… a lot of descriptions. What is the colour, the smell, the touch… it is very important to them. I incorporate a lot of this especially as I'm talking of the past. Sights, sounds, smell—everything gets in.

Is an oral style important?

Yes, you have to write it in an oral way. I always imagine a child to whom I tell the story.. makes the process better, easier.

What kind of stories do children prefer?

Children prefer stories if they are connected to familiar things, for example, nowadays computers are very common, so they could connect to one of my stories about a ghost in a computer.

Although my stuff is not always about familiar things—it is usually about palanquins and swords. I mean, I keep up with kids, and I can write about what is familiar to them like ipods.

What about morals?

It is not that I don't bring up questions, I do. Always sugar coated within a good plot, so they read it anyway. Evil of every kind appears, and so does goodness, but I do not preach—that makes kids puke.

I also weave in things like tolerance and equality but I do it very lightly. The protagonists always belong to different religions. They are often poor. People expect historical fiction to be about nawabs and princesses, so I have children of tongawallas and sabjiwallas going out and solving mysteries. This is also to break the cliched belief many middle class kids have that poor kids are dumb.

While writing for kids you are always conscious of the fact that you can influence them much deeper than you would an adult. That's what I enjoy, playing with their devious little minds.

Should certain topics, like rape, violence, be avoided when writing for children?

I have been thinking about this for a long time. But I don't think I am capable of handling it, at least for pre-teens.

I hear a lot from children—about peer pressure, divorced parents, physical/ mental abuse, all these things need to be talked about—it is very necessary. But for me, it is very difficult to talk about these things... it is difficult to write about them.

I've been thinking about it for some time. If I deal with it, it will have to be in the first-person, because the point-of-view decides how the story comes across.

Evil should be incorporated, makes for great plots! It doesn't shock kids. But I prefer an upbeat ending.

Tell us about how you work. Do you think feedback to work-in-progress is important?

I start early, and work till about lunch. You can't say 'I'll wait for inspiration,' you just have to write. The hardest part is to start writing.

Research is essential, even for modern stories, it gives them texture. Doing a story about three anonymous kids and a dog in an anonymous town doesn't work.

It is important to write. It is also important to get the stories read... you need to know if it works. The feedback is important. Sometimes the criticism can really destroy you, but it has to be done... and the more you write, the sharper it gets.

You have written a lot of stories which are set in the past...

Having a niche like history helps. The publisher needs to be convinced.

ACTIVITY 23

1. Make a list of 10 Indian books for children and specify which age-group each is intended for.
2. Write about your favourite book as a child of twelve. Why do you think you liked it so much?
3. On the basis of the material provided above write a paragraph about the difference between writing for children and adults.

Create a Person

Would you like to play God? For the next two class periods we will encourage you to create a human being based on someone you know; in your own image; or completely imaginary.

In the first workshop we ask you a series of questions that will help you form an image of the person in your mind. In the second workshop some of you may read out your answers to the class and answer questions that come from your class-mates.

The good news is that the teacher is not allowed to express an opinion.

Workshop 4

Let's create a person ***Answer the following questions without discussing them with anyone:***

1. What is the name of the person?
2. How tall is s/he?
3. How old?
4. Hair? Long or short, straight or curly?
5. Colour of eyes?
6. Does s/he work? What does s/he do for a living?
7. Is or was s/he married? If yes, describe the spouse in two lines; if not give the reason in two lines.
8. Does or did s/he have a lover? If yes, describe the lover; if not give the reason in two lines.
9. Does s/he have friends? Describe her\his closest friend in two lines or tell us the reason for her\his isolation.
10. What is her\his strongest desire? What does she\he hope\long\pray for?

11. Describe a dream s/he had last night in two lines.
12. Does s/he have an enemy? Why\why not?
13. In two lines describe a childhood incident that made a lasting impression on her\him.
14. Describe in two lines an accident s/he had as an adult.

Note: If the person is a child, leave out questions 6, 7, 8 and 14. Replace with:

1. Does s\he go to school? If yes describe the school; if not give the reason in two lines.
2. Describe her\his parents in two lines.
3. Describe her\his class teacher or any other adult s\he comes in daily contact with.
4. Describe the most frightening incident of his\her life.

After you finish tear out the page and hand it over to your teacher. You will get it back.

Note to the teacher: Please go over the answers the students have provided and select four sheets for classroom discussion.

Workshop 5 Tutorial Format

Discussing the person

1. The student reads out the questions and the answers.
2. The answers are open for discussion. However, the student who wrote the answers has to be silent until allowed to speak. The teacher too is not allowed to speak.
3. The discussion focuses on the following points:
   a. Appearance of the person.
   b. The kind of relationships s/he has. Is there a pattern to the relationships?
   c. Is the person ambitious? What kind of problems s/he might have in attaining the goals?
   d. The kind of life s/he is leading.
4. Defend the creation. The house puts questions to the writer of the answers. The writer explains her\his point of view. The teacher is silent.

*Note to the teacher: The minimum time for discussion of four sheets is 55 minutes (one period). You may include more sheets for discussion and extend the time of the workshop or have it over two to three days depending on the response of the students and your convenience. Please do not return the sheets to the students till the end of workshop 5.

Workshop 6

The Person Interrupted Imagine a situation in which the person you created does one of the following:

a. Meets a very unusual man\woman.
b. Gets a job abroad or has to move out of town.
c. Overhears a conversation that stuns and shocks her/him.

If your person is a child substitute with:

a. Meets a very unusual girl/boy.
b. Has to leave town because the parents are transferred.
c. Overhears classmates planning something that would shock parents and teachers.

Write up this situation in 500 words focusing on:

a. the feelings of the person
b. the place and time
c. the events as they take place

Workshop 7 (Optional)

Discussion of the situation constructed in Workshop 6 using the same format as workshop 5. It would be possible to discuss two to three situations in a 55 minute class period.

Home Work for the Portfolio

At the end of workshop 6/7 you may have an idea for a short story. If you do:

a. Keep away your worksheets.
b. Begin on a fresh page.
c. Try not to use any of the phrases and sentences that you have used in your worksheets.
d. Let the ideas you have come up with simmer at the back of your mind while you write.

At the end of workshop 3\4 you may feel that your person and the situation are not working. In that case:

a. Keep away the worksheets.
b. Begin on a fresh page.
c. Avoid everything you wrote and thought in workshop 1, 2, 3 and 4.

Both the outcomes are equally valuable.

SECTION III: DRAMA

What is Drama?

The Concept and Characteristics of Drama

All of us have constructed plays at same point or the other. As children, we play 'doctor-patient', 'teacher-student' or 'robber-police' and so on. We imagine ourselves with a completely different identity, we place ourselves in a fictional situation and evolve a sequence of events that culminate in some kind of a climax (it could be the doctor curing the patient – or in macabre instances, the patient dying; the teacher punishing a naughty child; and the thieves being caught or gunned down). The elements of these simple games that children play, are much the same as the great (or not so great) plays we read and watch; but writing a play is as complex a craft as writing a poem or a work of fiction. It is the one form that depends upon not just the writer for its success but also a whole lot of other people such as the actor, the director, the technicians (those involved with sound, lights, sets, props, scenery, etc), the costume designer, and so on It also involves the audience and its response. This is because though a play may work well as a written piece of literature, the ultimate aim of drama is that it must succeed when PERFORMED before an audience. So, when we write a play, we must always keep in mind the performative aspect.

The word drama is derived from the Greek word drao which means to 'do' or 'act'. Most dictionaries define drama as a general term used for performances in which the actors imitate the speech and actions of characters (fictional, historical, or non-human entities) in order to entertain an audience, either on stage or through a broadcast or by a particular example of this art i.e. a play (Baldick 1990:61).

Writing a play is not completely different from writing fiction. In both, there is a dependence on plot; a revelation of character through action and dialogues; a distinctive tone; and some kind of central concern or theme. (Minot 1982:215). However, drama has some special attributes that set it apart from fiction. Let us have a look at these.

Table 3.1 Attributes of Drama

Characteristics	Description
A spectator art	A play differs from a work of fiction in that it is addressed not to the readers but to the spectators. There is a direct and dynamic relationship between the playwrights and their audiences.
A dramatic art	A play generally has an emotional impact or force established early in it with a dramatic question that often develops into a specific conflict; such an impact is difficult to sustain and so the playwright works out a pattern of rising and falling action to regulate the emotional peaks of the audience. Irony, satire, and shock are some of the devices that add to the dramatic aspect of a play.
A visual art	Action or the movement of the characters on stage is as significant as the lines spoken by them. The set, lighting, experiments in mixed media such as the addition of projected images and even movie sequences, all appeal to the visual aspect of drama.
An auditory art	A play appeals to the ear; every word (except for stage directions) is a dialogue and is meant to be spoken aloud. Thus the sound of the language, be it in realistic plays or otherwise, is important (The sound of the pauses, too, need attention).
A physically produced art	In drama, sets have to be constructed and it is not always possible to shift from one scene to another as quickly as one does in film and fiction. The impact that this has on live performers is that it lends a kind of intense credibility, regardless of whether the play is realistic or not. It also allows a variety of techniques that help to blur the distinction between actors and audience.

(Contd.)

(Contd.)

A continuous art	When reading works of fiction and poetry, one can linger where one wants to; turn back a page or review an earlier scene. But in drama, the audience has to follow the pace set by the playwright. A portion of a scene might well be far more rapid than another. So, the playwright has to be evermore conscious of pace.
Popular form in theatre for example, puppet theatre for children	**Not all plays use dialogue; a *Pantomime*, for example, is a play without words, also called a *Dumb Show.* In ancient Rome, a pantomime meant an actor who single-handedly played all the parts.

Source: Minot (1982: 216–17)

To reiterate, drama has a lot in common with prose fiction in its use of character and plot, stimulation of emotion, and in the way it deals with life. Like poetry, drama draws upon all the resources of language including verse; a lot of drama is poetry. However, the one specific and special feature that sets it apart from all other forms is that it is written primarily to be *performed* rather than read. So, the action of drama is generally presented by performers/actors upon some sort of stage and before an audience: these aspects have an important bearing on the nature of drama and serve as a source of potential or limitation to the playwright.

In theatre workshops, one of the exercises is that the director asks the actors to imagine and then enact how they would behave in a certain situation. For example, how would they act if they were to be imprisoned inside a dark cell no larger than a coffin in height, length and breadth. So while one actor may scream out aloud 'Help! Help! Save me someone!' and thus play the role of a hapless victim, another may yawn, stretch and go off to sleep playing the role of the indifferent, 'couldn't-care-less' captive,and so on. The situation and the personality of the character work together and lead to the kind of emotions projected or the language used. To capture the attention of the audience the playwright must therefore find an interesting concept, that is, a basic situation in which some kind of a conflict or struggle, and an outcome or resolution (technically termed *Denouement*) occurs.

To work with an example, let us read the following episode from Act I of Mahesh Dattani's *Dance Like A Man*, a commercially popular urban Indian play in English; now also converted successfully into a screenplay. Dattani in his Foreword to the play has actually underlined the concept. It is not necessary, however, for the playwright to do so. Audiences can decipher the intention of the playwright through their own understanding of the concept as it gradually unfolds in the play.

> AMRITLAL Don't preach to me! I know what I have to do.
> RATNA. I have always been taught to speak to my elders with respect, but since I haven't done anything wrong there's no reason why I shouldn't speak up. Chenni amma is the oldest living exponent of the Mysore school and is the only link we have with the old school. She doesn't have a single student who is dedicated enough to absorb her knowledge. She is seventy-five and dying. There's nobody who even visits her, not even her relatives or her children. Oh, she does get the occasional journalist or a curious foreigner knocking at her door. But they don't do much for her, except maybe give her a few annas out of pity. But she doesn't mind all this. She doesn't mind at all being poor and lonely. What she is really frustrated about is that in her youth she did not have the freedom to express her art. All her childhood years were spent

in training. Training which she could never use. All a waste—for her. She spends her time now at the temple steps, selling flowers. When she came to know that I was a dancer, she greeted me and pleaded, yes, pleaded with me to learn the art of abhinaya from her. She even tempted me by offering to teach me some old dance compositions which she knew by memory. It was important for her that she should impart her knowledge to someone worthy of it. And it was important for me to learn what she had to offer. So, instead of going to the temple every Monday, I go to her house.

AMRITLAL. And practice in her courtyard for all passersby to see.

RATNA. Only those who are curious enough to peep over her wall to see where the sound of dancing-bells are coming from.

AMRITLAL. Your bells. The sound of your bells.

RATNA. Yes.

AMRITLAL. The sound of your bells coming from the courtyard of a prostitute.

RATNA. She is seventy-five years old.

AMRITLAL. And people peer over her walls to see my daughter-in-law dancing in her courtyard.

RATNA. Yes. Dancing the divine dance of Shiva and Parvati

AMRITLAL. And you feel what you are doing is right?

RATNA. Yes. My husband knows where I go and I have his permission.

AMITLAL. Your husband happens to be my son. And you are both under my care. It is my permission that you should ask for.

RATNA. You would not have given it to me.

AMRITLAL. And I never will.

RATNA. If you don't allow me to visit her, then—then I'll have to ask her to come here!

AMRITLAL. Never. Not to this house, ever.

RATNA. What objection do you have to a withered old lady coming to your house? It is my dancing in her courtyard that you mind.

AMRITLAL. You will not. That is all. I need not give you any reason for it.

RATNA. You can't stop me from learning an art!

AMRITLAL. I don't want you seeing that woman again, that's final. And that is all I have to say. You may go. I'm sorry I've kept you from jingling your bells. My request is that you finish with your session as quickly as you can and see that your guruji leaves before my visitors arrive. God forbid that they should bump into one another.

(JAIRAJ enters with the tray.)

JAIRAJ. They've finished their coffee. Why didn't you serve them sweets? One of them hinted he wanted to eat sweets. You know how they love to feel insulted. (To AMRITLAL.) I have to pay the musicians.

RATNA. It's nice to know they are already feeling insulted. They can't feel any worse when we ask them to leave. Give me the tray.

JAIRAJ. I'll take it to the kitchen. He wants you to do a padam now. (Looking at AMRITLAL.) The older they get, the crankier they become. (To RATNA.) And who said anything about them leaving? (To AMRITLAL.) Four rupees. (He exits to the kitchen.)

AMRITLAL (to RATNA.) I'm leaving it to you. I'll give you ten minutes before I personally request them to leave.

RATNA. Don't worry. I'll think of an excuse.

AMRITLAL. Good. And if you promise me not to visit that woman again, I won't feel it necessary to restrict your movements. (RATNA looks at him. She laughs suddenly.) What's so funny?

RATNA. I really feel sorry for you!

AMRITLAL. That's a strange way of showing that you feel sorry for me. Laughing like that.
RATNA. I really do feel sorry.
AMRITLAL. Why?
RAINA. Tomorrow, Jairaj starts learning another dance form—Kuchipudi.
AMRITLAL. So?
RATNA. (triumphantly). In Kuchipudi, the men dress up as women!
(RATNA laughs again triumphantly and enters the dance hall where she speaks to her guru. JAIRAJ enters and makes his way to the dance hall. He stops.)
JAIRAJ. Can I have the money now?
AMRITLAL. Yes I'll give you the money now.
JAIRAJ. Four rupees.
AMRITLAL. Yes. You can pay them four rupees and tell them never to set foot in this house again.
[Pause.]
JAIRAJ. You can't do that
AMRITLAL. I'm sorry, son.
JAIRAJ. But you promised.
AMRITLAL. Years ago
JAIRAJ. You promised you would allow me to continue with my hobbies.
AMRITLAL. That was when you were a boy and dance was just a hobby. Grow up, Jairaj.
JAIRAJ. I don't want to grow up! You can't stop me from doing what I want.
AMRITLAL. As long as you are under my care—
(RATNA enters as if leading guruji and the musicians to the door. She stands with folded hands near the door as they go out.)
JAIRAJ. Guruji! Why—(He watches them leave. Then he speaks to RATNA.)—why did they leave? Did my father—?
RATNA. It's alright. They didn't feel offended. I told them we were tired and he said it was time he left. He will come back tomorrow.
AMRITLAL. He will not come here tomorrow. I will send him a personal letter of regret.
JAIRAJ (to AMRITLAL.) As long as we are under your care — (He moves towards the bedroom).
RATNA. Where are you—?
JAIRAJ. As long as we are under his care! (He exits)
RATNA. I won't bother asking you what happened.
(AMRITLAL goes to the phone—the old-fashioned one—and dials.)
AMRITLAL (into the phone). Hello? Patel? … Yes. I want a favour from you … The woman you saw my daughter-in-law with. Yes, that one—could you send a doctor to see her? I believe she isn't well .. Yes—— and Patel? Please give-her a donation of five hundred rupees on my behalf. I will send you a hundi… Please. I shall be very grateful to you … thank you. (Puts the phone down.)
RATNA. That was very generous of you.
AMRITLAL. That was in compensation for depriving her of her only student.
(JAIRAJ enters with a bundle of clothes tied in a sari.)
JAIRAJ. (to RATNA). Come on. I've packed some of your clothes. We're leaving.
RATNA. Where?
JAIRAJ. We'll decide that later. (Gives RATNA the bundle.) First let's get out of here.
RATNA. But Jai, you haven't taken everything-

JAIRAJ. Never mind. (He takes RATNA by the arm and leads her to the door.)
RATNA. At least we could take all our belongings. We could leave tomorrow.
JAIRAJ. We don't need anything fancy. (He turns around and speaks defiantly.) As from now we are no longer under your care. And will never be again. Never. (He exits, followed by a bewildered RATNA.)
RATNA (as she exits). Jai! Jairaj!
(As soon as RATNA exits, the garden becomes the present day living room. AMRITLAL becomes the older JAIRAJ as he removes the shawl.)
The older RATNA's voice from the bedroom picks up from where the younger one's trailed off.)
RATNA [off]. Jairaj? (She enters.) Jairaj? Oh! You are still here? I didn't see you in Lata's room—I was wondering where you were. You haven't been drinking too much I hope. Come to bed. I've asked Lata to go back to her room. She tosses and turns too much. It disturbs my sleep. And you can't share a blanket with her, she grabs it all for herself in her sleep. I pity that Viswas. (Yawns.) Come on... (JAIRAJ slowly exits followed by RATNA. This part of RATNA's speech comes till it trails off with her exit.) You know, I don't think it is such a good idea asking Chandra Kala to lend Seshadri. They might plot to sabotage Lata's dance. He might give her the wrong tala. People can't make out whose mistake it is and they always blame the dancer. It happened once before when Nalini had taken Saraswati's cousin for her show...
(Lights fade out.)

ACTIVITY 24

1. What is the origin of the word 'drama'? What are the similarities between drama (i.e. a play) and fiction?
2. What is the one special attribute of drama that sets it apart from all other forms of art? Discuss.
3. What do we mean when we say that a play is a dramatic art? What are some of the devices that add to the dramatic aspect of a play?
4. How is drama a visual and an auditory art?
5. What are the advantages of the construction of sets in a drama?
6. What is the difference between the way we read fiction and poetry and the way we respond to drama?
7. How does a playwright begin writing a play to capture the interest of the audience?

After reading the episode, what do you think is the concept or situation that Dattani puts forward in this episode of the play? Do you find it interesting or not? Give reasons for your answer.

The Plot in Drama or Dramatic Structure

Once the concept is clear the next step is to develop the idea into a sequence of events of specific characters involved in some sort of conflict (*Crisis*)—a clash of actions, ideas, desires, or wills. The central character (*Protagonist*) struggles against (i) some other person or group of persons, (ii) some external force—physical nature, society, or fate (man against environment) or (iii) Some element in his own nature (man against him/her self). All the forces against which the protagonist struggles are referred to as *Antagonists*. The conflict(s) in which the protag-

- *In the episode from* Dance Like A Man, *who do you see as the protagonist(s) and who the antagonist(s)?*
- *What is the conflict between the two all about?*

onist is involved may be clear cut, single and identifiable or subtle, multiple and various i.e. the protagonist may be in conflict with one or more or all of the antagonists lined up against her/him. Sometimes the protagonist may not even be aware of his/her involvement in a conflict. The final and most significant crisis is called a *Climax*.

A good plot makes spectators ask 'what next?' or 'How will this turn out to be?' Suspense (concerning not only actions but psychological considerations and moral issues) is the element that generates such questions. Some of the common devices for achieving suspense are Mystery (an unusual set of circumstances which arouses curiosity in the audience and makes them eager for an explanation), Dilemma (the situating of characters especially the protagonists between two alternative courses of action), and Dramatic Irony, outlined in the previous unit, where the audience knows something that the character doesn't. Do you observe any of these devices in the Dattani episode?

Can you comment on the conclusion of the episode from Dance Like A Man*? Does it appear contrived?*

A good plot also contains Artistic Unity, i.e., it contains only those elements which further the central intention of the story; incidents, and episodes that are not only selected carefully but also arranged effectively. The various stages of the creation, progress, and reduction of conflict should be linked together so that it does not appear as if the playwright is managing the plot. In fact, poor cases of plot management where it is clear that the dramatist has given the story a turn unjustified by the situation or the characters involved,that is, any instance of unmotivated action, makes the author guilty of Plot Manipulation. In ancient Greek drama, one often noticed such plot manipulation wherein the dramatists had a god descend from heaven (by means of a stage machine in the theatre) to rescue the protagonist at the last minute from a difficult situation. This kind of a resolution is referred to as Deus Ex Machina (God from the machine). Such contrived ending or cases of plot manipulation, though not regarded with much respect today on the grounds that the plot loses its sense of conviction and inevitability; worked well till recent times with communities that believed in fate and miracles (Perrine 1978 for this section).

While there are several basic types of dramatic structure or plot, the two major forms are the Climatic (as with Sophocles' *King Oedipus*—the Greeks adopted this form; or Ibsen's Ghosts) and the Episodic (the plays of Shakespeare are a good example). Of course both plot forms can be combined effectively as can be seen in the plays of Anton Chekhov and Arthur Miller. Given below is a list of the differences between the two forms.

The following table outlines the chief characteristics of the two major forms and illustrates the differences between them.

Table 3.2 Comparing Climactic and Episodic Forms

Climactic	Episodic
1. Plot begins late in the story, towards the very end or climax.	Plot begins relatively early in the story and moves through a series of episodes.
2. Covers a short space of time, perhaps a few hours, or at most, a few days.	Covers a longer period of time: weeks, months, and sometimes many years.
3. Contains a few solid, extended scenes, such as three acts with each act comprising one long scene.	Many short, fragmented scenes; sometimes an alternation of short and long scenes.

(Contd.)

(Contd.)

4. Occurs in a restricted locale, one room or one house.	May range over an entire city or even several countries.
5. Number of characters severely limited, usually no more than six to eight.	Profusion of characters, sometimes several dozens.
6. Plot is linear and moves in a single line with few subplots or counterplots.	Frequently marked by several threads of action, such as two parallel plots, or scenes of comic relief in a serious play.
7. Line of action proceeds in a cause-and-effect chain. The characters and events are closely linked in a sequence of logical, almost inevitable development.	Scenes are juxtaposed to one another. An event may result from several causes, or no apparent cause, but arises in a network or web of circumstances.

Source: Wilson (1980: 262–63)

Two of the dramatic devices that are used in conjunction with the climactic and episodic plots are:

(a) the use of the *Dialectic* or *Counterpoint* between the characters in the central action of the play and a party outside the action. In Greek drama, the Chorus served this purpose. It was rarely a part of the plot but stood outside the action, argued with the main characters and forwarned them about impending obstacles, made connections between present events and the past, and commented on whatever had occurred. In modern drama, some plays have a Narrator who is the equivalent of the chorus and comments on the action. Brecht is one playwright who uses the narrator with great dramatic effect.

(b) the use of an intellectual debate. This occurs primarily in a Play of Ideas where the main conflict is an intellectual or conceptual one. If carried to an extreme, such intellectualization can completely ignore the experience embodied in the actor-audience relationship.

Apart from the traditional climactic and episodic forms of dramatic plot, there are other forms that can be seen in theatres such as the Theatre of the Absurd; the Modern Avant Garde; Ritual or Pattern; and the Musical. In Absurd Drama, events do not logically follow one another; the characters are frequently not only ridiculous in their actions but also embody an existential point of view; the dialogue too exhibits the same illogical/absurd pattern—one line does not necessarily follow from what is said before). Perhaps the most famous example of Absurd Drama is Samuel Becketts' *Waiting for Godot*. The Modern Avant Garde theatre exponents aim at abandoning plot or dramatic structure altogether as they believe in a multifocus theatre. They believe that since life itself is unstructured, art too, should be. Thus, they string together a series of unconnected activities or events; sometimes combining various arts like painting, film and music. Michael Kirby and John Cage are two famous Avant Garde theatre practitioners. In some instances, various theatre events are joined together to make a programme. This could include a group of skits and songs in a revue and a group of unrelated one act

To continue with the analysis of the episode from Dance Like A Man,

- *Do you think, keeping the excerpt in mind, that* Dance Like A Man *has an episodic or a climactic plot structure?*
- *What is the action that takes place in this episode?*
- *Is there any logical development in the line of action in this episode?*

plays. The different activities (each of which has its own dramatic structure) may or may not share a common theme. Ritual, which is the repetition or reenactment of a symbolic event or action often forms the basis of dramatic structure. In a ritual, actions are repeated in a set fashion with a beginning, a middle and an end and events progress naturally. Playwrights like David Storey (as in his *The Changing Room*) have made the structure of ritual a part of the structure of their plays. Some plays also have a Pattern of events that steer the plot. For example Beckett's *Waiting For Godot*, has two acts in which the incidents are duplicated; there is a ritualistic quality to this pattern. Most Musicals alternate scenes of spoken dialogue with musical numbers which vary from solos to duets and from choral numbers to dance numbers. Musicals range from the grand opera in which nothing is spoken but everything is sung to such forms as operetta, musical comedy, musical revue and a play with a few songs. (Wilson 1980).

When constructing the plot of a play, the word Scene is used to describe those divisions that are actually written into many scripts; these are generally subdivisions of the Acts. For the dramatists (and the actor) the word Scene refers to each unit of action which begins with an entrance or an exit and ends with the next shift of characters on the stage. These exits and entrances provide structure without breaking the attention of the audience (see Minot 1982).

While we have seen different plot forms used by dramatists, it is true that different experiences, our observations of people like/unlike ourselves help in deciding the tenor of the plot. In other words, depending on whether our experiences/observations are tragic or comic, the plot too builds up the idea of tragedy or comedy. It would be useful, then, to study briefly what writing a tragedy or a comedy involves.

Tragedy:

- asks basic questions about human existence like: why do men and women suffer? Is there justice in the world? What are the limits of human endurance and achievement?
- presupposes an indifferent and sometimes malevolent universe in which the innocent suffer and there is inexplicable cruelty
- assumes that certain men and women will confront and defy fate even if they are overcome in the process

Traditional tragedy:

- chief characters are kings, queens, persons of stature, and nobility
- central figure is caught up in a series of irrevocable tragic circumstances
- hero/heroine is willing to fight and die for a cause
- written in verse
- examples, *Hamlet, Medea, Macbeth, King Lear, Antigone*

Modern tragedy:

- involves ordinary people
- written generally in prose
- deeper meanings of tragedy explored by non-verbal as well as verbal elements
- examples, *Long Day's Journey into Night, The Iceman Cometh, Death of a Salesman*

Non-Tragic Serious Plays

Heroic drama

- frequently deals with high born characters
- often written in verse
- marked by either a happy ending or an ending in which the deaths of the main characters are considered a triumph and not defeat
- examples, *Saint Joan, Richard II, Cyrano de Bergerac*

Melodrama

- Exaggerated characters and events
- Creates horror or suspense or presents a didactic argument for some political, moral or social point of view
- Examples, *The White Devil, The Duchess of Malfi, The Little Foxes*

Bourgeois or domestic drama

- Ordinary people
- Stresses the problems of the middle and lower classes
- Examples *A Raisin in the Sun, The Sheep Well, The Weavers, The Lower Depths* (Source: Wilson 1980)

Comedy

- sees the humour and incongruity in people and situations
- accepts social and moral order and suspends natural laws (the man who falls flat on his face but does not really hurt himself)
- Develops in several spheres:
    - verbal humor: turning words upside down; creating puns, malapropisms and inversions of meaning (notice the humour through language in ACT I of *Dance Like a Man* when Viswas speaks to Chagan Lal)
    - comedy of character: men and women take on extreme positions, make fools of themselves or contradict themselves
    - physical comedy: slapstick and horse play
    - plot complications: mistaken identity, coincidences, people turning up unexpectedly in the wrong house or wrong bedroom.

All of these are elements in the following:

Various kinds of Comedy

- Farce: relies on strong physical humour and is designed to entertain (like Burlesque)
- Comedy of Manners: relies on verbal wit; dialogues are full of word-play and humour, e.g., plays by Wycherley, Congreve and Goldsmith; Oscar Wilde and Noel Coward.
- Satire: aims to correct vices by making fun of the evil in society, e.g., *Tartuffe*.
- Tragi comedy: fuses the serious as well as the comic elements; we laugh and cry at the same time, e.g., *Alls Well That Ends Well; Troilus and Cressida; Measure for Measure.*

Getting back to Dattani, into what category would you place Dance Like a Man, *in the light of the episode given and why?*

- Comic Relief: in tragedies/serious plays, humorous scenes and characters are interspersed in serious material)
- Comedy of Ideas: use of comic techniques to debate intellectual propositions, e.g., plays by George Bernard Shaw.(Wilson, 1980)

PLOT is far more significant in drama than in any other art form. It is what keeps the audience glued to their seats. A good dramatist must be aware of the different kinds of dramatic plots and the various dramatic tones that can be used to create a dramatic impact. This aspect is the starting point in the writing of a play; it forms the Dramatic Concept that shapes the play.

ACTIVITY 25

1. What does 'plot' in drama refer to?
2. What do you understand by (a) protagonist (b) antagonist (c) climax in a play?
3. What makes the audience ask 'what next' in a play? What are the two devices used by the dramatist to make the audience do so?
4. What do you understand by artistic unity in a plot? When is a dramatist guilty of plot manipulation?
5. Define the meaning of deus ex machina.
6. Briefly describe the climactic form of drama. How does the episodic form differ from it?.
7. In you own words, describe the two dramatic devices used in conjunction with the episodic and climactic plot forms.
8. What happens in Absurd Drama?
9. What is the aim of the Modern Avant Garde theatre practitioners and how do they go about achieving this aim?
10. Explain the Ritual quality of some dramatic plots.
11. How are most Musicals structured?
12. To a dramatist or an actor, what does the word 'scene' imply?
13. What are some of the fundamental questions asked by tragedy? What are the differences between Traditional tragedy and Modern tragedy?
14. What are the different aims of (a) Heroic drama (b) Melodrama and (c) Bourgeois drama.
15. What does comedy do? What are some of the means of achieving comedy? What kinds of comedies do these lead to?
16. Write the outline of a plot for the following dramatic situations:
    (a) A love triangle
    (b) A murder
    (c) Booth capturing during election

Characterization in Drama

Any character in a play is as much a creation of the actor and director as it is of the dramatist. The audience is not aware of the dramatist when watching a play (as against reading the play as literature) and so a lot depends upon the skills of the professional actors to make the characters appear credible and effective. However, it is also true that a play is a work of art carefully crafted by the playwright who devotes lot of time, skill, and thought to the selection and arrangement of language (*Dialogue*) and action. It is primarily through *Dialogue* and *Action* that a playwright evolves characterization though costume also has a role to play. At this point it would be pertinent to remember that *Dialogue* can, on occasions, include a *Monologue* or a *Soliloquy*, a speech in which a character, alone on stage, addresses him/her self; a 'thinking aloud' or a dramatic means of letting an audience know a character's thoughts and feelings. (Perrine 1978). It also includes silences, actions, gestures as well as changes of expression.

Characters serve specific functions in a story or plot of a drama. The *Major* characters of a play are those around whom the action revolves. The *Minor* characters are those who contribute only a little to the total action; they play a small part in furthering the story or supporting more important characters. One generally sees only a single facet of their personalities. Some characters fall halfway between the major and the minor characters; generally such characters have a distinctive personality and though their part in the play is small, it is significant.

Broadly speaking, characters in a play can be divided into (a) Extraordinary characters ; (b) Prototypical characters; (c) Stereotypical or stock characters (also, characters with a dominant trait); (d) Non human characters.

BOX 3.8: CHARACTERS

Extraordinary Characters

(a) In traditional theatre:

1. The heroes/heroines stand apart from ordinary people;
2. Are generally kings, queens, etc. and so are extraordinary in terms of their position of authority, for example, Macbeth, Lady Macbeth.
3. Such characters are either at their best or their worst, that is, at some extreme of human behaviour, for example, Lady Macbeth's ambitiousness.
4. Comic characters also show extremes of behaviour, such as the chief character of Ben Jonson's play *Volpone*.

(b) In modern theatre:

1. The heroes/heroines are exceptional people but without the trappings of position and authority;
2. They display their best or worst traits: for example, in Brecht's *Mother Courage*, the central character is a woman willing to sacrifice anything to survive; Strindberg's *Miss Julie* is a neurotic and obsessive woman at the end of her tether.

Prototypical characters

1. Not to be confused with a stereotype, these are fully rounded three dimensional characters.
2. Exceptional in that these characters are the embodiment of an entire group: Nora Helmer, the heroine of Ibsen's *A Doll's House*, is a prototype of all the housewives who refuse to be treated unfairly; her slamming of the door is symbolic of the emancipation of the modern woman.

Stereotypical characters

1. Such characters symbolize a particular type of person or some outstanding characteristic of human behaviour.
2. appear in all forms of drama but particularly in comedy and melodrama

(Contd.)

3. some examples of stock or stereotypical characters can be found in the daily soaps such as the manipulative 'other' woman; the principled 'do gooder' wife, etc.
4. the attitudes and actions of such characters are generally predictable.

Characters with a dominant trait

1. Closely related to stereotypical characters; these are characters with a single trait or 'humor'.
2. Such characters are often named after their particular personality trait such as Lady Sneerwell, Mrs Candour, Sir Benjamin Backbite, etc.

Non human characters

1. Sometimes dramatic characters appear in the guise of animals, birds, robots or inanimate objects.
2. Either they serve a functional purpose much like a prop in the play; or they serve to highlight the human quality of the animal (or vice versa). Eugene Ionesco has men turn into animals in his play *Rhinoceros*.

To continue with the case study of the Dattani play,
- *Can you see the emergence of any stereotypical/prototypical characters in the episode?*
- *In the stage directions at the end of the episode, Dattani switches from past to present. How does he show the switch over?*

It would be useful for a budding dramatist to have some idea about the range of characters that one can choose from to achieve maximum impact in the theatre.

Dramatists place characters in certain combinations in order to make them effective such as a *Protagonist* being opposed by an *Antagonist; Major Characters* being supported by *Minor Characters* and the *Orchestration* or bringing together of the characters under a common theme. Naturally the characters 'do' something; they 'act' or they 'perform'. It is what they do and say that unravels the plot and allows the audience to understand them. (For further details, see Wilson 1980).

ACTIVITY 26

1. Is the character we see on stage solely the creation of the dramatist?
2. How does a playwright evolve characterization?
3. Define (a) Dialogue (b) Action and (c) Soliloquy in drama.
4. Who are (i) Major characters (ii) Minor characters and (iii) Characters who fall in Between, in a play? Give examples from your own reading of plays.
5. Define the chief attributes of Extraordinary characters in traditional theatre. What is the major change that has taken place in such characters in modern theatre?
6. Explain what you understand by Prototypical characters.
7. What characteristic do stereotypical characters display?
8. What are 'humors'?
9. What purpose do characters playing the part of non humans serve in a play?
10. In what kind of combinations do dramatists place characters?
11. Refer to Question 16 in Activity 2. Describe the characters in any ONE of the situations that you created. Keep in mind that you must include all the characteristics associated with the kind of character you create.
12. Write a soliloquy for any one of the characters you have created.
13. Write a dialogue for any two of the characters you have created.

Verbal and Non-Verbal Elements in Drama

In the previous section we have seen that characterization evolves through *Dialogue* (and *Action*) in a play. Dialogue, in fact, serves various purposes in a play in that it can be (a) a response to the situation (b) a reaction of the characters to each other (c) a form of comic relief (d) advancing the plot (e) helping in characterization and (f) a connective statement that leads into the next scene (Dancyger 1991).

In real life, people often misunderstand or interrupt each other, even get distracted by others or by things they hear and see. Besides, words are not the only mode of communication; facial expressions, gestures, and non-verbal sounds also called non- fluencies (represented in written dialogue by mm, hm, er, ah, etc)also serve as effective means. The nature of communication changes according to (a) the role being played at a given moment (b) the feelings of the role player (c) the environment and (d) the relationship of the role player with the people/persons with whom the communication is being made.

Real life conversations/speech is very different from spoken prose; it is often noticeably non-grammatical or non-fluent. Some of the features of spoken language that should be kept in mind while writing a dialogue are:

(1) Non-standard intonation patterns
(2) Variations in tempo
(3) The use of pause
(4) Stammers and errors in articulation
(5) Incomplete sentences
(6) Repetition
(7) 'Silence fillers' such in 'well', 'you know', 'sort of', 'mm', 'er'.
(8) Silences which are filled by facial expressions and gestures
(9) Gestures which amplify the meaning of words.

The first seven of this list constitute the vocal features of oral communication while the last two are the non-vocal features, including gestures, facial expression and movements. While writing a play, the writer must keep in mind the repertoire of communication. (Holden 1981).

There are other non-verbal elements that a dramatist must keep in mind; these are the visual images of scenery, lighting and costumes, and the very environment created by a particular theatre space. All these along with the play itself completes the theatre experience for the spectators whose focus may be on the performers but on whom, all the other elements of drama that are present, create an equally strong impact.

Stage Spaces

Proscenium theatre:

- picture-frame stage; audience faces directly towards the stage, looks through the proscenium opening at the picture
- potential for elaborate scene shifts and visual displays because it generally has a large backstage area and fly loft
- sets up a barrier between the performers and audience
- example: musicals like *Jesus Christ Superstar, The Wiz* are staged in such theatres

Arena stage or circle stage:

- playing area is in the centre with audience in a square or circle around the outside
- opportunity for greater interaction between spectators and audience
- full visual displays of scenery and scene changes cannot be offered.
- Example, Greek theatre

Thrust stage:

- platform stage with three quarter seating on three sides
- exits and entrances are made in the rear
- opportunity for some amount of scenery
- combines scenic features of Proscenium theatre with the intimacy of the Arena stage
- plays by Shakespeare were mostly performed on a thrust stage

Created or found spaces:

- takes several forms, such as
  - use of non theatre buildings
  - adaptation of a given space to fit individual productions
  - use of outdoor settings
  - street theatre
  - multifocus environments

(Wilson, 1980)

Scenery

- Scene design creates an environment and an atmosphere
- It also helps to:
  - set tone and style
  - establish time and place
  - develop a design concept
  - provide a central design metaphor
  - coordinate with the other elements
  - deal with practical considerations.
- Special effects are those elements of scenery, lighting, costumes, props or sound that appear miraculous or highly unusual; require technical expertise to develop properly.
- When dealing with found or created space, the designer has to plan the total environment; the audience area as well as the stage area.
- The Scene Designer works closely with the director and other designers.

Lighting and Sound

- Lighting is the most mechanically sophisticated of stage elements today

- Lighting design is intended to – provide illumination on stage
  - establish time and place
  - set the mood and style of production
  - focus the action
  - get a rhythm of visual movement
- Lighting should be consistent with all other elements
- Lighting designer uses a variety of instruments, coloured gels and control dimmers and panels to achieve his/her effects.
- Sound effects are created by mechanical means or through tape. Microphones enhance speaking or singing.

Costumes

Clothes we wear in daily life are a form of costume indicating station in life, occupation and level of formality. On stage, costumes convey similar information about the people wearing them; are consciously chosen and designed to provide the audience with important facts. Costumes,

- set tone and style
- indicate time and place
- characterize individuals and groups
- underline personal relationships
- create symbolic outfits when appropriate
- meet practical needs of performers
- coordinate with the total production

Costume designer works with line and shape, colour and fabric of the costumes. Makeup, hairstyles and if need be, masks, are also the designer's concern. (Wilson 1980.)

Sample from *Dance Like a Man*

Stage directions inform about (i) kind of theatre space (Proscenium) being used; (ii) lighting; (iii) sets and (iv) entrance of character,

Act one (*Italics added*)

(A dimly lit room in an old-fashioned house in the heart of the city; Upcentre is the entrance to the room—a huge arched doorway: When the play starts we see a rather modern looking rear panel behind the entrance with a telephone and a modern painting on it. When specified in the script the rear panel is slid to reveal a garden. Upstage left, a dance practice hall. Upstage right a staircase going to the bedrooms. Downstage right exits into the kitchen. All the furniture in the room is at least forty years old. (Lata and Viswas enter from the doorway).

Viswas: So this is where I get killed.
Lata: They should have been here by now.
Viswas: They are not in? You said it was all arranged. Wait a minute. *They* said 7o' clock.

Lata: I know, but they had to go out. Emergency.
Viswas: Only doctors and firemen go out on emergencies. Dancers stay at home till it's show time. They also stay at home when they have invited their future son-in-law to their house.
Lata: Don't be so sure. They have to meet you first.

Sample from *Harvest* by Manjula Padmanabhan

Characters

Notice the details given by the playwright regarding characterization, especially, the description of the costumes

Donors:

Om

Twenty years old, he has been laid off from his job as a clerk and is the bread-earner of his small family. He is of medium height, nervy and thin. He would be reasonably good-looking if not for his anxious expression.

Jaya

Om's wife. Thin and haggard at the outset, she looks older than her nineteen years, but is passionate and spirited. Her bright cotton sari has faded with repeated washing, to a meek pink. Like the others, she is barefoot at the outset. She wears glass bangles, a tiny nose-ring, ear-studs, a slender chain around her neck. No make-up aside from the kohl around her eyes and the red bindi on her forehead.

Ma

Om's mother. She is sixty years old, stooped, scrawny and crabby wears a widow's thread-bare white-on-white sari. Her hair is a straggly white

Jeetu

Om's younger brother, seventeen and handsome. The same height as Om, he is wiry and conscious of his body. He works as a male prostitute and has a dashing, easy-going like-able personality.

Bidyut bai

An elderly neighbour, very similar in appearance to Ma, but timid and self-effacing.

Also ***urchins*** *and the crowd outside the door. The crowd is audible rather than visible.* ***guards*** *and* ***agents****.*

Guards

The guards are a group of three commando-like characters who bear the same relationship to each other whenever they appear. Guard 1 is the leader of the team, a man in his mid forties, of military bearing... Guard 2 is a young and attractive woman, unsmiling and efficient. Guard 3 is a male clone of Guard 2. Only Guard 1 interacts with **donors**.

Agents

The **agents** *are space-age delivery-persons and their uniforms are fantastical verging on ludicrous, like the costumes of waiters in exotic restaurants. Their roles are interchangeable with the Guards, though it must be clear that they do not belong to the same agency.*

Receivers

Ginni

We see only her face and hear her voice she is the blonde and white skinned epitome of an American-style youth goddess. Her voice is sweet and sexy.

Virgil

He is never seen. He has an American cigarette-commercial accent—rich and smoky, attractive and rugged.

The playwright must visualize the performance of the play in its entirety and so it is imperative for the novice playwright to have a thorough knowledge of all the aspects that go into the making of drama.

In the episode from Dance Like A Man
- *discuss the tone of the dialogues in this episode?*
- *Do they tell us more about the characters concerned?*
- *Do they advance the plot?*

ACTIVITY 27

1. What are the various functions of dialogue in a play?
2. What are the other modes of communication, besides words?
3. Why does the nature of communication change?
4. What are the vocal and non-vocal features of communication?
5. Name the different kinds of stage spaces that a dramatist can use.
6. What does scenery achieve?
7. What are special effects?
8. What is lighting design intended to do?
9. How are sound effects created?
10. What do costumes on stage convey about the people wearing them?
11. What are the other functions of costumes?
12. What are the extended functions of the costume designer?
13. Dress any three of the characters that you created.
14. Describe the stage space and the scenery for the situation that you created.

A Brief Overview of English Language Theatre in India*

The history of English language theatre in India has been a varied and interesting one. In the beginning such theatre was based on the dual movements of resistance and subversion. It positioned itself against the colonial powers that dominated the country, speaking to the rulers in their language, but using its own words. However it also pandered to the desired image of 'Westernisation', of aping Europe in manners, style and language, providing an easy and 'desirable' form of entertainment for those Indians who aspired to be 'like' their British masters.

* This section was contributed by Angelie Multani. Anjelie Multani teaches English in the Department of Humanities and Social Sciences at the Indian Institute of Technology, Delhi. Her areas of research include theatre, Indian Writing in English and Culture Studies. She has published widely on Indian Writing in English, contemporary fiction and the plays of Mahesh Dattani

After Independence too, English language theatre followed this double role—while Hindi and other Indian language theatre groups and dramatists found government patronage and a 'national' identity, English language theatre remained on the margins of intellectual and critical attention while simultaneously retaining its control of the cultural space, in terms of audiences and practitioners. While mainstream English language theatre flourished mainly in the metropolitan centers, it did spread from outside its traditional cities like Bombay and Chennai to other metros like Bangalore and Delhi.

Until the 1990s, English language theatre and its performances in India were dominated by Western texts—plays by European or American playwrights were performed regularly by amateur and semi-professional groups and watched by audiences. (India does not really support professional theatre groups outside the repertory companies of government sponsored institutions such as the National School of Drama, the Shri Ram Repertory, etc. Most theatre practitioners are people who try as much as possible to 'do theatre' in their spare time, outside their 'paying' jobs or professions). This does not mean that the theatre itself was repetitive or derivative - in Bombay for instance where theatre has had a long and well and established history, the performances were experimental, original and vibrant.

Despite the status of English as a language of power and prestige in our society, original Indian theatre in English was not really successful. There have been Indian playwrights writing in English for many years. Names such as Asif Currimbhoy, Partap Sharma, Gieve Patel and Gurcharan Das are well known pioneers in the history of English language theatre in India. The plays written by these playwrights were largely cast in the established mould of western proscenium theatre. Based in the realistic tradition of European masters, these texts centred around the family as a microcosm of society, using the 'private' lives of their characters to comment on the 'public' spaces of society, state and community.

While some of these playwrights openly tackled overtly political subjects,like Currimbhoy in *Goa* most of the others chose to make their statements through the private lives and loves of individual people. One of the reasons for the failure or absence of a strong tradition of Indian English theatre most often cited by critics is the lack of a vibrant and alive spoken idiom. One of the most obvious aspects of the earlier English language theatre really is the fact that the language spoken by its characters sounded 'stilted' and 'not real'.

The serious plays were the ones that suffered most directly from this handicap. They attracted small audiences on various counts—they were perceived as 'intellectual' rather than as 'entertaining'. Successful Indian English theatre was present—in the sex comedies and farces written and performed mainly in Bombay. These 'light entertainment' plays were very successful commercially as they referred to topical and contemporary issues and did so in a language that was 'real' and accessible. The English used by Bharat Dabholkar, who wrote and produced the *Bottoms Up* series in Bombay was a mixture of Gujarati, Marathi, 'street Hindi' and English. In short, it was more or less the kind of language that the audience themselves would use in their own lives.

Perhaps it was this growing self confidence vis-á-vis English as a language of daily use and perhaps it was also because of the slow infiltration of different registers of English into every day situations in Indian lives, there was a boom in Indian English Theatre in the 1990s, the period of economic liberalisation. This may not be the right space or time to delve deeply into the relationship between liberalisation and the growth of original Indian English Theatre, but there is a real and strong link.

The 1990s saw the emergence of one of the strongest and most influential voices in Indian English theatre—Mahesh Dattani. Dattani himself epitomizes the 'English speaking subject' in modern India. A Gujarati by birth, he has lived in Bangalore his entire life, and has recently started living and working in Bombay. Dattani's plays are an engaging mixture of the Western and Indian, yet completely original and rooted. He has written all kinds of plays—family dramas, comedies, political theatre, and won both commercial and critical acclaim, including the prestigious Sahitya Akademi Award.

One of the strongest points in Dattani's work is his style of language, which is completely natural and rooted in an urban Indian ethos. His characters speak like the urban Indian audience member would, without any pretensions or accent aspirations. The phrases employed by his character are again rooted in their own cultural contexts and do not sound false or constructed. Even when he has characters that 'would not' necessarily speak English, such as an auto driver or a constable, or even an eunuch, the language used is not 'perfect' English nor is it deliberately awkward.

Other playwrights who have been successful recently also display similar strengths—Manjula Padmanabhan, Dina Mehta and many others have successful written plays in English which have been produced successfully in various cities in India.

The big 'boom' of theatre may have died down somewhat in the 21st century, but that is true of theatre in general, not only of Indian English theatre. Some playwrights and theatre practitioners have moved from the stage to the medium of cinema. More and more Indian English films are being made and released every year now, on different themes, ranging from the comic to the serious. The most important thing is to have something to say, and to say it in our own words.

Some Different Styles of Contemporary Theatre in Indian English

Supper Theatre

Plays of this genre are performed in cafetarias and restaurants of various hotels allowing easy interaction of the stage with the audience. For example, the performance of *The Unexpected Man* written by Yasmina Reza, directed by Sita Raina and performed by Prime Time Theatre in Radisson Hotel. This is about the journey of two strangers, Mr Parsky (a writer) and Martha (reading his latest book) making their way from Paris to Frankfurt in the same train compartment. Again, the performance of *See Saw*, a play by theatre director Bubbles Sabharwal at Ashok Hotel; Sohaila Kapoor's company Hungry Hearts also presented its play *Suppressed Desires* in Ashok Hotel. Stage light's production *Under the Covers* was staged in hotels. The idea is: Eat while you watch!

Proscenium Plays

Such plays maintain a clear demarcation between the acting space (stage) and the audience space. The plays by Mahesh Dattani would fit into this category. The translated version of Badal Sircar's play : *Baki Itihas* – The other side of History (translated by Dr. Saumitra Chakraborty) would also fall in this realm, as would the play, *Hayavadana* from Girish Karnad's play of the same name.

There are a whole host of other theatre styles that one can see in India on the drama front. But these are primarily in regional languages, or if in English, adapted or borrowed fully from playwrights from the West.

For example, take Street Theatre: This is primarily leftwing open air theatre of protest aiming to agitate the people and mobilize them behind fighting organizations, as defined by Safdar Hashmi who till his murder in 1989 led such protest plays through his theatre group Jana Natya Manch (JANAM). Badal Sircar's work too is of great significance; he experimented with open air theatre and brought to the spotlight, the discontent of the rootless urban middle class. Theatre Union which included members like Anuradha Kapur, Maya Rao, Rati Bartholomew did a lot of street theatre while it existed (1983 – 89). In the south, groups like Samudaya (Karnataka), Praja Natya Mandali (Andhra Pradesh) and Chennai Kalai Kuzu (Tamil Nadu)—are all skilful exponents of the street theater form. Feminist groups and NGOs too perform excellent street theatre. However, almost all these plays are in regional languages.

Pantomime

It is a form of musical drama in which elements of dance, puppetry, slapstick and melodrama are combined and thus an entertaining theatrical experience. Often designed specially for children, it is a common enough theatre form in India. But again, these are translated or adapted from western pantomimes or are performed in a regional language.

Comedy

Comedies too, are popular on the Indian stage and the plays by Bharat Dhabolkar would fit the bill (especially his *Bottoms Up* series). Such plays are not always funny—they centre on a problem that leads to a catastrophe of some kind but then conclude happily. Even in this sphere, however, a lot of the comedies that are performed are borrowed (either fully or adapted) from the west. Take for example the play *Beauty Brains* and Personality written by the American playwright, Emmett Loverde. Vandana Sajnani of Moksh Creations obtained the performance rights from Loverde to produce the play in India. The play, which is about three very different modern women and their friendship, ran to packed houses.

Theatre for a Purpose or a Specific Intent

One form of Indian English theatre that is gaining currency, is *theatre for a purpose or a specific intent*. This could either throw light on some specific issue or serve to illustrate a particular aspect (of say, a newly launched product in the market). The target audience for such theatre is generally a pan Indian one and English works well with such an audience.

Theatre for Social Change

This takes up a social issue and uses performance as a way of illustrating injustice to the audience and is fast gaining ground in the Indian English theatre front. For example,

Going Solo 2, a set of one act plays presented in Mumbai, Delhi, and Pune, in which directors Anahita Uberoi, Vikram Kapadia and Rahul da Cunha had the characters delivering monologues about road rage, rape and marital discontent—issues that the urban Indian is faced with.

Indian English theatre may not have fully grown roots but it is surely and steadily progressing.

Some Well-known Practising Indian English Playwrights and a Few of their Plays

GURCHARAN DAS (playwright and nonfiction writer)

- *Larins:* About the British in Punjab; the story revolved around Rani Jindan, Sham Singh Attariwala and Henry Lawrence. Won a Prize from OUP; was on BBC.
- *Meera Bai:* Staged in Lamama, New York; the bhajans in Meena Bai were set in rock music.
- *Nine Jakhoo Hill:* Still being staged by Yatrik;basically about the changing middle class.

MANJULA PADMANABHAN (novelist, short story writer, comic strip writer, writes for children, playwright and artist).

- *Fires:* A collection of five dramatic monologues tackling issues of violence, intolerance of others, narrow concepts of community and nation, each with a twist.
- *Harvest:* About the sale of organs between rich and poor nations which becomes a sly metaphor for other types of transactions as between husband and wife, son and mother, lover and beloved made into a feature film called *Deham* directed by Govind Nihalani; adapted and broadcast as a radio play on BBC; Won the First prize in the 1997 Onassis Award for Theatre.

PARTAP SHARMA

- *Begum Sumroo*: A historical play about an Indian woman who was a dancer and took over a military brigade of European mercenaries and led them to fortune and philosophy.
- *Sammy!*: A historical play about the irrepressible Mahatma Gandhi, the inner voice he could not ignore. The play depicts the conflicts within Gandhi.
- *A Touch of Brightness:* A contemporary, sociological play about a girl who is sold into prostitution and a young boy who thinks of her as his sister and tries to save her but she refuses to be rescued.
- *Zen Katha:* A historical play, the Zen Katha of Bodhidharma is about the founder of Zen who was also a master of martial arts. He went from India to China in 425 A.D.(press!small caps) He fled from the demands of a throne but could not so easily escape the woman who loved him.

DINA MEHTA (short story writer, novelist, was fiction editor with the *Illustrated Weekly of India*, playwright)

- *The Myth Makers*
- *Brides are Not for Burning*

- *Tiger Tiger*
- *A Sister Like You*
- *When One Plus One makes Nine* (later broadcast on All India Radio as *Joke About Rabbits*)
- *Getting Away with Murder*

GIEVE PATEL (doctor, poet, translator, painter, playwright)

- *Mister Behram*
- *Princes*
- *Savaksa*

BHARAT DABHOLKAR (adman-wrote and handled the Amul butter ads for 15 years, actor, playwright)

- *Just Another Rape:* An adaptation of Jaywant Dalvi's Purush, the play deals with the rape of a school teacher who is also a social worker by the local politician with whom she gets into an ideological dispute.
- *Monkey Business:* A two act comedy about a Gujarati wedding caterer who along with his dominating wife and a pretty teenage daughter visits a not-so-friendly neighbourhood country where they get embroiled in some complicated, hilarious situations.
- *Also known for his Bottoms Up, Son of Bottoms Up, Grandson of Bottoms Up, Oh No! Not Again, Funny Thing called Love, Tamasha Mumbai Ishtyle, Last Tango in Heaven, Carry on Bindas, and Mind your Stethoscope.*

MAHESH DATTANI (stage director, playwright)

- *Where There's a Will:* The promise of a will and inheritance binds together the fates of a business tycoon, his family, and his mistress. But what happens when a cunning twist changes everything?
- *Dance Like a Man:* Received the Sahitya Kala Parishad award in 1997; is about the battle against society that prevents us from reaching out to our roots
- Has also written *Tara; Bravely Fought the Queen; Final Solutions;* a short play called *Night Queen; Radio plays for the BBC—Do the Needful; On a Muggy Night in Mumbai; Seven Circles Round the Fire; The Swami and Winston; Thirty days in September*

ASIF CURRIMBHOY

- *Dumb Dancer*
- *Goa:* Set in Goa when it was still a Portugese enclave and raises questions of nationality and independence.
- *The Hungry Ones*

ROYSTEN ABEL

- *Othello: A play in Black and White:* About the politics in a theatre group when a dark skinned Assamese entrant is cast in the title role which is coveted by a fair skinned senior member of the troupe.
- *Goodbye Desdemona:* About two actors doing their verson of Romeo and Juliet—with two men in the lead.
- *The Spirit of Anne Frank*

Also noteworthy are Poile Sengupta (*Thus Spake Shurpanaka, So said Shakuni; Body Blows; Good Heavens* [A set of one act plays for children] *Mangalam;* Sunny Singh (*Missing*)

Conversation with a Creative Writer

Mahesh Dattani

On Writing plays: A chat with Mahesh Dattani (excerpts of the interview with the author in May 2006)

When did you begin writing?

I wrote my first full-length play in 1985. Before that I had attempted writing short plays but wasn't very happy with the outcome.

How did you begin writing?

The Deccan Herald Theatre festival was on and they had invited my theatre group to perform. I did not have a play to offer and decided to write my own. My cast and I had a reading of the few pages I had written. They encouraged me to complete it. If it wasn't for the encouragement of my cast, I don't think I would have had the courage to write a play.

What forms/themes of writing did you experiment with early on?

None at all. I was never really interested in writing. I was keen on drama.

What drew you towards writing drama?

The dearth of good material in Indian English. Having become tired of the Neil Simon comedies that were staple fare then on the English language stage, I thought maybe I should try my hand at writing a play about 'us'.

Do you think that certain forms of writing lend themselves to the expression of certain themes? Could you conceptualize this with reference to your own work?

I think psychological conflicts where characters interact non-verbally while saying a whole load of things, lends itself better to text based theatre. If I need to follow the action rather than have the action in a certain time-space frame work, then I think I would rather make a film on that subject. But ultimately it is the form that a writer is most comfortable with and can express himself/herself freely that matters. If the writing is suitable for other mediums, they can be adapted. For instance, when I had the opportunity to make my first film, I felt *On A Muggy Night* in Mumbai would also lend itself to a low budget film. When I first thought of the subject of *Morning Raga*, it came primarily as a film in my mind.

What tells you that the moment has arrived when you are ready to begin a new work?

It is hard to tell when that moment first arrives. Ideas float in and out and the ones that stay may have the potential of being your new work. Putting your thoughts down is not the first step towards writing. I think it is your response to an incident or a moment in life on a subliminal level that could be the starting point of your story. In that sense, everyone has a story to tell. Whether we choose to tell it or not is the difference between a writer and non writer.

Do you work with a fully worked out plan and schedule/Do you always know where you are going? Do tell us your experiences.

No. I don't always know where I am going, but it helps. It saves a lot of time but takes away the pleasure of discovery if you know where you are going. But even in my most confident writing I have always had discoveries along the way. For instance, *Tara* earlier was just a memory fragment in the mind of her brother Chandan's journey but in the writing she claimed her space. I was confronted with my own prejudices. Was I making it Chandan's journey but claiming to be writing about Tara? The true theme of the gendered self and self imposed favoritism emerged after I had written it.

What role does research/background information play in your writing?

It plays a significant role in my later works post *Final Solutions.* I took two years to write *Final Solutions.* I had interviewed several people and studied what sociologists and intellectuals had to say on the subject of the Hindu Muslim divide.

30 Days in September was based entirely on the stories that were told to me in confidence by six survivors of childhood sexual abuse. Without that research it would not have been possible for me to write that play.

How many times do you revise your work before publication and are you ever fully satisfied?

I am never fully satisfied and sometimes I am not even partly satisfied. I hate publishing my plays because it sets them in stone. I think that theatre has taught me to relook at my work every now and then. As I change and grow as a person, so will my writing.

How do you deal with responses of readers and critics?

Not very well if it is negative. But then, I have a lot to thank those critics who have taken the time and trouble to critically evaluate my work. I may not take it well, but I have benefited a great deal out of it. But that also depends on who the critic is.

Who is your ideal audience?

The ones who take the trouble to turn off their mobile phones and watch the play in silent appreciation and only make their appreciation felt through applause and laughter.

What is your advice to aspiring young writers?

If you believe in yourself and what you want to write about, don't seek advice. If you are lazy and give yourself excuses for not writing, may be you don't want to write after all. Just do it. Or don't waste your time.

Writing Film Scripts

When one shifts from playwriting to script writing for the television or motion pictures, one finds a lot of similarities in the basic approach. However, there are a significant number of specific differences which certainly must be kept in mind. Arvind Joshi's essay on 'How to Write a Film Script' addresses these technicalities.

A Film Script by Arvind Joshi

Every age evolves or chooses a form of expression that speaks its tongue. The Drama spoke the language of a resurgent England in the Elizabethan age and the Movie speaks the language of new world orders, new lives, forming and re-forming in the 20th and 21st century.

Utterance was a world hatched from the Story and the Song, it walked as the Epic and the Play, it matured and peopled great cities as the Poem and the Novel, and now, in a world with few rules and a multiplicity of forms, it has all come alive as the protean carnivalesque giant called the Motion Picture.

Here is a brief overview for the beginner interested in the craft of writing a screenplay. From how to format a motion picture script to important dos and don'ts, this intends to act as a beginner's guide to creating the blueprint of a movie.

The most important thing for a screenplay writer to remember is that unlike a story or a novel, the screenplay is more than just a 'performance' on page. It is really a signboard of what will be a performance on screen. Write for the eye and the ear; write for movement and action!

A playwright writing for stage is already aware of the importance of dialogues, action and settings. On stage, the spoken word is the chief method of indicating action; body language, facial expressions and settings are secondary to the spoken word. For the screenplay writer, however, there is an embarrassment of riches to choose from. Elements like dialogue, expressions, action, setting or stylized visuals are at her disposal. The screenplay constitutes of a skillful selection of one or two of these elements over others as the chief mode of story telling for the movie.

The screenplay should do three things: It should provide the story and the plot; it should be able to provide sufficient indications of the immediate setting and feel of the 'scene'; it should provide dialogues that help build character and propel the story, and it should be easy to use for anyone involved in the movie.

Story and Plot

The story of a movie is an assortment of characters and events that would feature in the movie. The plot, on the other hand, is the sequence in which the story is told. And this classical definition of the plot is most relevant in the case of a movie script. While the story for a movie is comparatively easy – all you need is a basic idea and a few characters that come from it – it is the plot that really needs to be laboured upon. The plot calls for careful attention to factors that dictate the flow of a tale meant for the screen: action scenes, climactic points, rhythm and treatment.

Action Scenes

An action scene is a scene that verges on action more than dialogue. Usually these scenes are created and interpreted best by the director. The screenplay writer should be careful not to overdo the detailing of an action scene; at best, the writer should stick to a skeletal description that allows sufficient space for interpretation. Remember, the director might interpret the movie differently; a 'fixed' scene description that is integrated with the story might require the director to rework the entire story to integrate his vision.

Climactic Points

As in a play, so in a movie, the emotional and dramatic movement of the story is interspersed with climactic points, some minor, some significant. The number of such points and the distance at which they are placed depends on the pace and rhythm that the screenplay writer wishes to impart to the story. For example a comedy would require a large number of climactic points, almost one per scene or sequence, a larger dramatic movie story, like *Gone with the Wind* might have fewer climactic points, spread across the length of the tale (Scarlett's vow just before intermission and Rhet Butler's parting shot at the end are the two crucial climactic points in the movie).

Rhythm

The rhythm of a movie might be dictated either by the plot or the pace of the visual narrative. Rhythm is created by the number of climactic points distributed across the narrative, by the size of scenes and sequences and by the nature of dialogues. It is, probably, the most difficult to master, but the most important in a screenplay. The screenplay writer should have an instinctive feel for rhythm and should be able to create a rhythm consistent with the genre, the style and the plot of the movie.

Treatment

The 'treatment' is actually the screenplay writer stepping out of his skin and trying out the director's jacket. It constitutes directions inserted into the screenplay about camera angles, perspectives, lighting details, 'in scene characters' and 'out of scene characters', sound and the like. The screenplay writer should 'treat' the screenplay sparingly, as overdoing the 'treatment' is likely to impede the flow of a natural read and might irritate headstrong directors.

Script Format

Why format? You can write a screenplay any way you wish to, but you must use standard formatting methods when it is meant for professional eyes. The reasons are two-fold: firstly, the professional reader of movie scripts is used to reading it through widely accepted signs - formatting it in the standard way allows for an easy read of the screenplay; secondly, correct formatting increases the credibility of the text and allows the writer to be viewed as an 'insider' of the film fraternity.

Font The standard practice is to use the font, Courier 12 pitch; it is a font that is a relic of the days of the typewriter.

Title Page The Title page should carry the Title of the movie project, a simple half line description of the project and your name. Carry the title in capitals and make sure it is underlined. Describe the movie project clearly: "A 60-minute Family Drama," "A 30-minute Existentialist Drama," or "A 20-minute Environmental Documentary". Below the project description, run the screenplay writer's name. The lower half of the Title page commonly carries the draft status (First Draft, Revised Version or Final Draft) and the lower right part the screenplay writer's contact address. The draft status should be included only if you are working with a director at developing the script, otherwise you can do without it.

General Margin Settings Settle for a 20-spaces left margin for stage directions, a 30-spaces one for dialogues (A line of dialogue can be from 30 spaces to 35 spaces long) and a 40-spaces margin for character name (just above a unit of dialogue). The character name should be in upper case.

Scene Opening: Convention A scene is a unit of a movie bound by place-setting and time-setting. A scene should clearly indicate whether it is an 'interior' (INT) setting or an 'exterior' setting (EXT), and time markers like "DAY" or "NIGHT".

Example

```
INT. ROOM—NIGHT
EXT. RICE-FIELD—DAY
INT. HOTEL LOBBY - AFTERNOON
EXT. INDIA GATE - DAWN
EXT. JANPATH - REPUBLIC DAY PARADE - STOCK FOOTAGE
INT. CALL CENTRE - MIDNIGHT - ESTABLISHING
EXT. MARINE DRIVE - DAY - CONTINOUS
```

Setting and Character Introduction After the Scene Heading (as described in point 4), leave double space; describe the setting and characters in single space. Use the 20-space margin meant for stage directions when doing this.

Action Do not get carried away when describing sequences of action. Remember, this is just the screenplay; it is not yet the vision of the director. Stick to bits absolutely essential to the plot. Let the action descriptions run, left margin to right, in single-spaced lines and in mixed case (upper and lower). Use the active voice – think of the sequence as something you are describing as it happens, and – stick to the present tense! Keep the sequence snappy and short, not more than 5 lines, unless absolutely necessary.

Example

```
She turns the pages rapidly. A picture holds her eye.

Not

She turned the pages rapidly

Nor

The pages are turned rapidly
```

Technical note A Technical Note (also called an Extension) is added to the right of the Character name. It states how the dialogue will reach the audience. For instance, an O.S (Off-Screen voice) could be a dialogue between two drunkards behind the wall, while the scene only shows a car parked on the other side of the wall. A V.O. (Voice over), usually a commentary, could also be a strain of memory or surreal voices. A pause in dialogue is usually marked by writing—BEAT.

Script Length It is extremely difficult to fix the 'right' length of a script, as the length of a typed script depends on whether the movie project is a comedy or a drama or an action flick, whether it is a dialogue-heavy or action-heavy script, whether the action verges on actually shot footage or also on well described written portions. The best way to check the 'correctness' of length is to actually time the dialogues and sequences as if they have been shot. A normal 2 hr to 2.5 hr script could range from 100 to 130 pages.

Shots and Transitions 'Shots' are suggestions for the camera, while 'transitions' are instructions meant for the edit table. These should be used sparingly since a good screenwriter should be able to do without them. Deciding upon a shot and making a transition choice is the prerogative of the director, unless it is integral to the basic element of the story.

A shot instruction is usually in uppercase and begins from the left margin with single line spacing before and after.

Example
MED SHOT
EXTREME CLOSE UP
P.O.V. (point of view shot, refers to a shot taken from the point of view of a particular character)
CU (close-up)
PAN TO

A transition is typed into the screenplay in uppercase; it follows an action and precedes a Scene Heading.

Example
CUT TO
DISSOLVE TO
FADE TO

Dos and Don'ts

Dos

Dialogues that you can see: Dialogues are the mainstay of a screenplay, but it's still a motion picture script! Do focus on visual details that matter to the story being told: a match stick dropped into a glass, a sleeping old woman's walking stick resting against the wall, the play of dust and leaves on a silent dusty road after a car has just sped through.

Every Script has invisible Acts: Most scripts have internal climaxes and can be divided into symmetrical movements. A one hour story can be seen as a 4-act play and a half hour project as a 2-act production. Do divide your screenplay into Acts that needn't be visible in the formal copy, but help you manage the rhythm of the story.

Dialogues that you can hear
The dialogue is still what stirs the audience most and stays with them the longest. Make sure you do it right. Keep the language, the register and the rhythm of your dialogue consistent with the character and the scene. Do stay away from 'literary' lines; in a movie, they sound phony unless justified by the character.

Use the Potter's Method
Work like a potter works a pot on the potter's wheel. Lay out the screenplay first, without the pressure of size or shape – keep that at the back of your mind. Once the first draft is done, start shaping the script by chopping, paring and pruning. Aristotle's method of elimination still works here. When deciding whether a particular section should stay in or not, do imagine the story without the section in question. If the story still holds, let the section go! Repeat this test till you get the pot right!

Do scenes for the screen

Allow scenes from your script to run on an imaginary screen in your mind while writing it. You will realize that scenes meant for a movie are remarkably shorter and crisper than scenes meant for the stage. The language of cinema is one of the eye and the ear. It is fluid and fast. Think out your scene, and then, try to cut it to half!

Do break the rules!

The rules of screenplay writing are, after all, just conventions meant to let your screenplay be accepted by the movie fraternity. They are not inflexible. No great work gets written without bending the proverbial 'rules'. So once you are confident of having mastered the dynamics of writing a script by the rule, feel free to break them if your story so demands.

Copyright it!

Copyright your script before you send it. You don't want someone to make your screenplay their own, when you can't make their movie your own!

The Abstract

Your script should be accompanied by a snappy covering letter that gives a very brief snapshot of your story and says what it is about.

Don'ts

Take liberties, but not with the format!

When you are confident of all the rules, you begin to take liberties with the form. But whatever you do, DO NOT play with the script format. The professional reader is used to reading it the 'right' way.

This is not a comic-book

This is meant to be a screenplay. Even if it 'feels' right stay away from illustrations and fancy embellishments. Do not do pictures, cartoons. Do not use colour paper, fancy paper. Do not stick in quotations and fancy lines. Avoid embellishments of all kinds. Anything that will distract from the script should stay out of it.

Don't do a roll-call of characters

A play begins with a character list and a bit of the context. This is a screenplay! Just tell the story. Don't do a roll call of characters. Your script should be able to build the past AND provide the context.

You don't have to be an Aeschylus

Aristotle's rules of unity of place, action and time were created for the stage where it was still a bother to change setting and scenes and makeup and costumes. So don't try to be an Aeschylus. Do not limit your script by time, action and place (unless that's the point of the story). A movie allows you to move from London to Delhi in a second. It allows you to move from the real to the surreal and back to the real. Play to the strengths of the medium.

Do not give up

Consider yourself lucky if you receive rejection letters from professionals. In most cases, the people you send your script to are unlikely to even reply. Be patient. Do not give up. When you strike gold, it will be worth the effort!

ACTIVITY 28

Here's a little exercise for you. Given below is a short story written with the cinematic eye. It eventually became the first scene of a short film called THE ROOM that experimented with the interplay of VO and dialogues. Try your screenplay writing abilities on it! Flesh out the scene, format it, add or delete characters and insert instructions. Use your imagination, but stick to the rules!

THE ROOM

She says that she loves me. My smile is priceless. My hair, curly.

She'd like to see me-someday-making love. But it's difficult. The eyes shut of their own accord. It's not voluntary.

Yeah, just like that!

A picture with my head half covering the breasts. Not above the neck. Not her face. Just me and the breast.

She says that she loves the colour of my skin. This colour is rare.

There's something else she'd like to tell me but feels shy. I'm very curious.

Is it something good or bad? I'd like to know.

It's something good, and it's about me.

But telling it might ruin every thing.

Nevertheless.

It turns out to be something uneventful. She thinks

I am god.

When she was a little girl she played with the god. He was a dark god. His bones were young. His limbs were gentle.

She'd wanted to marry the god. Hadn't she told her mother about him?

I think I could be a god too. Who knows? But I get clever. I never believe myself.

Will she ever have to live without me? She enquires.

How do I know?

But I say not unless I die. Just like in the films.

She looks sad since I just mentioned death. She doesn't think I'll die too soon. I don't try to convince her either. Just in case-death is dicey.

I ask her what she'd told her mother about me but she doesn't want to tell. She shakes her head.

Oh, come on! -I urge her.

The way you are-she says.

I'd like to know that. So I ask her.

-That you have dark hair.

I want to know exactly what she said.

She sighs.

-That-he has…curly hair…he's got beautiful eyes…hmm…a…a sharp nose…

-I'm nothing like that. Maybe a fraction. But that's it.

Yet she says that when I hold her it makes her feel like a child again.

She thinks it's the god holding her.

What's it got to do with me?

The writer can be contacted for suggestions and/queries at arvindjoshi@rediffmail.com; Arvind Joshi is a poet by passion and makes 'minute' films.

Writing a Screenplay

Given below is an except from the script *A Calamity in Kailash* by Subhadra Sen Gupta which is based on Satyajit Rays Bengali novel *Kailashey Kelenkari.* Subhadra Sengupta and Tapas Guha have further developed the screenplay script into a comic strip as one can see post the excerpted script.

The student will get an idea how different elements are incorporated into a comic strip. These include the visual/caption/speech blurb/thought blurb/sound effects.

What the students have to understand is that it is the writer who decides the visual in each frame and has to tell a large part of the story visually and the importance of writing realistic dialogues. Also, for students interested in film making, the storyboards for films are also done in the same manner.

Satyajit Ray's A *calamity in Kailash*

Script: Subhadra Sen Gupta
Art: Tapas Guha

Story so far: Malik's travelling to Aurangabad by train. He has the yakshi with him. We took a flight.

1. Long frame: Feluda, Topshe, Jatayu, standing before Bibi ka Maqbara (ref. *Blue Guide*, p. 112). Wearing dark glasses, Jatayu with an awful floppy hat. Feluda carries a camera and a jhola bag (make this bag eyecatching, it appears later). Feluda is reading a guidebook, Topshe grinning.

   Cap: Malik would arrive by the afternoon train. So we went sight-seeing next morning. Feluda: This is Bibi ka maqbara, the tomb of Aurangzeb's queen Rabia-ud-Durrani... Jatayu: Hmm... looks sort of familiar...

   Topshe: Like the Taj Mahal went on a diet hee hee!

2. Jatayu and Topshe sitting on the lawns of the maqbara.

   Cap: Jatayu is still thinking of Prof. Shubhankar Bose.

   Jatayu: At Bombay airport during check in, I was behind Bose. His suitcase weighed 35 kilos! Can you believe it?

3. Jatayu talking, Topshe puzzled.

   Jatayu: I checked. Yours weighed 14, mine 16 and Felu's 22 kilos.

   Topshe:What could he be carrying?

   Jatayu: HAMMERS! CHISELS!!

4. CU Jatayu.

   Jatayu: I'm telling you! He looks exactly like my latest villian Ghanashyam Karkat! Same pointy nose, indentical shark like teeth...

5. Topshe: Feluda, Jatayu says Prof. Bose's luggage weighed 35 kilos. Feluda: 37 not 35. So what?

6. They are at a soft drinks stall. Feluda grinning. Jatayu excited.
   Jatayu: Don't tell Bose you're a detective! He could be dangerous y'know!
   Feluda: What'll he do? Hit me with his suitcase?
7. Feluda, offering chips to Topshe.
   Topshe: Jatayu thinks he's carrying hammers and chisels to break the carvings.
   Feluda: Or he's got big, heavy art books! Calm down folks! Chips anyone?

The World of Children Through Film and Theatre

We are all familiar with theatre for children as practically everyone would have participated in plays performed at school for a number of occasions be it the Annual Day or Independence Day or even Childrens'/Teachers' Day ! The play would obviously be suited to the mood of the occasion. There is also a big market for Childrens Theatre the world over and the number of Theatre workshops/Summer Schools/Professional Theatre groups/NGOs/Theatre Projects and Community/street theatre groups that work with and for children, in India and the rest of the world, is evidence of this growing demand.

The range of childrens theatre and film is so vast that it is not possible to study it in great detail but it would be useful to make general survey through broad categorisation. So, perhaps what immediately comes to mind are the Fairy Tales, Fables and Fantasies such as the ever popular *Cinderella* or *The Wizard Of Oz*; another very common mode are Theme plays with songs/musicals/dance dramas and perhaps the film *Sound of Music* is a classic example of this mode; Comedies which includes circus acts and farces; Mysteries be they murder mysteries or the typical whodunnits and the serial based on Arthur Conan Doyle's *Adventures of Sherlock Holmes* is a good example; Tales of horror and suspense; Melodramas; Contemporary fairy tales; Educational Plays and Plays with a specific ideological standpoint or social intent.

Scripting for each of these kinds of plays would naturally involve entirely different sets of paradigms and the next section entitled Scripting for Children's Theatre written by Sanjay Kumar offers ONE such paradigm. This is in keeping with the objectives of Pandies Theatre Company of which Sanjay Kumar is the Director. The aspiring Children's playwright should however be aware that there are a number of other possibilities in this field.

Scripting for Children's Theatre

Sanjay Kumar*

Scripting for any kind of theatre involves focusing on who is your possible audience and who are your likely performers. While scripting for children, the first issue that needs addressing is defining Children's Theatre. Is it theatre where children are the performers or are they the audience? Who is conceiving the performance, whose experience will constitute the basis of the script? In our world where grown-ups tend not only to tell the young child what s/he should do but even interpret her/his experience, children's theatre often begins and ends up in conceptually false modes. A usual pattern for children's theatre in our public schools is as follows: A grown-up (often the teacher) chooses a script (often a canonized play from England or America), children are asked to mug up their parts, the performance is conceived of and directed by grown-ups (teacher or hired professionals), and the audience primarily consists of parents and teachers and hopefully fellow students (many of whom abscond).

A more authentic and rewarding way could be to base the script on children's experience itself. The scripting methodology below is culled out of the experience of Pandies'

* Sanjay Kumar is the founding President of **Pandies' Theatre** (1993). He has been teaching English Literature at the Hans Raj College, University of Delhi since 1984.

theatre, an activist theatre group that works with children from diverse backgrounds—reaching out to them through theatre, helping them create scripts based on their experience, culminating in a small performance. The scriptwriter can be an outsider, a member of the activist group or a relatively older child from within the group of children. A description of the general pattern of such script writing is followed by an illustration from a specific script-writing exercise.

Whatever be the sector, a group of 25 is an ideal number to have for a theatre workshop. Certain diversity—gender, religion, geographical background—is helpful as it adds to the fund of experience.

1. We begin with exercises—physical and theatrical. These experiences are a part of the repertoire of all theatre groups. (Augusta Boal's book *Games for Actors* and Non-Actors, 1992 on theatre experience gives numerous examples of both, and is a must for theatre enthusiasts). Physical exercises that make the children focus and help remove preconceived peer formations give way to theatre exercises. Image making provides a good transition. We give the children a word and in 10 seconds, using their face and bodies each child has to individually create an image that according to her/him reflects the word. Words are weighted, often in pairs or multiples (father-mother, Hindu-Muslim-Christian-Sikh) and the process of introspection has begun. Each child is looking within her/himself interpreting to cull images that correspond to his notion of the word.
2. Individual exercises are followed by collective image-making. At this point, the group is divided into smaller groups of about five each. Each group is now given a word/concept more complex than earlier (my family, my society/how I would like it to be, my city, grown-ups, my school). Each group collectively creates an image/picture corresponding to the concept given. In the image, each child must represent something and the total picture conveys their collective view of the concept. The process of collective introspection, of looking into each other's experience and creating a holistically clear picture has taken place. The scriptwriter has to be actively involved at this stage.
3. Collective introspection is taken a stage further by narrativizing. Each group appoints a writer and s/he along with the other delving into their memories create a chart narrative around the themes emerging in the workshop. This is then presented before the whole group. A short story has proven the most effective mode at this stage though other forms are also useful. An improvised short skit often works well with street-children and autobiographical, anecdotal narration, where each child comes up and adds to the topic from his experience, works well with small children.

   The scriptwriter has to work with these narratives. He has options, if the stories are disparate, he can use an episodic mode where each story forms an episode and the whole is connected by a sutradhar or by thematic ties. But where there is homogeneity of themes, the more challenging mode is to try and create one sequential script combining experiences from all the narratives.

   The scriptwriting example presented below is illustrative of the process. It is from a Pandies' workshop on Child Rights with Project Concern International (PCI), Delhi, as Networking partners for The British Council. The children were, runaway, abandoned street-children whom the organization keeps at its home and imparts formal education and vocational training.

At the narrativizing stage, four of the six groups had opted to make small skits and two had narrated their experiences. The stories consisted of children abandoned, more often running away from repressive 'homes' and employers, on the streets, vulnerable and abused, cycles of exploitation and running away. The script writer chosen was from among them. He was about 20 years old, himself a runaway. He had taken some training in performance arts and had joined PCI as a facilitator. Working closely with the children and their stories, he came up with a comprehensive sequential script.

The summary of the plot:

Based on what happens to abandoned children in many parts of Delhi, the plot focussed specifically around Red Fort. On cold wintry nights, the really poor—beggars, hawkers—sleep on the streets. Areas are demarcated and each is under a contractor. These contactors provide quilts/thick blankets on hire at two rupees a night. These are taken by the poor men and returned in the morning. In the midst of this is the story of a poor runaway boy who cannot afford the quilt. As night descends, it gets cold. A man takes him under his quilt. For the warmth of the quilt he has to make the 'payment' of being abused through the night. Stark though the storyline is, what the scriptwriter did was amazing.

Prologue

The contractor with a servant describing the process of renting quilts to pavement sleepers—imparting of information to the audience. The servant is forgetful and the master has a peculiar way of speaking—the two generate a lot of humour at their own expense.

I. The boy protagonist is located in a village around Delhi. Abusive father wants him to work in a shop, the boy shirks work, beaten and abandoned at the mercy of the master. Lot of humor as the clever boy tricks the 'bad' adults and escapes.

II. The protagonist in Delhi around Red Fort. He befriends a boy dressed as a monkey—prancing and begging, horseplay and buffoonery. As evening turns into night the 'friend' decamps with whatever the protagonist has, leaving him cold, hungry and penniless.

III. Night is really cold. The boy sits huddled in a corner. From below the quilts 'eyes' stare at him. A hand stretches and offers him a morsel of food. The boy accepts it. The man gently pulls him inside the quilt.

Epilogue

The contractor and the man (who was with the boy) are arguing. The contractor demands an extra 2 rupees because the quilt is 'dirty'. The man argues and they finally settle for an extra 1 rupee. As the man leaves, the contractor turns to the servant and says, 'It's a great day, so many quilts are dirty.'

Points to Note

1. The structure: Within the sequence, the scriptwriter has created a structure which ends where it began and contributes to the success of the script. Structuring is one of the most important aspects of script writing.
2. The Humour: Humour is an extremely important ingredient of theatre— specially Children's theatre. Humour, even buffoonery and slapstick, has the ability to

engage an audience. Even the most serious message (as above) gains with the use of humour.

3. Suggestion: Everything need not be shown, certainly not said. The strength of this script is that despite dealing with something gross and violent, it does not show any violence, does not even directly refer to it; the impact is stronger, not weaker.
4. The Ending: Always very important in a script. As the two 'adults' haggle, their grossness and above that, the callousness of the adult world towards children and their rights is highlighted.

Developing as a Playwright and Evaluating Your Script

In his book, Three Genres *The Writing of Poetry, Fiction and Drama*, Stephen Minot provides the aspiring playwright with a fairly comprehensive methodology to evaluate ones script. Based on his guidelines, this section aims to help you evaluate your own work and develop your strengths as a script writer. Since drama is intended for a large audience, it is actually useful to get a feedback from friends and advice from teachers or professionals. However, the final revisions will depend upon the playwright. The first step is to begin with a silent reading. Perhaps you have been doing that all along but this time do so without halting to make corrections of any kind. Give the script your complete attention. While reading, visualize all the action in each scene. Without analyzing, try to hear the lines as they would be spoken by actors and actresses. Once you have experienced the entire play in this way in your mind, imagine that you are the director and write as objective a critique as you can of the play.

After taking this first step read the script aloud. This will help you to note the timing of the play keeping in mind of course that you will also have to make room for those actions that occur without lines. Whether your play has Acts and Scenes or whether it is a television script, you will be able to see how long each segment is and thus be able to cut or expand where required. You will also be able to estimate the total performance time of the play. Apart from informing you about the timing, this spoken reading will enable you to judge the effectiveness of dialogue as very often what looks good when written, sounds awkward or unsuitable when spoken. Once you have made the corrections you deem necessary after your spoken reading, the next step would be to organize a small informal group reading which could even be taped if possible. Obviously the skills of the readers would partly determine how good or bad the parts appear but certainly, this will give you the first glimpse of what the play may be like when it is fully produced.

While you may prefer to have a small audience of friends apart from your readers, it is not an essential factor. What is important is that you are aided ably in transforming the written script into a successful performance on stage. A discussion regarding the impact of the play, after the reading would be a helpful device. Inevitably, those who participate in the reading have extremely pertinent insights to offer. Be careful that the discussion does not degenerate into mere conversation about the issues raised by the play; remind the discussants that the discussion should focus on the script itself.

Five Key Questions

Minot suggests five key questions which he feels are vital in the analysis of a dramatic script and which prevent a discussion from digressing. According to him, they serve as a perspective to one's work in its initial stages.

First, *does the play have dramatic impact?* To be more specific, does the play generate some kind of an immediate response and if so, is this sustained? Does the play become too melodramatic in certain scenes in case the dramatist is using shock or suspense? And if the dramatist is using wit or satire, does the play really appear funny or is it mere slapstick humour or farcical? What were the specific scenes and characters that made the play work effectively as a comedy/ tragedy etc.?

Second, *is the structure of the plot effective?* By questioning the audience on what they considered to be the high points of the play, the playwright can learn as to whether the plot worked in terms of rising action and periodic climaxes. This could help in restructuring the plot if required.

Third, *were the characters convincing and interesting?* When such a question is asked, the playwright learns a lot about the effectiveness of dialogue and action in the play as naturally the characterization depends a lot upon both these elements. The playwright should not be misled by comments voicing individual like/dislike for a character but should instead try to see whether the character came across as an effective one, be it a protagonist or a secondary character.

Fourth, *what themes are being explored and how are they developed?* What you as a playwright intend to convey and what the audience actually understands as the theme/s of your play, may be entirely different. So you should not try to explain your intentions to the audience and should instead try to see your play objectively from the point of view of your audience. In this way you will be able to gauge whether the ideas were too subtle or too hackneyed or whether the tone was preachy or pedestrian. Do keep an open mind and don't get defensive as that would not help you to improve your script.

The fifth and final question is linked to the previous two: *Does the play or script show originality?* Every playwright would like to produce a memorable script, one that holds the attention of the audience and is new as well as convincing. So it is important to try and find out which aspects of your play were a new experience for the audience.

Finally, to write a play or film script…read a lot of plays, recent as well as older plays.

Watch a lot of plays…if you are a college student, you could *act* or *serve as stage* crew and you will find yourself learning a lot about the art and craft of script writing. As with poetry and fiction, allow the works already written to reach out to you and teach you. Every script writer would have faced the kind of hurdles you might have done…so be bold and *embrace the medium*. You could begin with the following workshops!

Workshop 8

How to Develop a Situation

STEP 1: READ THE FOLLOWING FACT

It was a dark and stormy night.

STEP 2: KEEP THE FOLLOWING ASPECTS IN MIND:

1. Setting: location of the scene/place of action
2. Character(s): their physical and mental state
3. Action(s): the building up of SUSPENSE to a climax; the whetting of the appetite to know 'what next'
4. Language: both, verbal language as well as non-verbal language
5. Target Audience: if your play is for children, for example, the theme/language/tone etc. has to be very different from a play for a mature audience.

STEP 3: NOW SEE HOW THE FACT IN STEP 1 CAN BE EXPANDED INTO THE FOLLOWING DESCRIPTION:

The wind howled against wildly swaying branches of the trees and the moon tossed about helplessly in the sky. A sudden sliver of light snaked its way drunkenly over the rundown path: it was from the flashing headlights of a car inching forward. As the car came closer, Maya could make out two hazy figures inside it. The blood coursed through Maya's veins and with all her might, she struggled to get up. But her bruised and broken body was limp. She tried desperately to call out but not a sound escaped her lips. Vainly, she tried to lift her arm—it rose slightly and then fell like stone. Sweat poured down from Maya's scalp to her neck and back through these exertions. The car was now just a few inches away. In a frenzy Maya stirred her body as much as she possibly could and attempted to scream aloud, the sweet salty taste—of blood in her mouth. The car passed by. Maya shut her eyes. It was all over.

Inside the car, Jade turned to Anu and said: 'Hey there's something moving under those bushes. Look.' Anu peered into the rearview mirror and started, 'You're right. It looks…' Jade completed, grimly, 'Human.' Maya could feel strong arms lifting her, a soothing hand on her brow and soft, distressed voices. Then she lost all consciousness.

STEP 4: CHECK TO SEE IF THE ASPECTS OUTLINED IN STEP 2 HAVE BEEN COVERED; MAKE CHANGES IF NEEDED.

ACTIVITY 29

Here are some situations borrowed from Georges Polti's list of 36 dramatic situations. Polti names the central concern or theme and also the possible characters in each of these situations:

(i) Ambition: An ambitious person; a thing coveted; an adversary
(ii) Madness: a madman; a victim
(iii) Adultery: two adulterers; a deceived spouse
(iv) Obstacles to Love: two lovers; an obstacle
(v) Daring Enterprise: a bold leader; an object; an adversary
(vi) Conflict With A God: a mortal; an immortal.

Choose any two of the above and write a sequence of events following STEPS 1 to 4.

Workshop 9

Tutorial Format

(i) Read out your sequence of events to the class.

(ii) Questions will now be put to you; these would cover the aspects in step 2. So, for example, the questions on the description in step 3 could focus on

(a) Comments on the setting: where is this set—a forest? Is it realistic—can anything else be added—is there anything jarring?

(b) What do you think could have happened to Maya—Why is she lying here? What is she thinking and feeling? What kind of a relationship is there between Anu and Jade? What kind of people are they?

(c) What do you think happened before this scene? What do you think happens after this scene?

(d) Can you gauge anything about the kind of people that Maya, Anu and Jade are on the basis of the description and the dialogue?

(e) What kind of a reader/audience do you think would respond to such a scene?

(iii) Now, defend your situation; explain your perspective.

Workshop 10

Choose any one of your sequence of events in a scene for a play. Keep the following aspects in mind while writing;

(i) When writing the scene for the play, decide where in the story does the scene fit; the beginning, the middle or the end.

(ii) Then, if the scene is the opening episode, you need to narrate the sequence of events till the conclusion after writing the scene. Similarly, if the scene is an episode in the middle of the story, you need to narrate the sequence of events pre and post the episode; if the scene is at the end, you need to narrate all that went before it. The aim is to show how effectively the scenes have been arranged in terms of the structure of the play.

(iii) Write out the list of characters; you may wish to give some rudimentary information about them.

(iv) Write out the stage setting, i.e., the props/furniture, if needed; the background sound and lights that are required; number the scenes (Scene I or Scene IV or Scene X as the case may be—remember, when you narrate the sequence of events as asked in (ii), you have to do so scene wise) [This must be written in parentheses]

(v) Mark the entrance and exit of each character; if the character is already on the stage when the scene starts, mention that in the directions written in parentheses in (iv).

(vi) Be careful to indicate non-verbal language (gestures, expressions, postures, etc.) in parentheses along with the verbal language (monologue/dialogue/soliloquy etc.)

(vii) If lighting/sound needs to be changed during the scene, you may wish to inform the director of these changes; do so in parentheses wherever required.

(viii) If you are convinced that the way you envisage your characters (their costumes, their behavior, their nature) is the way you would like the director and the actors to depict them, then say so either in (iii) or in (iv)

(ix) Look back at Unit 2 of this book: 'The Art and Craft of Writing'. The various language registers; the intersection of language with race, class, cast, culture, gender, location, physical impairment etc; the figures of speech, for example, irony, may help in the construction of dialogue, tone, humour, wit, pathos, etc.

References

Achtert, Walter S. and Joseph Gibaldi, *The MLA Style Manual* (New York: The Modern Language Association of America, 1985).

Agha Shahid Ali(ed.), *Ravishing Disunities: Real Ghazals in English* (Hanover, USA: Wesleyan University Press, University Press of New England, 2000).

Ali, Agha Shahid, *The Half-Inch Himalayas* (Hanover, USA: Wesleyan University Press, University Press of New England, 1987).

Ayers, Tim and John Dayus, *Developing Writing Skills for Key Stage 3 Tests* (Oxford: Heinemann educational Publishers, 1999).

Bailey, Tom (Ed), *On Writing Short Stories* (New York: Oxford University Press, 2000).

Baldick, Chris, *The Concise Oxford Dictionary of Literary Terms* (Oxford: Oxford University Press, 1990-91).

Bearne, Eve, *Making Progress in Writing* (London: Routledge, 2002).

Benson, Gerard, Judith Chernaik and Cicely Herbert (eds.) *Poems on the Underground: Illustrated Edition* (London: Cassell Publishers Limited, 1992).

Chaudhuri, Amit, Note on Aamer Hussein's new stories 19.3.1998 http://www.salidaa.org.uk/salidaa/site

Dahl, Roald, *Songs and Verse* (London: Jonathan Cape, 2005).

Dancyger, Ken, *Broadcast Writing Dramas, Comedies and Documentaries*, (Butterwoth-Heinemann), USA: Focal Press, 1991).

Dattani, Mahesh, *Final Solutions and Other Plays* (New Delhi: MANAS affiliated to. East West Press Pvt. Ltd,1994).

Decker, Randall E. and Robert A. Schwegler, *Decker's Patterns of Expostion 12* (Glenville, Illinois: Scott Forseman/Little, Brown Higher Education, 1990).

Drew, Elizabeth, *Poetry: A Guide to its Understanding and Enjoyment* (New York: Dell Publishing Co. Inc., 1959).

Ezekiel, Nissim, Collected Poems: 1952–1988 (New Delhi: Oxford University Press, 1989).

Ferguson, Suzanne C, 'Defining the Short Story' in Michael J Hoffman and Patrick D Murphy (eds.) *Essentials of the Theory of Fiction* (Durham London: Duke University Press, 1988).

Flower, Linda, 'Writing for an Audience' in, Paul Eschholz and Alfred Rosa (eds) *Themes for Writers* (New York: St. Martin's Press, 1994).

Goldberg, Natalie, *Thunder and Lightning: Cracking Open the Writer's Craft* (New York: Bantam Books, 2001).

Holden, Susan, *Drama in Language Teaching*, (Essex: Longman Group Ltd, 1981).

http://www.elizabethlowell.com/popfiction.html. (Popular Fiction: Why We Read It, Why We Write It). http://www.english.soton.ac.uk/hussein.htm)

Hussein, Aamer, *The Blue Direction and other Stories* (Delhi: Penguin books, 1999.

IGNOU Audio-Video Catalogue,'DCE 1: Principles of Writing: Fundamental Norms of Writing 1', Delhi: IGNOU, School of Humanities, 2002.

Kennedy, X.J., *Literature: An Introduction to Fiction, Poetry and Drama* (HarperCollins 1991).

Madden, David, *A Pocketful of Essays Volume II: Thematically Arranged* (Fort Worth, USA: Harcourt College Publishers, 2001).

Mahapatra, Jayanta, *Dispossessed Nests: The 1984 Poems* (Jaipur: Nirala Publications, 1986).

Melrose, A. R., The Pooh Directory: The Complete Guide to the Words of Pooh and all the Animals of the Forest (London: Methuen, 1995).

Mills, Paul, *Writing in Action* (London and New York: Routledge, 1996).

Minot, Stephen, *Three Genres: The Writing of Poetry, Fiction and Drama* (Third Edn) (Englewood Cliffs: Prentice Hall Inc., 1982).

Oxford Advanced Learner's Dictionary of Current English (A S Hornby (ed), Sixth Edition).

Padmanabhan, Manjula *Harvest,* (New Delhi: Kali for Women, 1997).

Paniker, Ayyappa, (Ed) *Modern Indian Poetry in English* (New Delhi; Sahitya Akademi, 1991, 2004).

Parthasarathy, R., *Rough Passage* (Delhi: Oxford University Press, 1977).

Perrine, Lawrence, *Literature Structure, Sound and Sense* (USA: Harcourt Brace Jovanovich Inc., 1978).

Potlti, Georges, *The Thirty Six Dramatic Situations* (retrived from http://en.wikipedia.org.wiki/the thirty-six dramatic situations).

Preminger, Alex, Frank J. Warnke and O. B. Hardison, Jr. (Eds.) *Princeton Encyclopedia of Poetry and Poetics* (Princeton, New Jersey: Princeton University Press, 1965, 1974).

Pritchett, V. S., quoted by Francine Prose in 'What Makes a Short Story?' in *On Writing Short Stories* (ed) Tom Bailey.

Ramanujan, A. K, *Collected Poems* (New Delhi: Oxford University Press, 1995).

Riccio, Ottone M., *The Intimate Art of Writing Poetry* (New Jersey: Prentice-Hall Inc., 1980).

Sarang, Vilas, *Indian English Poetry Since 1950: An Anthology,* Disha Books (a division of Orient Longman Limited, 1994)

Sarang, Vilas, *The Women in Cages* (Delhi: Penguin Books 2006).

Target Annual 1988 (India Living Media).

—*The Country Without a Post Office: Poems* (New York: W. W. Norton & Co., 1997).

Webster's Encyclopedic Unabridged Dictionary of the English Language 1994).

Wheeler, Charles B., *The Design of Poetry* (New York: W. W. Norton and Co. Inc., 1966).

Wilson, Edwin, *The Theatre Experience* (USA: McGraw-Hill Book Company, 1982).

Websites:

Teams Educational Resources, http://www.teams.lavoe.edu

http://en.wikipedia.org/wiki/Creative_writing

http://www.gc.maricopa.edu

http://www.amazon.com

http://en.wikipedia.org/wiki/Impressionism

http://literaryexplorer.blondelibrarian.net/novel.html

http://www.maheshdattani..com

http://www.tribuneinda.com

http://www.hinduonnet.com

http://www.doollee.com

http://in.rediff.com

http://web.mit.edu

http://www.explocity.com

http://www.telegraphindia.com

http://www.india-today.com

http://www.wikipedia.org
http://www.chennaionline.com
http://forumthree.blogspot.com
http://www.indidub.com
http://web.mid-day.com

4

Writing for the Media

Introduction

In the previous sections, we have discussed the various forms of creative writing. Writing for the media may not seem to be in the same category. This is because we normally associate creative writing with fiction, poetry and drama, and the media with facts. But, as has been pointed out in the section on fiction in Unit 3, creative writing can be fact-based as well. Then how is writing for the media different?

The simple answer is that there is not much difference at all. Any difference which can be observed is generated by the specific needs of the various media in question. So, there will be differences in the way one would write for the print media, and for the broadcast media because of the formats adopted by them. There are, however, a few common factors among the various forms of media.

To begin with, media writing values brevity: short words, short sentences, short paragraphs, short stories. Why? Because, media compete for people's time. The more time you take to communicate, the less likely people are to hear what you have to say.[1] Also, within a given medium, there is a limited amount of space and/or time available for communication. Therefore, in writing for the media, brevity is a very important factor. In general, the longer a piece is, the fewer the number of people who will read it. This does not mean that you make everything extremely short. You will have to judge the maximum amount of time for which the audience will be interested in what you have to say. You have to strike a balance between expressing all that you feel is essential, and retaining the interest of the audience.

The other factor to be kept in mind is the subject. What will you write about? The choice of subject will depend on 'newsworthiness', which is measured by the number of 'news values' that the subject demonstrates. These news values, which would be more or less equally important to each other depending on the type of story, are:

- Impact — how many people does the event affect?
- Timeliness — how recently did it occur?
- Prominence — how well known are the people involved?
- Proximity — how close, geographically, did it take place?

[1] Adapted from Media Writing Tips. URL: http://mtsu32.mtsu.edu:11178/171/tips.htm#brevity

- Conflict — does it involve some kind of disagreement or fight?
- Weirdness — how unusual is it?
- Currency — is it related to something people are talking about or interested in?[2]

Following these news values will help you decide what to write about—the more newsworthy the story is, the better chance it has of being published.

To sum up, the three essentials when writing for the media are:

- Identifying the elements of the story that will be of greatest interest to the audience.
- Structuring the story to convey the information as effectively as possible.
- Presenting the story in a way that will make maximum use of the medium and engage the maximum number of the audience for the maximum length of time (Ward 2003:110).

The factor common to the various forms of media is that *they are all different ways of communicating news and information to the general public*. So, newspapers, magazines, television, radio and even the internet are forms of the media because they communicate, not to any particular individual but to anyone who reads, watches, or hears them. Because of the large reach of the media, the subjects that they deal with should be relevant and important to society. There has to be a deep social responsibility in all that the media report. It is the task of media to not just report, but to comment, to criticise, and above all inform the public about what is really going on. It is this spread of information which keeps public aware of what goes on in all social fields. As Ian Hargreaves (2005) remarks:

> Journalism matters not just to journalists, but to everyone: good journalism provides the information and opinion upon which successful democratic societies depend. Corrupt that and you corrupt everything. But, equally, let journalism ossify, or be economically undermined, and politics and public life will suffer.

This social responsibility of the media should be reflected in the work of the writers in the media—it is their writing which can influence public opinion. It is extremely important for you as the writer to be aware of your social responsibility.

The media can be broadly divided into three types, based on the method of transmission—the Print Media (which includes newspapers and magazines), the Broadcast media (Radio and Television), and the New Media (The Internet or The Worldwide Web). All of these types of media require different kinds of writing styles which are dependent on their medium of transmission. Each of the three types of media presents different challenges and opportunities for the writer.

The **Print Media** includes newspapers and news magazines. Within this medium, a large variety of writing styles exist, which are dependent on subject. The kinds of writing which are prevalent in the Print Media include basic reportage/ 'hard news' (where you are reporting the facts of an incident/ event from a relatively objective point of view), Feature writing (where you deal with a particular subject in wider/ deeper detail than in reportage, with a greater amount of subjectivity), interviews, book/ film reviews, travel writing, editorials, and personal columns. Some modes of creative writing present in this medium are not necessarily governed by the factor of 'newsworthiness'—

[2] Media Writing Tips. URL: http://mtsu32.mtsu.edu:11178/171/tips.htm#newsvalues

for example advertising. Creative writing in the field of advertising is not governed by the principles of journalism but primarily by commercial considerations.

All of these varieties of writing, within the Print Media, present different challenges to the writer. Perhaps the greatest challenge is to keep it concise, because you have only a limited amount of column space available (which is dependent on the newsworthiness of the subject) to convey the news effectively. The other challenge will be stylistic in nature. You have to be objective and factual when reporting an incident or an interview, but can be extremely subjective when it comes to something like a review, or an editorial, or a personal column. The Print Media offers the greatest scope for creative writers, in terms of the various kinds of writing that are required. So you may start as a correspondent who reports on any and every event, may eventually specialize in a particular field, and become a sports correspondent or even a regular columnist with your own column.

The Broadcast Media, like Television and Radio, present a different set of challenges for the writer. Almost the same variety of writing styles is present in the Broadcasting Media as in the Print Media with the addition of other types of writing as well. Interviews, reviews, reportage, all of these are present in television as well as in radio broadcasting, but the writing styles required in these media differs from the corresponding style in the print media. For example, in television, an interview would be an audio-visual recording, rather than a printed page.

As far as Radio is concerned, the verbal element is very important; the news items will still be in the written form and will be read out by the presenter or the anchor of the programme. What differs is the length—the entire report cannot be very long, as a programme that is too long will test the patience of the listener. The important thing is that the report must not seem to be written or read but must appear to be; at the same time the style must not be too loose or casual. The kind of programming available will dictate style. An entertainment-based show, on music for example, would require the host of the programme to be comparatively relaxed, and somewhat informal; the script for this kind of programme would have to written carefully to convey that feeling. Radio also has educational programmes, interviews, as well as those programmes which involve a greater amount of creativity like radio-plays. Advertising will also be primarily verbal, and succinct, conveying the message in as short a time as possible.

Most of what applies to Radio holds true for Television too. In fact the actual verbal content of a Television news-report might be significantly less than it is for Radio. This is because the report is almost always accompanied by visuals. The presence of the visuals means that a lot of description which has to be included in a newspaper report will not be required. Television also offers other opportunities for creative writing; serials and documentaries are also prominent on television. Of course, the writing for these will be in the form of scripts or screenplays—conversation supplemented by action between the characters. In this medium, there are a lot of opportunities for the creative writer. The major challenge is to be able to write as concisely as possible, especially when reporting news. Advertising on Television is also script-based.

The New Media is the newest medium of all—the Internet or the Worldwide Web. This medium does not have any fixed form of writing. It is open to all forms of writing, including fiction, poetry, drama, creative non-fiction, news, interviews, and advertising. And all of this can exist not only in written form but also in audio or the audio-visual format. Writing for the web requires the same skills as writing for the Print Media, but also requires the additional skill of attracting potential readers to the page. Brevity is important, because not many readers will be willing to scroll down a long page to read all that you have written. The Internet offers the greatest amount of liberty to the writer in terms of what can be written. You can write anything you want and there will be someone to read it. Apart from the sites which supply news and analysis, there are a variety of sites which publish creative work.

The various media offer different opportunities and present differing challenges for the creative writer. The format and technology that are used by the different types of media demand a lot of flexibility and adaptability on the part of the creative writer. If you decide to write for the media, then you will have to decide which medium attracts you the most, and then sharpen your writing skills in order to communicate most effectively in that particular medium.

The Print Media

The Print Media includes newspapers as well as magazines. The two branches within the Print Media—newspapers and magazines—tend to have different characteristics.

The prime function of newspapers is to provide information. So, most of the articles in a newspaper will be concerned with events that have taken place within the last twenty-four hours. This is because the newspapers are concerned with delivering the maximum amount of news at the earliest possible time. The newspaper on any working-day is primarily news-oriented with perhaps only the editorial functioning as a commentary on events. Generally the reader will not read interviews, profiles, travel-oriented articles, and similar features, on a working-day. This is because on a working day, the average reader does not have enough leisure to be able to read the analysis and commentary on many topics. The only thing that matters is that the news must be communicated as efficiently as possible.

On weekends, however, the reader has the leisure, and the inclination, to read about things beyond the immediate news. So, most newspapers include supplements on weekends. These supplements include travel features, person-profiles, interviews, book/film reviews, columns on art and literature, commentary on social issues and other leisure reading. The main paper also undergoes some transformation; personal columns are also generally published in the main newspaper.

Magazines are different from newspapers in one aspect—they are more concerned with analysis, commentary, and investigation than newspapers. There is no rush to meet the deadline, so writers for magazines have more time on their hands to produce a well written piece. Magazines allow for much more space for the writer to explore and analyse issues compared to the space available in newspapers.

The number of issues or subjects which are dealt with in a magazine is fewer, but these few subjects are analysed in a critical and investigative manner, with extensive commentary being provided. The article should try to provide a balanced opinion, rather than a one-sided comment. Both sides of an argument can be extensively discussed—the writer's task is to provide as much information as is available. Magazines may also cater to special-interest groups; women, sports, photography, business, fashion. All of these magazines deal with specific subjects, but the format of writing does not change—they include, news-articles, interviews, reviews, profiles, and other types of articles of interest to specific groups of readers. Newspapers and magazines share a common pool of journalistic styles; the only difference is the level of analysis and debate, as well as column length.

Before we take a look at the different kinds of writing in the print media, let us take a look at a few general guidelines for writing for the news media.

The Language of News

The language of news is not the language of other kinds of writing. It is not a natural form of writing—it has its own particular stylistic qualities, with its own rhythm, words and phrases (Keeble 1996: 86). Like any other style, journalistic writing has to be learnt.

The most essential rule is to 'keep it short and simple'. Every word in a news story has to count, has to be relevant to the subject as news value is what matters. The simplest method of keeping the article short is to cut down the number of words. Never use two or three words (like break of day) when one (sunrise or dawn) will do. Try to use short words (like short) rather than long ones (like diminutive). Avoid using 'thing', when referring to an object; it is vague. Above all, use language precisely—don't confuse affect/effect, effete/effeminate, luxurious/luxuriant. (Keeble 1996: 89)

The most important rule of sentence construction: don't use the passive form of a sentence. Instead of: 'The seminar will be conducted by the teachers tomorrow,' use 'The teachers will conduct the seminar tomorrow.'

You should also avoid the use of the clichés. Phrases like 'part and parcel', 'by leaps and bounds', 'nose to the grindstone', 'pouring rain', 'storm in a teacup', have been so overused that they contribute nothing to the effect of the story.

Another kind of language which is difficult to understand is jargon. Each social group, especially in terms of profession, has its own jargon, which functions as a kind of shorthand aid to communication. Journalism too has its fair share of jargon. News writers must avoid jargon in their own writing, and try to translate other people's jargon into language which is understood by the majority of people.

You should try and avoid any kind of language which will make it more difficult for the reader to understand what you are trying to communicate. Remember, the reader has a limited amount of time to spend in reading the news. If your language is difficult, the reader will not read your article. But the task is also to attract the reader and keep him interested in what you have to say. One of the ways of doing this is through word-play. For example:

> You must take care that the word-play does not become irritating to the reader. So maybe once or twice you could use terms like 'Ton-dulkar' in a headline of an article on Sachin Tendulkar's centuries, but a phrase like 'Ton-dulkar plucked the Pigeon' within an article on Sachin and Glenn McGrath[3] might be too much.

You must also avoid the use of abusive, rude, or vulgar language when writing.

Types of Media Writing

Many different kinds of writing are available in the Print Media. The most common is of course *the news-report*.

[3] The Australian fast bowler Glenn McGrath's nickname is Pigeon.

The news-report is concise in form, and based on facts, outlining the major issues/people involved. The news-report can be either hard news or soft news. 'Hard news is the reporting of issues and events in the past or about to happen.'(Keeble 1996: 105). The beginning should have the most important details. Analysis, description, commentary and subjectivity should either be excluded or included very briefly. (Keeble 1996: 105)

The following report in Box 4.1 demonstrates how hard news is written.

BOX 4.1: TRUCK OVERTURNS AT VEGETABLE MARKET

A truck carrying potatoes overturned at the corner of the road leading to the New Vegetable Market, at about 11:30 at night yesterday. The driver suffered minor injuries; no one else was hurt. The police reports that the accident occurred because the truck was overloaded, and that the driver was driving too fast. The driver has been booked for negligent driving.

In this article, there is absolutely nothing that is extraneous, and the very first line answers the vital questions of 'What, When, How, Where, Who, and Why.' There are no descriptions, no quotations, nothing beyond the factual details.

Soft news differs from hard news in terms of what it deals with, and how it is written. Soft news includes broader aspects of the story; it may contain background information, extensive description, as also an analysis of events and situations. The article may not even necessarily begin with the main issue; it may begin with background and then move on to the main story. Here is an example illustrating 'soft news'.

BOX 4.2: BREAKTHROUGH IN ROBOTIC BRAIN RESEARCH

The scientists at the Asimov Robotics Laboratory are a happy bunch nowadays. Their lot has always been to bear the scorn of the public for having been unable to fulfil their own technological aims of creating new-generation, thinking robots. There was frustration among the scientists at their inability to achieve a breakthrough. An added tension was the rumour doing the rounds that their government funding was going to be withdrawn. But two months ago, one of the scientists, who had been working on the problem, stumbled onto the technique for creating a stable brain for these robots. 'I am a great fan of football, and it was during a game I was watching on T.V. that the solution occurred to me—the brain had to be hard and soft, simultaneously, like a football is. We had been trying to make it as hard as possible,' said Doctor Oliver, the scientist responsible for the breakthrough.

And, as a result of that brainwave, the engineering department of the Laboratory today unveiled the first working Non-Organic Brain (NOB for short), which will soon be fitted into already existing robotic bodies. If this experiment is successful, it will mean a giant leap in the scientific understanding of the workings of the human brain.

Meanwhile, Doctor Oliver is back watching his favourite team battle it out with its rivals on the football field. 'I might get another brilliant idea!' he laughs.

Notice how the focus is different from that of 'hard news'. There is background, description, and even quotations gathered around a central fact.

The other kind of writing which is present in the newspaper every day is the *editorial.* This is an article that is written by the editor of the newspaper, which voices an opinion on a subject of vital interest. The editorial, in a way, presents the opinion of the newspaper on a topic which it considers vital. Editorials are not in the style of ordinary reportage, but are critical in nature. The editorial tends to present a very strong argument for or against a particular opinion; the editorial does not necessarily present both sides of the argument equally. The editorial is personalized, but purports to deliver a more general perspective on issues.

ACTIVITY 1

Find and read editorials from different newspapers. Do these differ in opinion and/or style from each other? If so, what is the difference?

If we look at editorials from different newspapers, we will see that they all depart from the writing style of ordinary reporting. The style is serious and factual, and rather than being mere reporting of facts and events, there is a short analysis. The style is that of an argument, with opinions being presented, and one opinion being favoured over the other. A solution is presented for the problem under discussion.

Somewhere in between the 'soft news' and editorial, in terms of style, comes *the news feature*. News features contain more analysis, comment, background, and also, in terms of subject, draw their sources from more areas than news stories do. It is especially in the introduction (not to mention the title) where the tone of the article is set, that the news features tend to be more colourful and individualistic. There might be very strong opinion, with the author's views being prominent, but the emphasis is still on the news. While context, analysis, description, narrative, dialogue, quotations, opinion and historical contextualising might all be important, but factual detail and news sense must predominate. The feature must adhere to the news around which the analysis is based.

ACTIVITY 2

Take any newspaper, and locate the news features in it. Keep in mind the above requirements of the feature. Also remember that 'soft news' and 'news feature' are not mutually exclusive categories!

Other types of writing are not as common in the weekday paper, but are generally present in weekend editions of newspapers, as well as in magazines. Interviews, travel-writing, book/film reviews all appear in the weekend supplements of most newspapers and magazines. These are published on weekends, because the perception is that the readers have more leisure to read longer, analytical, and descriptive pieces on a variety of subjects.

Interviews

Among news features, the interview is perhaps the least creative, because the writer does not have the luxury of writing the words of the person being interviewed. The reporter has to report the words exactly as spoken; no addition may be made. However, you might need to edit some parts of the interview to make the final version coherent and focussed. The process of the interview is the most important factor which affects the final written piece.

An interview is intentional conversation (Keeble 1996: 66). The most important aspect that the interviewer should keep in mind is the purpose of the interview: whether it is information, or opinion; whether there is a subject, topic or theme being investigated, or whether some wrong-doing is to be exposed. On the other hand, the subject being interviewed also has a purpose. They may want to convey opinion or information, hide something, or maybe just express their mood. However, the interviewer should keep a few things in mind:

- The subject might be lying or trying to convey misinformation.
- The subject might be nervous, or afraid, or confused and thus be unable to say or express what they really mean.
- They may forget or hide details.

Also, the interviewer's personal biases or attitude may affect the subject and, thus, the responses that are received may be different from what they might have been. A different interviewer may elicit different response; factors of identity, like age, sex, and even race, may affect the interview. The reporter must remain aware of all these possibilities.

BOX 4.3: NEW DESIGN FOR A NEW AGE

The Asimov Robotics Laboratory has recently created the Non-organic Brain (NOB) that they had been trying to develop for the past few years, without any success. Robotic Science interviews **Dr. Daniel Oliver**, *the scientist who is responsible for the idea which provided the breakthrough.*

RS: Dr. Oliver, you are the person responsible for the creation of the new generation of robots. How does it feel to have achieved such a breakthrough?

DO: I am not the only person involved in this project. My colleagues in the Engineering Department have been the people who have made the NOB possible. My contribution was merely at the level of design. But yes, it does feel great to be part of the team which has made this technological breakthrough possible. We, at the Asimov Laboratory, are all excited at the potentialities of the new robots.

RS: So, what was the new design that was evolved by you?

DO: The basic problem was both structural, as well as to do with consistency. I merely suggested a design that would allow both rigidity and flexibility, as also give the NOB the ability to sustain physical shocks.

RS: And how did this idea come to you? Was it a result of intensive research?

DO: (*Thinks*) Well, yes, in a way… (*Laughs*) We were researching at the Laboratory, of course, but the actual idea came to me while I was at home, watching T.V.

RS: That sounds interesting!

DO: It is rather funny.. (*laughs again*). You see, I was watching a football match on T.V. It was when Gikard took a free-kick that the idea for the brain came to me. The shape and consistency of the football, as well as its shock-bearing capabilities—for instance, when it is kicked—seemed to be the ideal solution for our problem at the Laboratory. I took the idea to our engineering team, who were quite excited with the idea. It was them that came up with the actualization of this rather wild idea.

RS: Wow! That's quite a story! Don't you think it is rather unusual to get ideas like that?

DO: Not as unusual as you might think. It is a well-known phenomenon that the mind keeps thinking of the solution to a problem at the sub-conscious level, even when we are not actively thinking of it. It is this kind of background processing of information that connects such apparently different things as robotic brains and footballs. It is just that one should cultivate a scientific temper.

RS: So, Dr. Oliver, what do you propose to do next? What other problems are left?

DO: Hmmm... Some things are still in the planning stage, as far as the new robots are concerned. As for me, I will probably get back to watching my favourite team play in the World Cup. I might get another brilliant idea! (*Laughs*)

ACTIVITY 3

(a) In the above interview, how does the interviewer maintain continuity? What is the purpose of the interview?

(b) If you were to interview your friend, with the purpose of finding out his views on contemporary cinema, what questions would you include?

Reviews

Reviewing can serve many purposes. It informs people of the event and where it is happening, it provides an informed opinion for people to form their reactions for or against it and in many cases, provides people with an experience which they might never directly have. So, it is very important for the reviewer to provide details and perspectives on as many aspects as possible, while keeping the reader entertained.

Reviews are also important to the creators of the work under review; the opinion of the reviewer can greatly influence the reception of the work among the public. For the publication, reviewing is important because it can become a source of revenue through advertising; a newspaper that carries book reviews is more likely to get advertising from publishers, than one which does not. A few things must be kept in mind while reviewing:

- Titles of works/performances/productions must be accurately presented, as also the names of performers/characters, producers, writers.
- Quotations must be accurate.
- Plot/ contents must be summed up clearly in easily understood language; also any elements which are not generally understood, should be explained.
- Special sensitivity is required in some cases; a school play and a play by professional actors cannot be judged by the same benchmark Also, revealing the twist in the plot may spoil it for the reader/ viewer.

- The journalist must not stray into libel while criticising.
- The introduction must attract the reader. It needs to be stylistically unique.
- Reviewers must learn to express themselves concisely, within a given word count.

Generally reviews are compact, with the focus being on the entertainment value of the work. Language is to-the-point; sensational and human-interest angles are highlighted. The review must also cater to the particular kind of readership that subscribes to the publication—a Times of India film review might be different from the review of the same film in The Hindu. Of course, the review may be of a film, a play, a book, or even a musical/ dance performance.

■ BOX 4.4: RETELLING AN EPIC: ASHOK BANKER'S RAMAYANA SERIES

It is never easy to tell a story that has been already told and retold an uncountable number of times. More so when the story is one that is known to generations of readers and listeners, and one which has had many famous recounters. Ashok Banker sets out to tell us a story that has been made famous by the likes of Tulsidas, Kamban, and more recently, C. Rajagopalachari.

So, what is new about Banker's version of the Ramayana? The most noticeable difference is the style—more contemporary and fast-paced than the other versions. Banker's narration focuses, almost insistently, on action and description—the heroes are bold, the monsters are terrifying and the action breathtaking. It is a story that incorporates all elements of a modern-day thriller—action, adventure, and suspense, with delicate touches of emotion interwoven through it.

Banker's Ramayana series might not appeal to the older generation of readers, given the way in which he seems to sensationalize the story. But the good thing is that he makes this epic accessible to a generation which has been brought up in an age dominated by religious scepticism. Banker does not, however, lose his moorings and allow the series to become a mere pot-boiler. Questions of morality, duty, obedience, loyalty, love, and even definitions of good and evil are dealt with, in a compact package, which makes this modern retelling of the Ramayana a compelling read.

ACTIVITY 4

(a) Read the above book and review carefully. Would a film review be substantially different?

(b) Write a review of a movie you have seen.

Personal Columns

Personal columns—regular columns written by individuals—are another extremely creative form of writing which are available in the print media. These are highly subjective articles in which the subjectivity is more overt than in most other news. There is no attempt to hide the individual behind a façade of truth, balance, or objectivity. The narrator is obviously present, with individuality being completely apparent in the tone of the column. Nastiness, humour, warmth, irony, sarcasm, irritation, confession, authority, all can be displayed in a personal column.

The column generally appears with a picture or caricature of the columnist, which helps the reader to relate to him—positively or negatively. The important thing is that the columnist should not be ignored. The columnist can pick up any topic which interests him/her, not necessarily the dominant news of the time. Some pointers to writing columns:

- The columnist should have a few favourite topics, on which s/he holds strong opinions. But these should not be overdone.
- The columnist's opinion should be an honest one; insincerity is always obvious.
- The columnist should allow the readers a restricted view into his/her private life.

ACTIVITY 5

Look at personal columns by different people—Jug Suraiya, Bachchi J. Karkaria, Swaminathan Iyer, Shobha De, Khushwant Singh—and see how each writer has an individual style of writing which sets them apart from others. Does the personality of the columnist affect your opinion? If so, how?

Profiles

Another, personalized kind of writing is the Profile. In profile writing, the writer's task is to describe a person, his life, thoughts, and actions. This description is generally very personal, with the profile writer describing his or her opinion or perspective of the person. Even here, the profile need not necessarily be of a person—schools, colleges, organizations, monuments may all be profiled. However, people profiles are the most common. Even in these there can a variety of ways in which the profile may be written:

- A profile concentrating on a recent achievement.
- A profile concerned with a specific opinion held by the person on a specific subject.
- A profile giving an overview of a life.
- An obituary is also a form of profile.

BOX 4.5: THE ORNITHOLOGICAL INDIAN: SALIM ALI

My first introduction to Salim Ali was when I was ten years old. All I wanted to know was the name of the tiny, bright, shining purple bird which I saw flitting among the yellow flowers in my grandparents' garden. And the only person who could help was Salim Ali; or more accurately, his pocket guide to Indian Birds. And like numerous other bird lovers, I too was charmed by his style and impressed by his vast experience.

For many decades Salim Ali was the authority on all birding in India—he was the man to consult on any questions on Indian Birds; he was called the 'Birdman of India'. Not only was he a specialist on birds in the field, but also in terms of the science involved—he was instrumental in the reclassification of many bird species. But perhaps his most important

contribution was not limited only to the field of Ornithology; he took over the Bombay Natural History Society, and saved the institution from closing down, by writing to Jawaharlal Nehru for funds. It is due to this initiative that the conservation movement gained ground in the country.
He was nominated to the Rajya Sabha in 1985, and it was in this position that he was instrumental in saving both the Bharatpur Bird Sanctuary in Rajasthan, as well as the Silent Valley National Park in Kerala. These were important landmarks in the conservation efforts in the country.
But perhaps the greatest impact that Salim Ali had was on people like me, who found out the name of 'that bird'—a Purple Sunbird, incidentally—and would never have known, had it not been for him.

Travel Writing

Although not very different from other kinds of feature writing, travel writing has its own unique flavour. Travel writing is partly reporting, partly like a diary and provides information to the potential visitor. There are variety of writing styles available to the travel writer, but there are certain common elements:

- The style should be clear and convey the information as directly as possible.
- The piece should convey that the writer speaks from personal experience, such that the reader is able to identify with it. Humour, satire, unabashed admiration all increase the impact.
- There should be practical and accurate information about the place, which would be useful to the reader.

Other topics like sports, and fashion also find a place in the Print Media, but they are written in a variety of styles. There are no hard and fast rules when it comes to writing about these topics. The report might be hard news, or a news feature, or a profile, or even a personal column.

In general, whatever writing style is adopted, it may be the same for various types of writing, whether it is for a newspaper or for a magazine. The only difference is that magazines give more space for each piece, and the tone is generally more analytical. In that sense, hard news is never published in a magazine; it will at least be a feature.

A large variety of writing styles is used in the Print Media, and it is here that the largest number of opportunities are available for creative writers.

The Broadcast Media

The broadcast media has traditionally included only two forms—the radio and television. These two media are very different from the Print Media. The writing for these formats is essentially in the form of scripts, which are either read out or enacted. The kinds of programmes which are aired decide the kind of script to prepare. You could write news reports, the script for a serial or play, the script for the host or presenter of a programme. There are some modes of writing which would be completely unavailable in this media; if you interview anyone, the audience is going to hear and/or see it. Profiles will be either in documentary or interview style, again giving primary importance to the script. The rules that govern writing for Radio and Television are not the same as for Print.

Writing for the Radio

Radio is exclusively restricted to the spoken word, while television depends heavily on visuals. Difficult words and long sentences must be avoided. Each sentence of the script must be clearly understood or the listener/ viewer will lose the context. The speed at which the script is read also matters; too slow and the listener will lose interest, too fast and the listener will be lost. Using simple words and sentences is important—the listener has generally no means of 'rewinding' the speech for clarification. Also remember, someone is going to read out the script, so there should be absolute clarity in what you write. A few rules for writing for the Radio:

- Sentences should not be too long or confusing; keep them short and conversational.
- Do not use abbreviations in the script; use 'and' instead of '&'.
- Most importantly, be sure to mention how long, in minutes, the piece will be when read.

There are three types of sentences: simple, compound and complex. A simple sentence contains a subject and a verb. A compound sentence is composed of two simple sentences joined by a coordinating conjunction (for example: and, but, or, nor). A complex sentence is composed of two simple sentences joined by a subordinating conjunction (for example: when, because, although).

You may probably remember this lesson from school, but the distinctions remain quite relevant to news writing for broadcasts. In your scripts, simple sentences are the best. You will, of course, regularly use compound and complex sentences, but the clarity achieved by simple sentences is much greater.

Another thing to remember, as far as the grammar of the sentence goes, is to avoid relative clauses. Words like 'who', 'which', and 'where' must be avoided in broadcast writing. In a text which is communicated visually, the reader has words on a page to guide him back to the main sentence after the diversion caused by the relative clause. The radio listener has no such guide, and must rely on the script to provide information in short and uninterrupted clauses. The following would be an unwieldy sentence structure:

> 'Mr. Sharma, who is a candidate for the municipal elections, was arrested today for tax evasion.'

A better way of expressing it would be:

> 'Mr. Sharma was arrested today for tax evasion. He is a candidate for the municipal elections.'

Radio scripts have to be much more dependent on the spoken word than Television; there will be no visuals to lay out the scene. For a radio script, all action will have to be indicated through words. The news, for example, is generally read more or less in an even tone, conveying no particular emotional bias at all. So all the impact must be conveyed through the words and phrases used in the description of the incident.

As far as scripts for hosts and presenters of music or entertainment-based programmes go, a more dynamic script needs to be prepared. There has to be enough material for the presenter to make the programme as enjoyable as possible. Though, of course, care has to be taken to have an optimum mix of the spoken and presented material. If the presenter speaks too much on a music programme, the audience will simply switch channels. The breaks, too, have to be organized efficiently.

Radio plays rely entirely on the capability of the actors who read the lines; emotion must be expressed through words. The script-writer must take care to specify the emotional tone of what is being spoken in the play. The task of the writer is to imagine what the words would sound like when they are read out. A few rules for general radio writing are:

- Write accurately, and impartially.
- Make each sentence a new paragraph.
- Write simply and with clarity, so that the newsreader and listeners will be left in no doubt as to the meaning. Avoid presenting more than one main idea in one sentence.
- Avoid strings of adjectives; for example, 'good, strong, healthy, and powerful'. They're often hard to read in one breath, and they take the listener's mind away from the main point.
- Use conversational English (for example, 'It's been said' and not 'It has been said').
- Do not use quotation marks, and do not use 'I' or 'we' unless it means the person reading the item or the radio station.
- Avoid words that are hard to sight-read (like communiqué, mystique).
- Use first names instead of initials. (Professor Vishwamohan Bhatt rather than Prof. V. Bhatt).
- Do not use abbreviated forms of words that have to be read in full. (India versus Australia, and not Ind. vs. Aus.).
- Spell out numbers if more than two figures (for example, 1048 may be written as one thousand and 48. If necessary, round off a large number. Instead of saying '1289 students joined the protest march' you may write: 'Nearly 13 hundred students participated in the protest march').
- Generally, first sentences should not be more than about 20 words. Other sentences should also not be much longer. Also, vary the length of the sentences.
- Use active verbs wherever possible and not passive verbs. Also, write in the present tense.

ACTIVITY 6

Read a news article and see how the piece sounds like when it is read out. Does the piece sound more effective when read in any one particular way—for example, when read with pauses and emphasis—as opposed to when it is read in a monotone? Would any change be required to make it more 'audio-friendly'?

Television Scripting

Television adheres to almost the same set of rules, with one important exception. The writer should always remember that in Television visual is the most important. And it is one thing which changes the whole writing style, making it different from the style of the Radio. The visual is the most important element of a news story, around which the written script must be structured. The audio-visual elements must be in tandem with each other.

A good Television script-writer should keep the following things in mind:

- The script should be clear and logical.
- The script should be of appropriate length, and proceed at a pace that would sustain the interest of the viewer without being too content-centric.
- The script should be structured around the visuals—the narration should not overwhelm the visual.

The script-writer is also the person to organize the complete presentation. The script-writer should prepare the story, the scene, as also the division of the sequences into shots, keeping in mind the themes and issues to be dealt with in the programme. The programme should be laid out in terms of the visuals and the narrative that goes along with them. It is important that the script is properly organized before the programme goes into production. Since the production is totally based on the script, it cannot be altered without causing serious problems.

The basic rule is that the focus should be on people. This means that in any film, documentary or news report, the human angle needs to be emphasized. The sequence of the narrative needs to begin with either dramatic action or with attention on a person involved in the narrative. Let us presume that the report/ documentary is about a housing scheme for poor people. The commentary could begin with the action itself—'The construction of houses for the poor has been nearly completed'—or perhaps more effectively with the people for whom it is intended—'Sita Ram, a homeless labourer, is looking forward to the completion of the construction of his house, an initiative by the government.' From there the story begins and goes into the details.

The important part about writing commentary is that there should not be too much of it. The commentary must not stifle the visual—the idea is to let the visual speak for itself, with the words only complementing or supplementing what the viewer can already see. The co-ordination between visuals and words is the essence—words and pictures must work together for the best effect.

Because of the strong visual element, one aspect that the television script writer should take care of in script preparation is the co-ordination of the audio with the visuals for maximum impact. If, for example, the visual is a shot of a crowd of people at a theatre festival, then it is no use saying:

> 'Dr. Lena Roy, the Director of the Centre for Film Arts, was also in the audience at the festival.'

The viewers would not be able to identify the person in the crowd, and when the person eventually is shown up close, they would not be sure of the person's identity. A much better method of saying the same thing would be to write:

> 'Among the audience was the Director of the Centre for Film Arts, Dr. Lena Roy.'

This sentence would have to be co-ordinated with the film footage in such a way that the reference to the audience would be in tandem with a long shot of the crowd and reference to Dr. Lena Roy would coincide with the appearance on the screen of the person. It is not necessary to use phrases like 'as we can see', 'behind me'; if the visuals and the words coincide, then the viewer will link them up. But this is a very finely tuned operation—if there is a second's gap between the two the viewer will be confused. Used skilfully, words and pictures can heighten the effect created by each other. The words must not overpower the visuals—the picture must be dominant.

Writing specifically for the news on television is not as organized as writing for a film or a documentary. For one, the news writing has to be done in a rush, and it often covers only some portion of the whole news. Also, in many cases, the actual footage of the event may not be available. The report may be about a road accident, for which action footage would not be available; the writer would have to work from reports of the accident, and organize them around the visuals of the scene of the accident. The initial sentence of the story would contain the facts of who, what, where and when. Then the visuals would take over, as the script attempts to work around it and explain the 'how' of the accident.

Let us look an example of how things would change for Television, with reference to the article which we have already used (on page 11):

BOX 4.6: OPENING SHOT OF THE OUTSIDE OF ASIMOV ROBOTICS LABORATORY

The Asimov Robotics Laboratory today announced (*cut to inside of laboratory; people working at computers*) that they have created the first ever Robotic Brain.
(*Cut to shots of robotic brain on display*) This brain will be fitted into (*cut to robots being manufactured*) the new generation of robots.
(*Cut to Doctor Daniel Oliver walking out of the laboratory, getting into his car, surrounded by media-persons, and then driving away*) Doctor Daniel Oliver, the scientist who came up with the idea of this robotic brain, refused to comment on the specifics of the brain.
(*Cut to busy street shot*) The development of this brain means that soon we will see robots walking among us.

This is only a very rough outline of what the final production script would look like. We can see that even though the verbal content is very low (about 60 to 65 words), the visuals generate their own meaning, in combination with the words. Also notice the overlapping of the words and the visuals—the right visual and the right word together clarify, as well as complement each other.

Writing for the broadcast media, especially television can be a frustrating task—the scriptwriter has to keep a lot of other elements in mind. How the script sounds, how it is read, how it coordinates with visuals, all of these become important.So the writing style adopted has to be in accordance with the situation.

The New Media

The new media is also essentially electronic in nature. The difference is that it is newer than the other two electronic media. The Internet, or the World Wide Web, is proving to be revolutionary in the speed at which it has spread across the world.

The Web offers every opportunity for writing that is present in any other medium. You can publish fiction, poetry, and drama on the Web; at the same time news, in written and/or audio-visual format is freely available on the Web. So the Web has opportunities for traditional creative writing as well as for the mass media.

The web is emerging as a useful resource for newspersons as well as a tool for dissemination of news. Virtually all the major newspapers, magazines, journals and media channels have a presence on the Internet. The attraction is not just because it is a new medium, but because the kind of audience that the Internet provides access to. More than 1 billion people (nearly 20 per cent of the population of the world) use the Internet. The Internet provides the opportunity to the traditional media to transcend their local boundaries, and reach an audience that is widely varied.

This large audience means more advertising which is the revenue earner for the media. Advertisers earn more on websites that are visited by millions of people. So, as with all other media, the struggle, on the Internet, too, is for maximum readership. The only way of attracting more readers, and therefore more advertising revenue, is to ensure that the readers spend more time on the website. The readership can be increased if what the website offers is different and appeals to a majority of the visitors to the site. Also the idea is not just to attract the maximum number of individuals accessing the site, but the maximum number of visits. The intention is that people should be persuaded to return to the site after visiting it for the first time.

The writing style for the Web is similar to that of the Print Media; the major difference is the way in which the material is presented. The same kind of news reportage can be written for the web—soft news, profiles, interviews, personal columns, all are part of the web. At some level it might be easier to think of the Web as an extremely dynamic print format. The words are visible as printed matter, but the text is interactive—you can move from within the text to other pieces of text to which it is linked.

The fundamental theory is that of non-linear story construction, rather than the linear construction, that is part of writing for the print media. It takes longer to read from a screen than it takes to read a printed page. If the story is very long, then readers are more likely to move away from the page; one solution is to break up the story into sections. So, the story on the robotics laboratory will get broken into segments (Figures 1 and 2).

But this breaking into segments may create more problems—the reader, in moving from one page to another, might lose track of what has already been said; whatever 'it' refers to on page 2 or 3 might have its referent on page 1. So, the writing style needs to change along with the presentation style. As we can see in Figure 2, in the second part of the article, instead of continuing where the first page had left off, there is a clarification of who the person is, and what he achieved.

This is merely a rough example of what an article on a website would look like. Ideally, the longish paragraph in Figure 1 should have been broken up into smaller paragraphs. If you look at Figure 2, where the text has been divided into smaller paragraphs, the screen looks less cluttered and more readable. The average Internet user is more used to scanning the page than reading closely—the text on the page must be presented in such a manner as to make scanning easy. So instead of long blocks of paragraphs, the text should be broken up into smaller paragraphs, which are more screen-friendly.

A few rules with regard to writing for the Internet:

- Get straight to the point.
- Make the headline simple and informative.

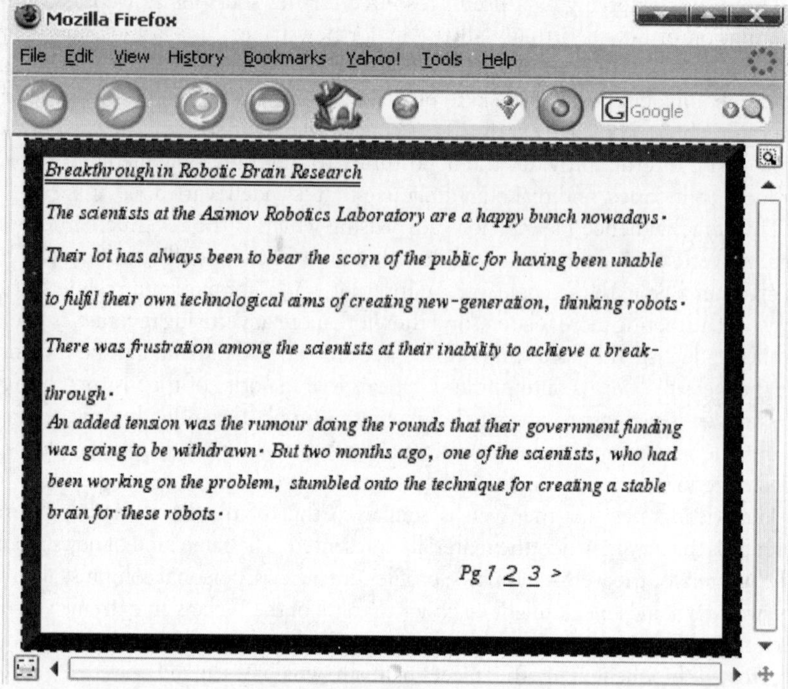

Breakthrough in Robotic Brain Research

The scientists at the Asimov Robotics Laboratory are a happy bunch nowadays. Their lot has always been to bear the scorn of the public for having been unable to fulfil their own technological aims of creating new-generation, thinking robots. There was frustration among the scientists at their inability to achieve a break-through.

An added tension was the rumour doing the rounds that their government funding was going to be withdrawn. But two months ago, one of the scientists, who had been working on the problem, stumbled onto the technique for creating a stable brain for these robots.

Pg 1 2 3 >

Figure 1

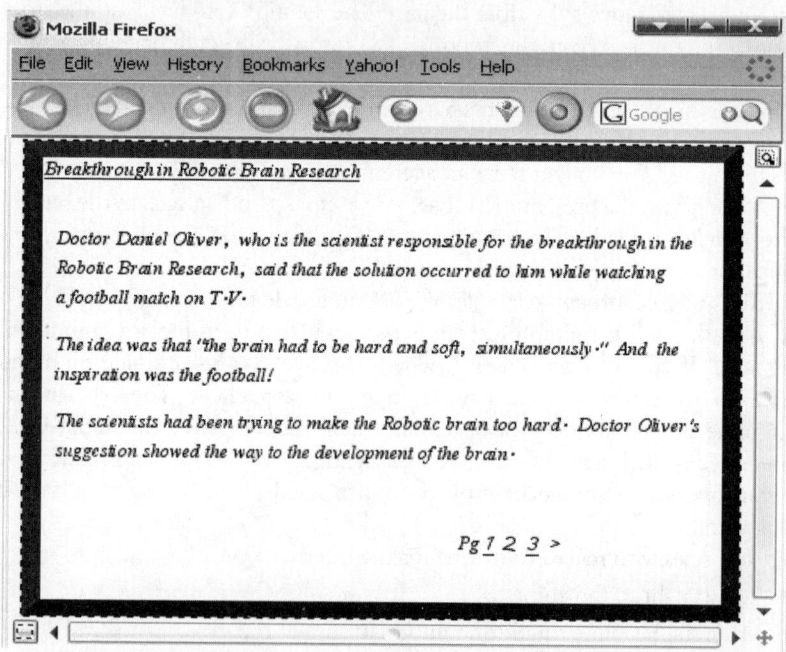

Breakthrough in Robotic Brain Research

Doctor Daniel Oliver, who is the scientist responsible for the breakthrough in the Robotic Brain Research, said that the solution occurred to him while watching a football match on T.V.

The idea was that "the brain had to be hard and soft, simultaneously." And the inspiration was the football!

The scientists had been trying to make the Robotic brain too hard. Doctor Oliver's suggestion showed the way to the development of the brain.

Pg 1 2 3 >

Figure 2

- To attract the visitor to stay further, the headline could also be a question—a specific question like, 'Has the US been hasty over Iraq?' rather than 'Have you seen this?'
- Break the story into interesting chunks, which make sense even when read separately.

The unique part about the Internet is the ability to move from one page on the net to another, merely by clicking a link. By clicking on a link, the reader can go to an entirely different page. It is perhaps this quick accessibility to other pages in the same medium, which makes the Internet radically different form all other media. There are two kinds of links, internal and external.

- Internal links take the user around the same website—to other sections of the story, to related stories, to additional features like video/audio files, or just to other areas of the same website.
- The external links take the user to other parts of the Internet, either to pages with related material, or to advertising sites.

So, to make sure that the reader visits other parts of the website, one must provide links to related stories within the same website, and also links to additional services provided by the site. Advertising links are also present.

On the whole, there is not much difference between writing for the Internet and writing for the print media. The only difference is in the structuring and organization of the article, as well as some modification in the language used.

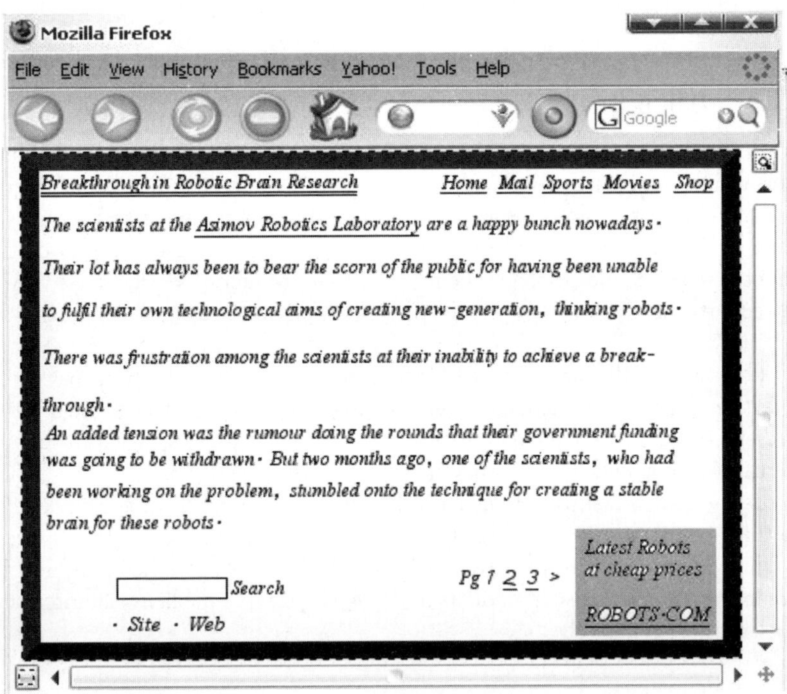

Figure 3

ACTIVITY 7

Take a look at Figure 3. How does the page differ from a news page in the print media? What options does it provide to the viewer?

The Internet is not solely limited to news reporting. It offers multiple opportunities for other kinds of writing too. Fiction, poetry and drama are published on the Internet on a variety of sites. There are sites which are devoted to very specific kinds of writing—detective fiction, fantasy, short stories, poetry, humour; in fact, virtually every kind of writing. Considering that the Internet is estimated to contain some 80 million websites (as of April 2006),[4] it is no surprise that virtually every person can find a website that caters to their specific tastes. Academic articles, journals on various subjects are also available on the Internet—like the Internet Public Library.[5] The internet also allows the space for a variety of personal expressions like online diaries in the form of blogs—a user-generated website where entries are made in journal style (Wikipedia)—in the form of photographic albums, galleries and so on. The variety offered is virtually unlimited.

The Internet is also predominantly in English—estimates range from 50 to 80 percent—thus making knowledge of the language an important asset. The chances are that if your website is in English, more people will visit it. So, whether you are an aspiring poet, or journalist, or just want to tell the world what you feel, get on to the Internet!

Advertising

Advertising does not constitute a separate medium. It is present in all media, but the factors which control it are different from other modes of communication. Advertising is commercially oriented—it spreads information about products and services. The motive of advertising is to make the audience aware of the existence of a particular product or service, and persuade them to use that product or service. At a very basic level, advertising tries to create a need in the consumer for the product which is being advertised.

Advertising is the main source of income for the media. Advertisers pay for space and time in the different media, in which to advertise their products. Since advertising is present in all three media, the styles of writing for these will vary widely. The advertising campaign for a product will include all the media; the kinds of advertisements for each of the media will focus on different elements, while keeping something common (like the slogan).

There are various kinds of advertising, classified according to their purpose.[6] These range from those advertising products to those which serve public/social interests. Let us look at these separately.

---

[4] <http://news.netcraft.com/archives/2006/04/06/april_2006_web_server_survey.html>

[5] www.ipl.org

[6] Based on the classification by Aggarwal and Gupta (2002).

Standard Advertising

This is the kind of advertising that we see every day in the various media. This type of advertising aims to promote a particular product or service, with the intention of persuading the target audience to purchase them. Soaps, perfumes, clothes, soft drinks, and even advertisements for companies that offer bill-payment services, can all be included within this category. The advertising is paid for by the manufacturer/seller of the product or service, so the only purpose is to promote the product as efficiently as possible.

Public Service/Social Responsibility Advertising

Public service or social responsibility advertising answers a public need. It is generally produced and distributed by government agencies or non-profit organizations, in cooperation with private advertising and mass media companies. While the government or non-profit organization provides the information that is to be broadcast, the advertising and media agencies provide the creative services and the space and time for the display of the advertisement. Environmental messages, disease eradication campaigns, and announcements by police are kinds of public service advertising.

Counter-Advertising

Counter-advertising focuses on the alleged fraud and misrepresentation in advertising. The advocates of counter-advertising claim that standard advertising does not inform the public of everything, thus hampering the ability of consumers to make a really informed choice. Counter-advertising intends to counteract the allegedly false claims, to ensure that the consumer is made aware of certain aspects which are hidden. The anti-tobacco campaigns by various agencies, as well as the campaign for awareness of rights of consumers are part of counter-advertising.

Advocacy Advertising

This is closely related to social responsibility advertising as well as counter-advertising, except that advocacy advertising is a type of advertising placed by businesses and other organizations that is intended to communicate a viewpoint about a controversial topic relating to the social, political, or economic environment. It is concerned with the propagation of ideas and clarification of social issues of public importance in a manner that supports the position and interest of the sponsor. It expresses a strong point of view on behalf of an organization. Issues like drug addiction, alcohol consumption, rising crime rate, etc., which are perceived as conditions affecting public welfare, are taken up through advocacy advertising.

Image Advertising

This kind of advertising is designed by businesses to improve their image, rather than to promote a particular product. At one level, this kind of advertising is affiliated more closely with public relations rather than with marketing. This kind of advertising promotes the name, the image, the personnel, and also the reputation of the advertiser. The intent is to enhance the image of the company in the eyes of the target audience. The advertisement may choose to emphasize the various areas of human activity in which the company is involved; it may be creating awareness of the different products which they produce; the advertisement may also show how the company is a good place to work.

ACTIVITY 8

Locate the various types of advertising in different media; identify the purpose of the advertisements.

Parts of an Advertisement

Generally speaking, from the point of view of print advertising, an advertisement is created out of text and images. The organization of these two elements is itself an important part of the advertisement. The combination of the text and the images in the most effective way affects the way in which the advertisement appeals to the audience. So it is not only the components but also the layout of these elements that creates the effect of the advertisement. We are primarily concerned with the textual elements, rather than the visual one.

Under the general category of text, there may be descriptive information about the product. Other text serves the purpose of catching the reader's attention, as well as (typically) short phrases that act as a kind of slogan, and finally the name of the company and/or the name of the product. All of these elements are organized according the function that they perform in the advertisement—the slogan, the headline, the sub-head, and the descriptive text, all are placed at different positions within the advertisement, where they fulfil different functions. Let us look at these different bits of text which are used in an advertisement.

Slogan

The slogan is perhaps the most important element of the advertisement. This is what attracts the consumer, and is also perhaps the element that is recalled most easily by the viewer of the advertisement. The slogan is that word, phrase or sentence that describes the product in some way or the other—either its benefits or its most important qualities.

The slogan generally has two purposes: one, to establish, in the mind of the audience, the product and its qualities. The other is to provide continuity for a campaign for as long as it runs—whether it is for a few months or a few years. In India, phrases like 'Utterly Butterly Delicious' and 'Taste the Thunder' are slogans which have become part of our awareness of the brands which they represent. The slogan does not necessarily remain the same throughout—if the campaign's purpose changes, then the slogan should also change.To be effective, the slogan should generally have a few basic characteristics.

- It should be short, and easy to say and remember; rhyme helps the slogan to be remembered easily.
- Should be based on just one idea/ theme/ concept. Too many ideas in one line will dilute the impact of the slogan; for example, 'the anti-dryness, beauty-enhancing,

non-oily, skin-friendly, fairness lotion' would be a slogan that says too many things, (apart from being too long) and thus the effect is lost.

- Should highlight the product—either directly, or through the effect that it supposedly creates.
- Should not confuse the consumer as to what is meant.

ACTIVITY 9

In the various media, find different slogans—what do they emphasize? The product or the effect of the product? Do the slogans work? Come up with slogans of your own for popular products that already exist.

Headline and Subheads

A group of words may not necessarily have anything to do with the product or service that is being advertised, but serves to attract the reader/viewer. It is supposed to gain immediate attention for the advertisement, so that the viewer/reader is prompted to take some time to look at what the advertisement is about. The headline says only enough to arouse curiosity, and attracts the reader to find out more. There is no ideal length.

- The headline should have an immediate impact; therefore, it should be understandable at the first reading
- Should be specific and to the point; not too long.
- Must be linked to any other element of the advertisement.

However, there is no requirement for the headline to be necessarily present in the advertisement; if the slogan, or a visual element fulfils the function of attracting the customer, then the headline can be omitted. There are a large variety of headlines:

- Headlines which talk about the product/service itself; directly, indirectly or combining both of these methods.For example, 'Lose weight now!' is direct—it states the purpose of the product/service but does not tell you how.
- News headline kind of sentence, 'for the first time in India—a cure for baldness!' attracts the attention of the customer with that which is new.
- Question/Command headlines use the language of the headline to lead the reader into the text. In a question form the headline, 'What drives the leading Racing Car Drivers?', the reader is drawn to the copy of the advertisement in order to find out the answer. In the command form of headline, for example, 'Help the Girl Child Live!', the reader is almost ordered to do something, and must read the other information in the advertisement to find out what exactly he must do.

ACTIVITY 10

Look at advertisements in any newspaper, and identify their headlines, if any. How do headlines differ from slogans?

Some advertisements have many headlines, one of which is the main headline, while others only serve to expand on the idea; these are not a necessary part of all advertisements.

BOX 4.7: ILLUSTRATION/IMAGES

Photographs or illustrations are generally the most important part of an advertisement, because they can directly show the product/service to the viewer/reader. The advertisement may consist of an illustration of the product, or of an idea which the product represents.
We are not directly concerned with the kinds of images that can be used in advertising, except in the manner in which they are related to the copy in the advertisement. The main concern for the copywriter must always be that the copy and the image complement each other – the copy must be a verbal equivalent of the visual image, or vice-versa; they must both indicate the same idea which the company is trying to communicate about its product/ service.
For example, a builder's advertisement for a housing scheme called 'Gulmohar Apartments' would be illustrated by the picture of *Gulmohar* trees, while the text would probably refer to 'lush green trees' or the parks of the colony.
Remember: the text and the image must be in harmony.

Copy/Body Text

Copy or Body Text is the main textual content of the advertisement, which expands on what the slogan and/or the headline declares about the product. It provides all details, and answers all questions, which may be indicated in the slogan or the headline.

Writing advertising copy begins with defining objectives—of the campaign, of the marketing programme, and of the specific advertisement. These objectives will be unique to each company/institution, to each campaign, and to each advertisement. The copywriter should first develop a copy policy/platform that should describe the objectives, focus, and approach of the campaign. The idea is to know what the copy shall say, and how it shall say it, keeping in mind the following:

- The target audience.
- The media being used.
- The points to be made and their sequence.
- Should the copy be lengthy or brief?
- What tone is appropriate—serious or light-hearted?
- What is the message?

There are a few rules for copywriting that the writer should keep in mind:

- Keep the language simple; talk to the reader/listener/viewer in easy, familiar words—don't be too formal.
- Brevity is important—say what you want in the minimum words; too many and the reader will not be interested.
- Use the present tense and the active voice.
- Make the copy interesting; try to use bright, cheerful language that keeps the reader alert and maintains attention. Be enthusiastic and exciting.

Copy can be classified depending on content and style. The purpose of selling/ marketing is common to all, but the ways in which one can go about it can be very different.

1. *Straight Copy.* This states the content in a very simple and short manner.
2. *Descriptive Copy.* In this kind of copy, the main focus of the advertisement is an extensive description of the product or service being offered.
3. *Narrative Copy.* In this the copy purports to narrate a story.

Figure 4

4. *Testimonial Copy.* In this kind of copy, a celebrity endorses the brand or the product. This tends to make the advertisement more appealing and believable.
5. *Humorous Copy.* This helps to make the advertisement more appealing to the viewer/reader.

ACTIVITY 11

Scan the print, electronic and new media for examples of advertisements that use the five kinds of 'copy' defined above.

These are the elements that a good copy writer should include in the advertisement. The fundamentals of a good advertisement are:

- *It should grab the attention of the viewer/reader/listener.* There should be some element in the advertisement—slogan, headline, illustration or the layout—that arouses sufficient interest. And the copy itself must sustain that attention.
- *It should promise some benefit.* Something in the ad should promise the reader or the listener that they will benefit from what the advertisement asserts.
- *It should be credible.* The premise of the advertisement must be believable. Do not make any outrageous claims about the product.
- *The advertisement should be persuasive.* It should sell or generate the need for the service you offer, and project your service as better.
- *It should generate desire.* The advertisement must create a desire to want to avail of the product/service.
- *It should prompt to action.* The ultimate aim is to generate action on the part of the reader or listener; to cause the reader to want buy your product.

ACTIVITY 12

In the above advertisement, which is the slogan? Which is the headline? Do the text and the images complement each other? How does the advertisement create a want or a need in the reader?

BOX 4.8: JOURNALISM, NEWS CONTENT AND OBJECTIVITY

A re-appraisal

Somnath Batabyal

Journalism is about news. First, last, and all the way in between. This seems simplistic. But the basis of good journalism lies precisely in this: What constitutes news? Ask a journalist how s/he constructs news, what s/he leaves behind and what gets chosen and you will hear the familiar bluster, 'We do not construct news. We report facts.'

(Contd.)

But it is also a fact that not everything becomes news, most happenings do not. So who decides what will hog the headlines today, what will be prime time, what will be left behind in the middle pages and what will be entirely discarded?

News is socially and culturally constructed. If you find this hard to believe, let us take an example. Imagine three people reporting on the state of Bihar, former Chief Minister of the State Laloo Prasad Yadav, former US President Bill Clinton and a seasoned reporter from Patna. While Mr. Yadav will find excuses for whatever he sees, Mr. Clinton undoubtedly will be shocked. The reporter might be cynical because s/he has seen it all before. Three different versions will thus emerge, objectivity be damned.

Objectivity is a professional ethic, empirically impossible to achieve. As Shekhar Gupta, Editor of Indian Express once put it 'Talk to everyone, officials, people at the spot, and in the end trust only your judgement.' This is precisely where good journalism, good training and reporting skills come in.

To say that the news industry in India has expanded would be an understatement. In the past five years, television news channels have mushroomed with new ones coming up every second month. The opportunities are many. The hurdle remains in the quality of journalists.

Training schools have not been able to keep pace with this sudden spurt. Most vocational training courses are woefully short on theory and lack expertise in dealing with practice. While most journalists blame the political economy for the decline in the quality of news, the lack of quality journalists, especially in electronic media also is a huge factor. If journalists have not imbibed the understanding that news media along with being an industry is also a public service, content will and must suffer. A good theoretical grasp of the media thus becomes imperative for aspiring journalists.[7]

I was watching BBC World this evening. One of their main headlines was a UNICEF report, which stated that the highest number of undernourished children are in three Asian countries, India, Pakistan and Bangladesh. Fifty six million undernourished children live in India alone. None of the national news channels carried this report.

I did a bit more research. There are 70,000 Indian millionaires and growing. There are also 400 million families on the bottom rung in India whose fate would be much better in Africa's Botswana or in strife ridden Palestine, states the latest UNHDI report. The average family today is absorbing 100 kilograms of food less than it did in 1991.

Does this not make a story? Or, does the image of a shining, resurgent India that constantly finds its way into the front pages and evening bulletins get dented when confronted with an India outside the margins of this constructed news scenario. Is news only meant for the happy middle class?[8]

These are the questions confronted by journalists, media analysts and academics today. Even with the continuous proliferation of news channels, why is content so homogenous? Why can we not differentiate one channel from the other? Given the realities of political economy today, can news media find a space between the public service ethos of state run Doordarshan and the audience rating driven content that is doled out? Is there a middle way?

---

[7] I am not making a heroic statement for journalistic agency. Agency is a complex process and how much the journalist is a free agent is a matter of heated debate in academia. But I do believe that sound understanding of theory and practice can only empower journalistic agency.

[8] One can argue that there are indeed stories of poverty in national channels. Any decent book on media theory will show that the way these news stories are constructed shows the people and the areas as foreign, as out there, which makes us feel safe in our middle and upper class lodgings. It's a classic way of how for years the affluent West reported on the East. We have managed to marginalise entire sections of India.

The questions crop up far more frequently than the answers. Given the rapid changes in technology and media, there is hardly any time to ponder over issues, the situation changes.

I started as a reporter some ten years back with my first serious assignment being with The Pioneer as a crime reporter. Television cameras and glare of lights had still not entered the scene. The money was laughable but we, the reporters, were driven by only one thing, a bid to outdo each other, fight for the best story, get the most damaging information against the establishment (the police). A pro police story was looked down upon and any reporter filing such a story would be mocked at as a Delhi Police pet the next day. Competition was healthy and fierce and it resulted in some very good stories. But more over, it was all about fun, about new experiences, going to places one would not normally go, the thrill of covering shocking crime scenes, the high of taking on a mighty establishment. And as a twenty-something, fresh out of Delhi University, not much else mattered.

Within ten years, the pay packet has increased manifold for journalists, the fun perhaps has gone out a bit. Former colleagues instead of ranting at editors, talk of the problems of their latest car. But one thing that has not changed is the power of the media to influence discourse. With heightened readership and viewers, that has definitely increased. What we do with this responsibility depends on the journalists. As Tom Stoppard stated, 'I believe if you want to change the world, journalism is still the best short term weapon.'

(Somnath Batabyal is currently pursuing a doctoral programme at SOAS, University of London and works on news production practices in Indian Television. A former journalist, he has worked with NDTV, Hindustan Times, The Pioneer and The Week.)

ACTIVITY 13

Take a field trip to a newspaper or magazine office and press, and another to a radio or television studio, to see the media at work and prepare a report on how writing for the media takes place and is prepared for print/broadcast.

References

Aggarwal, Vir Bala and V. S. Gupta, *Handbook on Journalism and Mass Communication* (Delhi: Concept Publishing, 2002).

Hargreaves, Ian. *Journalism: Truth or Dare?* (London: OUP, 2003).

Keeble, Richard, *The Newspapers Handbook*, 2nd edition (London, New York: Routledge, 1994, 1996).

Ward, Mike, *Journalism Online* (Oxford: Focal Press, 2003).

Websites

Internet World Stats. http://www.internetworldstats.com/stats.htm

Netcraft. http://news.netcraft.com/archives/2006/04/06/ april_2006_web_server_survey.html

Wikipedia. http://en.wikipedia.org/wiki/Blog

5
Preparing for Publication

Revising and Rewriting

As soon as you have written your creative piece, get ready for the process of revising. To begin with, consider revision as part of the creative design. Technology has facilitated revision in a significant way and writers, unlike many other creative artists are privileged in that they can revise their work so easily, and unlike architects or painters can rearrange and alter at will. The ease in revising in writing is due in some measure to the separation of the text from its physical form. Until recently a text had to be captured on paper to be stored, read and revised. The computer changed all that. By displaying text on a screen in patterns of light that can be manipulated by simple key presses, the computer has made the act of revising easy. It is not just the physical process that is easy. We are all amateur critics. Most writers are able to find faults in another person's text and spot poor style or unintelligible jargon.

Despite the facility and ease of revision, there is a lot of difference between the revision undertaken by expert writers and inexpert practitioners. Expert writers revise more and the quality of their revisions is superior because they alter the overall structure of the text, whereas inexpert writers tend to make changes only at the word and sentence level. Good writers make revisions in the meaning of the text while poor writers tend just to correct spelling and grammar.

Revising a text involves a number of interacting processes, the most basic of which is pattern matching. While we read over a text, we match the shape of the words against stored mental schemas and the best match summons up the meaning. As we continue, the text becomes predictive: the new words fit into a pattern of grammar and style. If we meet a misspelled word or a badly constructed sentence it jars with our expectations and becomes a candidate for revision. From first learning to read, children begin to build up these patterns of correct and appropriate language, a process encouraged by school lessons in spelling and grammar.

Detecting and correcting badly-written sentences is an essential part of revision, but not the most demanding part nor the most productive. Expert writers revise for two main reasons: to make the text more appropriate and acceptable to their readers and to gain a new understanding for themselves. While the first is taught in most language classes, the second is learned through experience. In the process of revising for readers, we learn to see the text from the perspective of both the writer and the reader.

The first way of revising is a deliberate ritualized process. Corrections are done at the level of spelling and grammar and also at the level of the arrangement of sentences and phrases. At this stage the text may also be rearranged to ensure connectivity and logical progression. Writers act as their own best critics, and every time they re-read what they have written the cycles of interpreting, contemplating, specifying and editing the draft text are repeated.

BOX 5.1

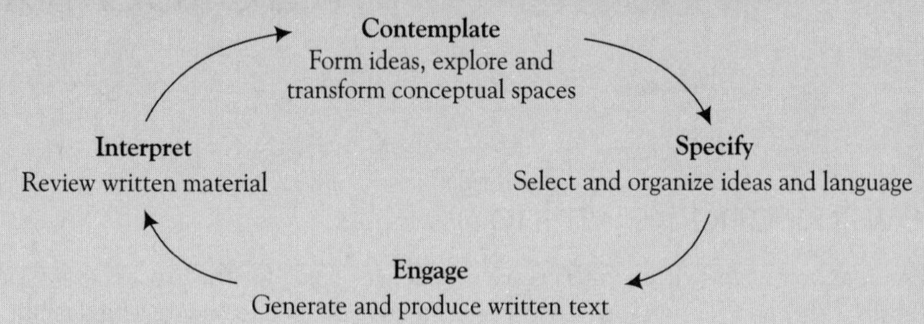

Interpreting goes beyond just simple pattern matching and is a constructive process. It involves reviewing the text as a reader who does not share one's perspective and also looking at the overall meaning and structure of the text. Interpretation is then compared against the mental constructs and schemas of the writer's intentions to detect mismatches that may range from a misspelled word to an overall style that is inappropriate or ineffective. As a result of this contemplation, the writer specifies changes to repair obvious faults and to construct a new version of the text that better expresses intentions. This leads directly or indirectly to annotating and editing the text. A writer can go through the cycle of revision in small chunks, paragraph-by-paragraph or sentence-by-sentence, composing the text and then revising it. Alternatively, the writer can perform the longer cycle of drafting and revision, revising while composing, and can perform her/his role of writer first and then switch to the role of reader. Whatever be the preferred mode of revision, this process continues until the writer is satisfied that s/he has done all s/he could to polish the text.

While we are revising for ourselves and/or for the reader, two basic types of revising can be identified, each with its attendant demands and problems. Revising for oneself demands that a writer be able to interpret the text in relation to plans and intentions and revising for another requires the writer to have a sense of audience, to be able to appreciate the reader's understanding while composing, and be able to re-read the text from the perspective of a possible reader while redrafting. The three most effective ways to overcome the demands and problems of revising are to:

1. *Offload thoughts on to paper*—instead of trying to think about multiple intentions and forms of expression, write them down as notes and alternative phrasings; instead of struggling to gain an overview of the text, mark up a draft with headings and sub-headings to indicate its overall structure.
2. *Delay revision*—instead of trying to imagine the audience while composing, read over the draft text some time later in a fresh context; instead of revising the whole text in one shot, make the easy revisions first and then think about the more major changes

3. *Use reference aids*—instead of coping with a half-remembered knowledge of language, look up a dictionary, thesaurus and grammar book. A style manual is also a useful guide to punctuation and grammar.

Revision is not the end of the line for the writing process. It forms an essential link back to planning and composing. In reading over a text for revision we gain new ideas that demand to be written down. Embedded within each part of the revision process is the seed for further complete cycles of writing. This notion, that one part of the process can become a new version of the entire process is called *recursion*. Recursion in writing is both daunting and empowering: daunting because any minor revision could be the gateway to a complete new round of composition; empowering because each piece of written text is a resource for composing. Seen this way, revision is the start of the writing process. As we read over texts written by ourselves, or others, we gain ideas for writing. No writing is truly original, because it relies on the ideas, language and literary styles of others. All writing is productive and creative, because we recursively build a complete work out of a series of fragments (Sharples 1999: 110–111).

Proof Reading

A draft text provides both the raw material for publication and a visual space for adding annotations. The head and the foot of the page, the back of each page, the margins and the spaces between lines and characters all have different relationships to the words. Each of these spaces can be filled with marks to guide the revision. The most convenient way to indicate revisions is to annotate the text with publishers' proof marks. These proof marks are not just part of the publishing process, but a valuable resource for the individual writer. As well as indicating revisions to be made, they also form a checklist: Can words be deleted? Are the words correctly capitalized? Is the punctuation correct?

By working through the text, testing each sentence or paragraph against the set of proof marks the writer can at least be sure to have thought about the errors of grammar and punctuation. (Ibid: 102–09)

Reproduced below is a list of proof reading symbols and a sample marked proof.

Delete	ℊ	Flush left	fl	Make subscript; insert here	∧
Close up; delete space	⁀‿	Flush right	fr	Insert comma	∧ ,
Delete and close up	ℊ⁀‿	Align horizontally	=	Insert period	⊙
Let it stand	stet	Align vertically	‖	Insert question mark	(set) ?
Insert space	#	Transpose	∽	Insert semicolon	;|
Make space between words equal	eq #	Spell out	sp	Insert colon	:|
Insert hair space	hr #	Wrong font	wf	Insert hyphen	=
Letter space	ls	Set in italic type	ital	Insert em dash	M
Begin new paragraph	¶	Set in roman type	rom	Insert en dash	N
Move right	]	Set in boldface type	bf	Insert parentheses	{|}
Move left	[	Set in lower case type	lc	Insert apostrophe or single quote marks	∨ ∨
Centre	][	Set in capital type	caps		
Move up	⊓	Check type image	×	Indent type one em. From left or right	□
Move down	⊔	Make superscript; insert here	∨		

Book Reveiw

It is never easy to tell a story that has deen already told and retold an uncountable numbers of times. More so when the story is one that is known to generations of readers and listeners, and one which has had many famous recounters. Ashok Banker sets out to tell us a story that has been made famous by the likes of Tulsidas, Kamban, and more recently, C. Rajagopalachari. So, what is new about Banker's version of the Ramayana? The most noticeable difference is the style—more contemporary and fast-paced than the other versions. Banker's narration focuses, almost insistently, on action and description—the *heroes* are bold, the monsters are terrifying and the action breathtaking. It is a story that incorporates all elements of a modern-day thriller—action, adventure, and suspense, with delicate touches of emotion interwoven through it. banker's ramayana series might not appeal to the older generation of readers, given the way in which he seems to sensationalize the story. But the good thing is that he makes this epic accessible to a generation which has been brought up in an age dominated by religious fanaticism. Banker does not, however, lose his moorings and allow the series to become a mere potboiler. Questions of Morality, Duty, obedience, loyalty, love, and even definitions of good and evil are dealt with, in a compact package, which makes this modern retelling of the ramayana a compelling read.

Editing

The word 'editing is derived from the Latin '*editus*', past participle of the verb '*edere*'—to put forth, to give out, to publish. The editor selects, sifts, cleanses and sorts out the material and then arranges it in the most effective manner. When you are editing your creative work you will primarily be editing at the level of grammar, spelling and arrangement of sentences, that is *copy editing*, and also doing some *general editing*—that is, concerning yourself with precision and accuracy in the presentation of your idea.

Reproduced below is an article, by a teacher of writing, on revising your manuscript.

'The Maker's Eye: Revising Your Own Manuscripts,' first published in slightly different from in The Writer, provides an example of directional process. The author presents his information in chronological steps, most of them supported by direct quotations from professional writers. Much of the advice is applicable to student writing as well as to professional work.

The Maker's Eye: Revising Your Own Manuscripts
By Donald M. Murray

When students complete a first draft, they consider the job of writing done—and their teachers too often agree. When professional writers complete a first draft, they usually feel that they are at the start of the writing process. When a draft is completed, the job of writing can begin.

That difference in attitude is the difference between amateur and professional, inexperience and experience, journeyman and craftsman. Peter F. Drucker, the prolific business writer, calls his first draft 'the zero draft'—after that he can start counting. Most writers share the feeling that the first draft, and all of those which follow, are opportunities to discover what they have to say and how best they can say it.

To produce a progression of drafts, each of which says more and says it more clearly, the writer has to develop a special kind of reading skill. In school we are taught to decode what appears on the page as finished writing. Writers, however, face a different category of possibility and responsibility when they read their own drafts. To them the words on the page are never finished. Each can be changed and rearranged, can set off a chain reaction of confusion or clarified meaning. This is a different kind of reading, which is possibly more difficult and certainly more exciting.

Writers must learn to be their own best enemy. They must accept the criticism of others and be suspicious of it; they must accept the praise of others and be even more suspicious of it. Writers cannot depend on others. They must detach themselves from their own pages so that they can apply both their caring and their craft to their own work.

Such detachment is not easy. Science fiction writer Ray Bradbury supposedly puts each manuscript away for year to the day and then rereads it as a stranger. Not many writers have the discipline or the time to do this. We must read when our judgment may be at its worst, when we are close to the euphoric moment of creation.

Then the writer, counsels novelist Nancy Hale, 'should be critical of everything that seems to him most delightful in his style. He should excise what he most admires, because he wouldn't thus admire it if he weren't ... in a sense protecting it from criticism.' John Ciardi, the poet, adds, 'The last act of the writing must be to become one's own reader. It is, I suppose, a schizophrenic process, to begin passionately and to end critically, to begin hot and to end cold; and, more important, to be passion-hot and critic-cold at the same time.'

Most people think that the principal problem is that writers are too proud of what they have written. Actually, a greater problem for most professional writers is one shared by the majority of students. They are overly critical, think everything is dreadful, tear up page after page, never complete a draft, see the task as hopeless.

The writer must learn to read critically but constructively, to cut what is bad, to reveal what is good. Eleanor Estes, the children's book author, explains: 'The writer must survey his work critically, coolly, as though he were a stranger to it. He must be willing to prune, expertly and hard-heartedly. At the end of each revision, a manuscript may look ... worked over, torn apart, pinned together, added to, deleted from, words changed and words changed back. Yet the book must maintain its original freshness and spontaneity.'

Most readers underestimate the amount of rewriting it usually takes to produce spontaneous reading. This is a great disadvantage to the student writer, who sees only a finished product and never watches the craftsman who takes the necessary step back, studies the work carefully, returns to the task, steps back, returns, steps back, again and again. Anthony Burgess, one of the most prolific writers in the English-speaking world, admits, 'I might revise a page twenty times.' Roald Dahl, the popular children's writer, states, 'By the time I'm nearing the end of a story, the first part will have been reread and altered and corrected at least 150 times ... Good writing is essentially rewriting. I am positive of this.'

Rewriting isn't virtuous. It isn't something that ought to be done. It is simply something that most writers find they have to do to discover what they have to say and how to say it. It is a condition of the writer's life.

There are, however, a few writers who do little formal rewriting, primarily because they have the capacity and experience to create and review a large number of invisible drafts in their minds before they approach the page. And some writers slowly produce finished pages, performing all the tasks of revision simultaneously, page by page, rather than draft by draft. But it is still possible to see the sequence followed by most writers most of the time in rereading their own work.

Most writers scan their drafts first, reading as quickly as possible to catch the larger problems of subject and form, then move in closer and closer as they read and write, reread and rewrite. The first thing writers look for in their drafts is information. They know that a good piece of writing is built from specific, accurate and interesting information. The writer must have an abundance of information from which to construct a readable piece of writing. Next, writers look for meaning in the information. The specifics must build to a pattern of significance. Each piece of specific information must carry the reader toward meaning.

Writers reading their own drafts are aware of audience. They put themselves in the reader's situation and make sure that they deliver information which a reader wants to know or needs to know in a manner which is easily digested. Writers try to be sure that they anticipate and answer the questions a critical reader will ask when reading the piece of writing.

Writers make sure that the form is appropriate to the subject and the audience. Form, or genre, is the vehicle which carries meaning to the reader, but form cannot be selected until the writer has adequate information to discover its significance and an audience which needs or wants that meaning.

Once writers are sure the form is appropriate, they must then look at the structure, the order of what they have written. Good writing is built on a solid framework of logic, argument, narrative or motivation which runs through the entire piece of writing and holds it together. This is the time when many writers find it most effective to outline as a way of visualizing the hidden spine by which the piece of writing is supported.

The element on which writers may spend a majority of their time is development. Each section of a piece of writing must be adequately developed. It must give readers enough information so that they are satisfied. How much information is enough? That's as difficult as asking how much garlic belongs in a salad. It must be done to taste, but most beginning writers underdevelop, underestimating the reader's hunger for information.

As writers solve development problems, they often have to consider questions of dimension. There must be a pleasing and effective proportion among all the parts of the piece of writing. There is a continual process of subtracting and adding to keep the piece of writing in balance.

Finally, writers have to listen to their own voices. Voice is the force which drives a piece of writing forward. It is an expression of the writer's authority and concern. It is what is between the words on the page, what glues the piece of writing together. A good piece of writing is always marked by a consistent, individual voice.

As writers read and reread, write and rewrite, they move closer and closer to the page until they are doing line-by-line editing. Writers read their own pages with infinite care. Each sentence, each line, each clause, each phrase, each word, each mark or punctuation, each section of white space between the type has to contribute to the clarification of meaning.

Slowly the writer moves from word to word, looking through language to see the subject. As a word is changed, cut, or added, as a construction is rearranged, all the words used before that moment and all those that follow that moment must be considered and reconsidered.

Writers often read aloud at this stage of the editing process, muttering or whispering to themselves, calling on the ear's experience with language. Does this sound right—or that? Writers edit, shifting back and forth from eye to page to ear to page. I find I must do this careful editing in short runs, no more than fifteen or twenty minutes at a stretch, or I become too kind with myself. I begin to see what I hope is on the page, not what actually is on the page.

This sounds tedious if you haven't done it, but actually it is fun. Making something right is immensely satisfying, for writers begin to learn what they are writing about by writing. Language leads them to meaning, and there is the joy of discovery, of understanding, of making meaning clear as the writer employs the technical skills of language.

Words have double meanings, even triple or quadruple meanings. Each word has its own potential for connotation and denotation. And when writers rub one word against the other, they are often rewarded with a sudden insight, an unexpected clarification.

The maker's eye moves back and forth from word to phrase to sentence to paragraph to sentence to phrase to word. The maker's eye sees the need for variety and balance, for a firmer structure for a more appropriate form. It peers into the interior of the paragraph, looking for coherence, unity, and emphasis, which make meaning clear.

I learned something about this process when my first bifocals were prescribed. I had ordered a larger section of the reading portion of the glass because of my work, but even so, I could not contain my eyes within this new limit of vision. And I still find myself taking off my glasses and bending my nose towards the page, for my eyes unconsciously flick back and forth across the page, back to another page, forward to still another, as I try to see each evolving line in relation to every other line.

When does this process end? Most writers agree with the great Russian writer Tolstoy, who said, 'I scarcely ever reread my published writings, if by chance I come across a page, it always strikes me: all this must be rewritten; this is how I should have written it.'

The maker's eye is never satisfied, for each word has the potential to ignite new meaning. This article has been twice written all the way through the writing process, and it was published four years ago. Now it is to be republished in a book. The editors make a few small suggestions, and then I read it with my maker's eye. Now it has been re-edited, re-revised, re-read, re-re-edited, for each piece of writing to the writer is full of potential and alternatives.

A piece of writing is never finished. It is delivered to a deadline, torn out of the typewriter on demand, sent off with a sense of accomplishment and shame and pride and frustration. If only there were a couple more days, time for just another run at it, perhaps then …

Finally, here is some advice from Sandra L. Cook about polishing your manuscript to make it shine and reveal all its facets.

Polishing Your Manuscript

Sandra L. Cook

Tightening up your manuscript is always necessary. It is difficult in the beginning, but becomes easier with practice. As you consciously go through your manuscripts, you will develop an eye for whackable words. Soon you will be eliminating them from your writing before you put them on paper.

Whackable words are "Telling" words, "-ly" adverbs and lame adjectives. "Telling" words are often forms of the "to be" verbs. In the statement, "She was surprised", the word "was" tells the state she is in. What could you say besides "was surprised"?

She slapped her hand on her chest and gasped. By this action, we know she is surprised without being told. Using action is what editors mean when they say "Show, don't tell." To eliminate these telling words, search your manuscript and circle words such as:

was, were, is, has, had

Adverbs ending in –ly are whackable words. You may say, "He walked slowly towards me." By combining the verb and adverb into one more descriptive verb, you can cut your word count and be precise with your language. If a person is walking slowly, then they may be described as sauntering, meandering, or strolling. You could then say, "He strolled towards me." Maybe he sauntered towards you or meandered towards you. By controlling your adverb/verb combinations, you can set the tone or communicate emotion better.

Lame descriptors that don't tell you very much about the very thing you are trying to describe very precisely and can be eliminated very easily. Very often, a writer will be very non-committal and will use a word such as "very" to emphasize something they think is very important in their story. I hope using very very frequently will help make it evident how weak the word very is as a descriptor.

Instead of saying "very important", you could say "critical". Instead of saying "very often", you could say "frequently". "The very thing" can have "very" eliminated altogether since it doesn't enhance the meaning at all. "The very thing" IS the same as "the thing".

Eliminating a weak descriptor will strengthen the statement without adding additional words. Instead of saying "very lame", just saying "lame" is equally as effective.

Other lame words include "just" (she just wanted), or "that" (I told you that he left), "due to the fact" condenses to "because". Taking out "just" or "that" does not change the meaning of the statement, so zap them! There will be occasions where keeping the words will make the sentences flow. By being aware of need versus unnecessary usage, you can make your manuscript better.

Happy Writing,

Sandy
www.signaleader.com

BOX 5.2

a. Explain the idea and importance of reviewing and revising.
b. What is the difference between the preparation made by an expert and a novice writer, while preparing for publication?
c. How do you understand the process of 'interpretation' in the context of revising and rewriting of creative works?
d. Discuss some of the ways in which the process of revising can be facilitated.
e. Do you agree with the idea that no writing is ever completely original? Think about what all you have written and try and identify your sources of information and inspiration.
f. Proof read and edit the following piece of prose:

there once was in the contry of alifbay, a sad city, a city so ruinously sad thatit Had forget its name, the saddest of cities. It stoods on a mournful sea full o f glumfish, who were so miserable to eat that they made person belch with melancholy even though the sky were blue. And in the depths of the city, beyond an odl zone of ruined buildings that looked broken hearts, there lived a happy young fellow by the name of haroun,the only child fo the story – teller Rashid Khalifa, whose cheerfullbess was famous throughout the unhappy metropolis, and whose never-ending river of tall, small and winding tales has earned him not one but two nicknmames. In the north of the sad city stood mighty factories in which (so I'm told) sadness was actually manufactured, packaged and sent all over the globe, which never seemed to get enough of it. Black smoke came out of the chimneys of the sadness factories and hangs over the city like badnews. To his admirers he was Rashid the ocean of notions, as stuffed with cheery stories s the sea was glumfish to his jealous rivalries he was shah of blah. To his wife soraya ashid wsa for many years a love husband as any could wish for, and during these years haround grew up inahome in that instead of miser and frowm he had his father ready llaughter and his motehr's sweet voicesraised in dong. Then some thing went wrong.

(Rushdie :15)

Submitting Your Manuscript for Publication

While you are writing, you should also be reading a good deal and familiarizing yourself with the publications that may be interested in your work. Those who study the genre they have chosen, carefully, remain perpetual students who not only develop their writing ability, but also become aware of the potential avenues for their work.

The Appearance is Part of the Message

Before you actually send off your manuscript here are some pointers about the physical and mechanical details:

- Type and print your manuscript on a good grade of A4 size paper.
- Use a standard font.
- The margins should be 1.5 inches at the top and the left, and about 1 inch at the bottom and right, without excessive hyphenation.
- All material except name and address should be double-spaced.

- Place your name and address on the left about two inches down from the top and write the label 'Poem'/'Fiction'/ 'Play'/ etc. on the right.
- The title is normally placed in capital letters about a third of the way down the page.
- The text begins two spaces below this.
- The pages, after the first, should be numbered in Arabic numerals along with your last name in the upper right corner.
- Check the spelling and grammar very carefully.

(Minot 1982: 301–02).

How to Get Published

Here are some guidelines by Susan Page about getting published—ensuring that you take a very good shot at having your manuscript considered seriously by a publisher:

- Establish clear goals for your work.
- Have an answer to the question—'I am writing in order to ....'
- Dream big—where would you like to see your work?
- Establish the unique identity of your work—how is it different from all other books in the market? Who will read your book and why? What are you offering the world?
- Start working on a 'fabulous title' that will instantly say what the book is about or be so intriguing that the reader is compelled to read on.
- Decide which publisher(s) you will approach.
- Enlist a famous person in the field to write a foreword or an endorsement.

Where to Publish

Here is a list of some of the national newspapers, magazines and journals, along with publishing houses in India to whom you could send your work:

Newspapers: *The Times of India, Hindustan Times, Indian Express, The Hindu, The Pioneer, Tribune, The Telegraph, Asian Age, Tehelka, Deccan Chronicle*, etc.

Magazines and Journals:

- Current Affairs: *India Today, Outlook, The Week, Frontline*, etc.
- Business: *Business Today, Business Standard, Economic Times, Financial Express, Economic and Political Weekly*, etc.
- Entertainment, Fashion, Society and Women: *Filmfare, Stardust, G–Mag, Screen, Chitralekha, Music Today, Vogue, Cosmopolitan, Cine Blitz, Femina, Society, India Today Plus, Glamour, Harper's Bazaar, Woman and Home*, etc.
- Literature: *Little Magazine, Book Review, Literophile, Biblio, Chandrabhaga, Manushi*, etc.
- Children: *Amar Chitra Katha, Tinkle, Chandamama*, Nick.com, *Odyssey*, etc.

Publishers: Pearson Longman, Katha, Penguin India, Oxford University Press, Ravi Dayal, Rupa, Hamlyn, Har-Anand, Harper Collins, Sahitya Akademi, Sterling, Kalyani, Raintree, Macmillan, Orient Longman, Sulekha, Indialog, Shristhi, Permanent Black, Sage, Viking, Arnold-Heinemann, Roli, Ratna Sagar, Madhuban, Seagull, Picador, Random House, etc.

The list above is neither exhaustive nor prescriptive in any way, but an important starting point as you embark on your literary journey. You could look at the works published in and by them and find out which platform would be most suitable for you to launch your work in the public arena.

BOX 5.3

Since you would have already written a lot by now, make a tentative list of all the possible avenues where each of your pieces could find a place. For example, if you have written a travel piece, you might want to look at the Sunday edition of the Hindu newspaper or the latest issues of India Today Plus to see what kind of travel articles are published by them.

Summary

- Writing is an act of communication and the ultimate test of your writing is its readability.
- While writing, be well informed and passionate about what you are saying and convincing in your point of view.
- Choose your form carefully and make sure your structure matches with it, as do the words you have chosen to express your ideas and feelings.
- Choose your distinct style and medium.
- Make sure that you have mastered all the techniques that will facilitate your expression.
- Minimize the distance between your reader and yourself.
- Revise carefully and consciously with the clear aim of learning and improving.
- Use proof reading techniques judiciously to help you write better.
- Editing helps you to make choices and also arrange your material in the most effective manner.
- Pay attention to the content and the appearance of your manuscript when you prepare to submit it.

References

Achtert, Walter S. and Joseph Gibaldi, *The MLA Style Manual* (New York: The Modern Language Association of America, 1995).

Ayers, Tim and John Dayus, *Developing Writing Skills: for Key Stage 3 Tests* (Oxford: Heinemann Educational Publishers, 1999).

Cook, Sandra L., *Polishing Your Manuscript* http://www.signaleader.com, 2001

Flower, Linda, '*Writing for an Audience*', in Paul Eschholz and Alfred Rosa *Themes for Writers* (New York: St. Martin's Press, 1994 Pp. 404 – 07).

Hamilton, Alaine, *Professional Communication: Writing Matters* (London: Riba Publications, nd).

Hunt, Douglas, *The Riverside Guide to Writing* (Boston: Houghton Mifflin Co., 1991).

IGNOU, DCE 1: *General Principles of Writing* (New Delhi: Indira Gandhi National Open University, School of Humanities, 1989, 2002).

Madden, David, *A Pocketful of Essays Volume II – Thematically Arranged* (Fort Worth, USA: Harcourt College Publishers, 2001).

Minot, Stephen, *Three Genres: The Writing of Poetry, Fiction and Drama* (Englewood Cliffs: Prentice Hall Inc., 1982, Third Edition).

Murray, Donald M., 'The Maker's Eye: Revising your own Manuscripts' in *Deckers' Patterns of Exposition 12* by Randal M. Decker and Robert A. Schwegler. Glenview, Illinois: Scott Forseman/Little Brown Higher Education, 1990, pp. 153–59.

Page, Susan, *How to get Published and Make a Lot of Money: Everything You Need to Know in the Order You Need to Know it* (Great Britan: Piatkus, 1998).

Rushdie, Salman, *Haroun and the Sea of Stories* (New Delhi: Penguin Books India, 1990, 1991, 2003).

Sharples, Mike, *How we Write: Writing as Creative Design* (London: Routledge, 1999).

Index

Abel, Roysten, 156
    Goodbye Desdemona, 156
    Othello: A Play in Black and White, 156
    The Spirit of Anne Frank, 156
Acronym, 18, 31
Advertisement, 198
    body text, 200
    fundamentals of, 202
    headline and subheads, 199
    parts of, 198
    slogan, 196, 198–200, 200
Advertising, 179, 185, 193, 195–198, 200
    advocacy, 197
    image, 197
    kinds of, 197
    motive of, 196
    social responsibility, 197
    standard, 197
Aesthetic compulsion, 45
Ali, Agha Shahid, 53
    Rooms are Never Finished, 77
    The Country Without a Post Office, 77
    The Half-Inch Himalayas, 53, 77
Alliteration, 17–18, 30, 43, 60, 89
Alls Well That Ends Well, 143
Allusion, 18, 22, 43
Ambiguity, 18, 28, 40, 43, 89
Ammons, Archie, 6
    Four Poems of A.R. Ammons, 6
Antigone, 142
Antipathy, 25
Antistrophe, 68
Antithesis, 17, 18, 23, 43
Aphasia, 37
A Raisin in the Sun, 143
Archaism, 40, 44
Archer, Isabel, 98
Aristotle, 104, 112–13
Art, 1, 8, 48, 51–52, 54–55, 57–58, 63, 65, 76, 90, 92, 96
    auditory, 54, 59
    propaganda and, 8
Assonance, 17, 18, 30, 43
Audience, 46–47, 58, 81, 89, 177–78, 188–89, 191, 193, 196–198, 200
Audio-visual recording, 179
Austen, Jane, 97–98
    Pride and Prejudice, 97
Autobiography, 11, 15, 103

Ballad, 69, 77
Bannerjee, Sarnath, 99
    Corridor, 99
Barnes, Julian, 97
Barth, John, 97
Basho, 64
Beckett, Samuel, 141
    The Changing Room, 142
    Waiting For Godot, 141–42
Bellow, Saul, 8
Biography, 52, 65, 103–04, 109, 119
Birtwistle, Sir Harrison, 6
Bishop, Elizabeth, 49
Blake, William, 23
    A Poison Tree, 23
Bond, Ruskin, 117
Broca's aphasia, 37
Bronte, Charlotte, 98
    Jane Eyre, 98
Brooks, Gwendolyn, 49
Browning, Elizabeth Barrett, 67

Caesar, Julius, 27
Capote, Truman, 95, 98, 114
    Breakfast at Tiffany, 114
    In Cold Blood, 95, 98
Chakraborty, Dr. Saumitra, 154
Chandra, Vikram, 104
    Red Earth and Pouring Rain, 104
Characterization, 101, 111–12, 119, 144–45, 147, 150
Chaudhari, Amit, 104
Chekhov, 101, 140
Chernyavsky, 7
Chiasmus, 17–18, 31, 43
Children, 71, 83–85, 88, 95, 104, 117, 119–20, 130–31, 167–70, 172
    fiction for, 117
    film and theatre, 167
        big market, 167
        plot, 169
        script writing, 167
    stories for, 83
    verse for, 83, 88
        forms of, 46, 68, 78, 83
        themes and types, 84
Cinquain, 56, 83
Clarity, 45, 46
Classical poetry, 73
Clerihew, 65
Climax, 113, 134, 140, 159
Coleridge, Samuel Taylor, 4, 6, 28, 49, 55, 65
    Metrical Feet – A Lesson for a Boy, 56
    The Rime of the Ancient Mariner, 28
Colloquialism, 20
Comedy, 143–44, 154
Communication, 17, 37, 43, 45–47, 58, 89, 95
    modes of, 17, 44

nature of, 147
oral, 147
Complication, 115
Conflict, 178
Conrad, Joseph, 97
Heart of Darkness, 97
Lord Jim, 97
Consonance, 17–18, 30, 43
Cook, Sandra L., 212
Polishing Your Manuscript, 212
Copy writing, 200
classification, 201
rules for, 200
Correctness, 46
Counter-advertising, 197
Couplet, 60
Crapsey, Adelaide, 56
Triad, 57
Creative writer, 78
conversation, 78
Anuradha Marwah, 116
Mahesh Dattani, 157
R. Parthasarathy, 78
Subhadra Sen Gupta, 131
Creative writing, 3, 9–15, 17, 42, 45, 77, 95, 177–79, 192
discipline of, 13
forms of, 9–10, 177–79, 190
kinds of, 9
language of, 14
modes of, 45, 178, 188, 196
originality of thought and expression, 9
raw material of, 14
Creativity, 1–4, 6, 8–9, 14–15
art and literature, 2–4, 7, 9, 14
complex and varied phenomenon, 1
continuum of, 2
definition of, 1, 3
dimensions of, 3
emotion, 2
everyday phenomenon, 1
features of, 2, 5
function of, 8
image of, 5
ingredient of, 9
kinds of, 1–3, 10, 15
madness and, 8
measure of, 2–3
mental process, 1, 14
modern psychometric approach to, 2
pathological traits and, 9
process of, 5–6, 14
resistance and, 6
social-personality approach, 3
subjectivity, 2–3
tests of, 3
variety, 3
Creativity Quotient, 3, 14
Criticism, 7, 22, 45, 90
Freudian psychoanalytic, 22
Currency, 178
Currimbhoy, Asif, 152
Dumb Dancer, 156
Goa, 156
The Hungry Ones, 156
Cyrano de Bergerac, 143

Dabholkar, Bharat, 156
Bottoms Up, 152, 154, 156
Carry on Bindas, 156
Funny Thing called Love, 156
Just Another Rape, 156
Last Tango in Heaven, 156
Mind your Stethoscope, 156
Monkey Business, 156
Tamasha Mumbai Ishtyle, 156
Dahl, Roald, 85
Daruwalla, Keki N., 71, 74, 154
A Summer of Tigers, 77
Landscapes, 77
Night River, 77
Partition Ghazal, 74
The Keeper of the Dead, 77
Under Orion, 77
Winter Poems, 77
Das, Gurcharan, 152
Larins, 155
Meera Bai, 155
Nine Jakhoo Hill, 155
Das, Kamala, 77
My Story, 77
Summer in Calcutta, 77
The Old Playhouse and Other Poems, 77
Dattani, Mahesh, 136, 140, 143, 146, 153, 157
Bravely Fought the Queen, 156
Dance Like A Man, 136, 139, 143, 149, 151, 156
Final Solutions, 156
Night Queen, 156
Tara, 156
Where There's a Will, 156
Davis, Anna, 13
De, Shobha, 100
Death of a Salesman, 142
Debi, Rassundari, 11
Amar Jeeban, 11
Decipher, 46
Defoe, Daniel, 98
The Fortunes and Misfortunes of the famous Moll Flanders, 98
Derozio, Henry Louis Vivian, 77
Fakeer of Jungheera: A Metrical Tale, 77
The Enchantress of the Cave, 77
Descartes, Rene, 22
Dialogue, 145, 147
Dickens, Charles, 99
Hard Times, 34
David Copperfield, 99
Dickinson, Emily, 49
Dixon, Peter, 85
Teabag, 85
Drama, 8–9, 11, 15, 134–35, 139, 141, 144, 147, 152, 158, 177, 179, 192, 196
absurd, 141
attributes of, 135
character, 136, 139–47, 149–53, 155, 157, 159
sequence of events of, 139
types of, 145
characteristics of, 134, 140
characterization in, 144
climactic, 140–41, 159
comedy, 142–43, 145, 156
kinds of, 143–44, 153
concept of, 134
costumes, 147–50
elements in, 143, 147
episodic, 140–41
forms of, 141, 145, 157
lighting and sound, 148
musical, 142, 154
non-tragic, 143
bourgeois, 143
domestic, 143

heroic, 143
melodrama, 143, 145, 154
plot in, 139
manipulation, 140
scenery, 135, 147–48
serious, 143–44, 152, 153
stage space, 136, 140, 142, 145–49, 153–54, 156–57, 159
thoughts and feelings, 145
tragedy, 142
modern, 142
traditional, 141–42, 145, 152
types of, 140, 155
writing, 135–36, 142, 144, 147, 152, 157–59
Dramatic poetry, 72
Dutt, Toru, 77
A Time to Change, 77
Hymns in Darkness, 77
Latter-day Psalms, 77
Sixty Poems, 77
The Exact Name, 77
The Third, 77
The Unfinished Man, 77
Dysphasia, 37

Edison, Thomas, 6
Editing, 206–07, 210–11, 215
copy, 207
general, 207
Elaboration, 3
Eliot, T.S., 21, 45, 49, 78, 84, 91
Old Possum's Book of Practical Cats, 84
Preludes, 91
The Love Song of J. Alfred Prufrock, 21
Emotion, 2, 5, 22, 42, 51, 54, 63, 69, 90, 96
English, 34–37, 40–42, 46, 53, 55, 61, 66, 68, 71, 73–74, 76–78, 80–81, 89, 96–97, 136, 151–55, 157
status in India, 152
varieties of, 24, 30, 34, 42–43
dialects, 34–35, 40, 43
idiolects, 35
non-standard, 33–34
standard, 33–34, 42–43
writer's dilemmas, 46
Epic, 69, 78, 101, 159
Epigram, 65
Epiphany, 102
Epode, 68
Euphemism, 18, 28, 43
Experience, 2–3, 45, 51–52, 55, 59, 74, 79, 81–82, 91–92
Ezekiel, Nissim, 75, 76, 77, 81
A Morning Walk, 75

Fair tree of the void, 103
Fantasy, 84–85, 94
Faulkner, William, 101, 115
Feelings, 45, 48–49, 51–52, 58, 63, 68, 75, 83, 96
Ferguson, Suzanne C., 102
Defining the Short Story, 102
Fiction, 9–10, 89, 94–97, 99–05, 111–16, 119–20, 131, 135–36, 153, 155, 177, 179, 192, 196
definition, 49, 52, 94
flash, 101
formula, 100
kinds of, 59, 88–90, 96
literary, 96
popular, 96
realism, 96
romance, 96
literary, 99–101, 103, 119
modernist, 96, 97
popular, 99–100, 103, 119
post-modern, 77, 97
prose, 136
realistic, 96–97
Flexibility, 3
Flower, Linda, 47
Writing for an Audience, 47
Forster, E.M., 111
Fowles, John, 97
Francis, Richard, 13
Frost, Robert, 78

Ghazal, 74, 79, 81
characteristics of, 74
Ghosh, Amitav, 100, 104
The Hungry Tide, 104
The Shadow Lines, 104
Goldberg, Natalie, 12
Goldman, Lucien, 103–04
Gone with the Wind, 7, 100, 112
Graham, Harry, 27
Grammar, 40, 45–47
mechanism to convert, 46
mechanism to express, 46
stone-clad prescripts of, 46
tense and time, 41
Graves, Robert, 21
The Naked and the Nude, 21
Gray, Thomas, 68
Elegy Written in a Country Churchyard, 68
Greek tragedy, 27
Guilford, J.P., 2
Gupta, Subhadra Sen, 120, 131, 165
A Calamity in Kailash, 165
The Sword of Dara Shukoh, 120, 130–31

Haddon, Mark, 119
The Curious Incident of the Dog in the Night-time, 119
Haiku, 64, 91
Hardy, Thomas, 49, 98
Return of the Native, 98
Hariharan, Githa, 104
The Thousand Faces of Night, When Dreams Travel, 104
Hashmi, Safdar, 6
Halla Bol, 7
Hemingway, 101, 104
Hemingway, Ernest, 97
A Farewell to Arms, 97
For Whom the Bell Tolls, 97
Herbert, George, 62
Easter Wings, 62
Hindemith, Paul, 6
Homonym, 18, 20, 43
Homophone, 18, 30, 43
Hood, Thomas, 29
Faithless Nelly Gray, 29
Horace, 104
Huckleberry Finn, 119
Hughes, Langston, 19
Harlem, 19
Hugo, Victor, 99
Les Miserables, 99
Human intelligence, 3, 14
Humility, 51
Humour, 65, 169, 187, 196

Hussain, M.F., 7
  depiction of Hindu goddesses, 7
Hussein, Aamer, 105
  The Blue Direction and Other Stories, 105
    Sweet Rice, 105, 110–16
  This Other Salt, 105
Hyperbole, 17–18, 26, 43

Ibsen, 140, 145
  Ghosts, 140
Idea, 47
Iliad, 69
Imagery, 58–59
Imagination, 45, 51, 78, 84–85, 96
Impressionism, 96, 99, 102
India, 7, 11, 13, 151–56
  caste oppression in, 7
  contemporary theatre in English, 153
    styles of, 153
  courses in creative writing, 12–12
  English language theatre in, 151
Indian English playwrights, 155
Indian English Poets, 76
Indian novelists, 104
Innovation, 2, 14
Inspiration, 4, 12, 14
Intellectual leadership, 3
Internet, 178–80, 192–93, 195–96
  writing for, 177–81, 188–89, 192–93, 195–96
    rules for, 189–90, 193, 200
Interpretation, 2, 14
Interview, 178–80, 183–84, 188, 193
Invention, 59
Ionesco, Eugene, 146
  Rhinoceros, 146
Iowa, 13
  first writing school in, 13
Irony, 17–18, 27, 43, 187
Irving, John, 101
  The World According to Garp, 101

James, Henry, 98, 102
  Portrait of a Lady, 98, 102
Jargon, 33, 43
Joshi, Arvind, 158
  How to Write a Film Script, 158
Journalism, 178, 181
Journals, 193, 196
Joyce, James, 97, 101–02, 111
  Finnegan's Wake, 111
  Portrait of the Artist as a Young Man, 97, 102

Kafka, Franz, 104, 112
  The Castle, 112
Kapoor, Sohaila, 153
  Suppressed Desires, 153
Kapur, Manju, 104
  Difficult Daughters, Home, 104
Karnad, Girish, 154
Katha, 103
Keats, John, 11, 61, 69, 78
  Ode on Melancholy, 68
Keller, George, 2
Kennedy, John F., 50
Khan, Shah Rukh, 1
King, Stephen, 1
King Lear, 142
Kundera, Milan, 7

Lahiri, Jhumpa, 104
  The Namesake, 104
Language, 17, 28, 30, 32–38, 40–59, 66–68, 73–74, 78–79, 81, 89–92, 95, 99, 136, 143, 145, 147, 151–54, 157–59, 181, 185, 195–96, 199–200
  abnormal, 37
  borrowing, 35–36, 44
  code switching, 35–36
  constructs of, 51
  creole, 35
  discursive, 52
  disordered, 37
  drammatical differences, 42
  figurative, 17, 24
  functions of, 50
  gender and, 36
  grammar and lexical possibilities in, 47
  handling of, 45
  ideal, 40
  literal, 17, 22, 44
  medium of, 45, 51, 73
  memorable, 50
  normal, 37–38, 40
  ordinary, 17, 40
  process of, 51, 59, 81, 96
  properties of, 40
    grammar, 17, 35, 37, 38, 40, 42
  selection and arrangement of, 145
  sexism in, 37
  sexist, 36, 37, 44
  use of, 17, 19–20, 22–24, 27–28, 30, 33, 36–37, 40, 42, 53
  uses of, 52
  variations in, 35
Lawrence, D.H., 6, 95, 111
  Sons and Lovers, 6, 95
  The Rainbow, 111
Lesbianism, 7
Limerick, 65, 95
Literary artifacts, 45
Long Day's Journey into Night, 142
Lowell, Elizabeth, 99
Lucretius, 104
Lyric, 67, 91, 104
  forms of, 46, 68, 78

Macbeth, 30, 142
Mahabharata, the, 22, 69, 99
Mahapatra, Jayanta, 71, 77
  A Rain of Rites, 77
  Bare Face, 77
  Burden of Waves and Fruit, 77
  Dispossessed Nests, 71, 77
  Life Signs, 77
  Relationship, 77
  Temple, 77
Mangeshkar, Lata, 1
Marlowe, Christopher, 58
  The Passionate Shepherd to his Love, 58
Marquez, Gabriel Garcia, 1
Marwah, Anuradha, 116
  Idol Love, 116–17
  The Higher Education of Geetika Mehendiratta, 116
Matla, 74
Maugham, Somerset, 115
  The Appointment in Samarra, 115
Maxwell, Ann, 99
McCourt, Frank, 95
Meaning, 47
Measure for Measure, 143
Medea, 142
Media, 177–81, 186, 188, 192–93, 195–97, 200, 203
  broadcast, 177–78, 179, 197

forms of, 177–79, 190
Internet, 178–80, 192–93, 195–96
news, 177–84, 186–93, 197, 203
magazines, 178, 180–81, 183, 188, 193
newspapers, 178, 180, 183, 193
variety of writing styles, 178–79, 188
print, 178–81, 188, 193
social responsibility, 178, 197
types of, 177–81, 183, 188–89
types of story, 177
Worldwide Web, 178–79
Mehta, Deepa, 7
Fire, 7
Water, 7
Mehta, Dina, 153
A Sister Like You, 156
Brides are Not for Burning, 155
Getting Away with Murder, 156
Joke About Rabbits, 156
The Myth Makers, 155
Tiger Tiger, 156
When One Plus One makes Nine, 156
Meinke, Peter, 22
Progress, 22
Melodrama, 143, 145, 154
Metaphor, 17–19, 21, 24, 43
Metonymy, 17–18, 21, 43
Miller, Arthur, 8
Mills, Paul, 14
Milton, John, 69–70
Paradise Lost, 69
Minot, Stephen, 170
Three Genres The Writing of Poetry, Fiction and Drama, 170
Mistry, Rohinton, 104
Such a Long Jouirney, A Fine Balance, 104
Mitchell, Margaret, 7
Modern poet, 5
creativity of, 1, 5, 8, 15
Modern poetry, 4–5
self-reflective, 4
Monologue, 145
Moraes, Dom, 77
A Beginning, 77
Beldam And Other Poems, 77
John Nobody, 77
Poems, 50, 77, 79
Morrison, Nobel laureate Toni, 7–8, 97, 100
Beloved, 97, 100
Motivation, 4, 6, 45
psychological, 45, 54
subconscious, 6
unconscious, 4, 6
Murray, Donald M., 208
The Maker's Eye: Revising Your Own Manuscripts, 208

Nabokov, Vladimir, 6, 97
style of, 6
Transparent Things, 6
Nair, Rukmini Bhaya, 77
Ayodhya Cantos, 77
The Hyoid Bone, 77
Yellow Hibiscus, 77
Narration, 114
modes of, 103, 114
Narrative poetry, 69, 70
Naturalness, 11–12, 15
concept of, 2, 8, 10, 11
Neologism, 40, 44
Neruda, Pablo, 8
Newbery, John, 83–84
A Little Pretty Pocket Book, 83
News, 181, 183, 199
editorial, 179–80, 183
language of, 181, 199
Newspapers, 178, 180, 183, 193
editorial, 179–80, 183
Non-fiction, 95, 103–04, 120
definition, 49, 52, 94–95
Notation, 39
Novel, 69, 78, 94–97, 99, 101, 104, 159
19th century and, 97
character, 103, 105, 111–15, 117
combination of social chronicle and biography, 103
constituents of, 115
eighteenth century and, 97
elements of, 113
epistolary, 98
graphic, 99
historical, 98
milieu, 101, 115
picaresque, 98
prose romance, 98
realistic, 96–97
regional, 98
setting, 101, 105, 109, 113, 115, 119
short story and, 101–02, 114
types of, 97
Novelette, 101
Novella, 101

O'Reilly, John Boyle, 22
A White Rose, 22
Octave, 62
Ode, 61, 68
Odyssey, 69
Onomatopoeia, 18, 30, 43
Openness, 3
Orality, 38
Orchestration, 146
Originality, 1–3, 9, 14
Osborne, John, 23
Look Back in Anger, 23
Owen, Wilfred, 70, 71
Dulce et Decorum Est, 70
Oxymoron, 18, 24, 43, 89

Padmanabhan, Manjula, 153
Fires, 155
Harvest, 150, 155
Painting, 2
Palindrome, 18, 31, 43
Pamuk, Nobel Laureate Orhan, 7
Paradox, 18, 24, 43
Parthasarathy, R., 48, 73, 77
At Ghalib's Tomb, 79
Rough Passage, 73, 77
Homecoming, 73
The Arrest of the Last Mughal Emperor at Humayun's Tomb, 79, 80
Patel, Gieve, 152, 156
Mister Behram, 156
Princes, 156
Savaksa, 156
Pathetic fallacy, 18, 25, 43
Pawar, Daya, 7
Personality, 3, 9
Personification, 17–18, 24–25, 43
Picasso, Pablo, 1–2
the painter, 1
Pidgin, 35, 44
Pink, Daniel, 2
A Whole New Mind, 2

Plath, Sylvia, 19
Plays, 140, 143, 153, 155, 159, *see also* Drama
  pantomime, 154
  proscenium, 147, 152–53
Playwriting, 158
  action scenes, 159
  climax, 159
  story and plot, 159
Poem, 48–49, 51–64, 66–67, 69–75, 78–81, 83–85, 89–92, 103, 116, 159, *see also* Poetry
Poetry, 2, 4–5, 8–9, 11, 14, 22, 48–61, 65–73, 76–78, 81–82, 84, 89–92, 177, 179, 192, 196
  auditory art, 54
  contemporary life and environment, 51
  definition of, 49
  emotions and feelings, 51
  experience and enjoyment of, 55
  features of, 2, 5
  form of, 50, 56, 59, 61, 65, 68–69
  functions of language, 50
  imaginative language, 49
  ingredient of, 65
  integrated literary composition, 52
  metrical composition, 48
  modes of, 45, 67
  nature of, 54, 58, 67
  prose and, 52, 96
  reasons for, 47, 51
  sound device in, 59
  spontaneous overflow of power ful feeling, 22
  structural and technical features of, 51, 60
  themes, 54, 68, 74, 78, 84, 88, 90
    nature, 54, 57–58, 63–64, 67, 79, 90–91
    romantic, 73–74, 91
    social issues, 90
  thoughts and feelings, 48
  twentieth century, 78, 84
  word puzzle, 89
  writing, 48, 50–53, 55, 58, 65, 67, 73, 77–79, 83, 89–90, 97
    images and symbols, 58
    rhyme and reason, 59
    rhythm, rhyme, and meter, 55
    shape, form and technique, 54
    theme and atmosphere, 57
    voices, 66, 74
    way of, 53
Pope, Alexander, 2, 25, 55, 60
  Essay on Criticism, 55
  The Rape of the Lock, 60
Porter, Jimmy, 23
Pound, Ezra, 78
Precision, 45
Pride, 51
Print media, 178–81, 188, 193
  personal columns, 178, 180, 186, 193
Pritchett, V. S., 102
Prominence, 177
Pronunciation, 32, 38
Propaganda, 8, 15
Prose, 48–50, 52–53, 84, 96, 98, 136, 142, 147
  artful use of language, 52
  conventionalization of speech, 52
  ordinary speech, 52
  poetry and, 52, 56, 61, 65, 78, 91
Prose, Francine, 102
  What Makes a Short Story? 102
Prosody, 55
Provincialism, 40, 44
Proximity, 177
Psychoticism, 9
Publication, 205, 207, 213
  preparing for, 205
    editing, 206–07, 210–11
    interpreting, 206
    proof reading, 207, 215
    revision, 205–07, 209–10
    rewriting, 205, 209–10
    submitting manuscript for, 213
Pun, 18, 28–29, 43
Puppetry, 154
Puzzle, 89

Qafia. See Rhyme
Quatrain, 61
Quiroz, Rachel De, 21
  Husband's Revenge, 21
  Metonymy, 21

Radif, see Refrain
Radio, 178–79, 188–90
  rules for, 189–90, 200
  scripts for, 189
  plays, 179
Ramanujan, A.K., 72, 77, 81
  Relations, 77
  Rough Passage, 73, 77
  Second Sight, 77
  The Black Hen, 77
  The Striders, 77
Randall, Alice, 7–8
  The Wind Done Gone, 7
Rasika, 81
Ray, Satyajit, 165
  Kailashey Kelenkari, 165
Reza, Yasmina, 153
  The Unexpected Man, 153
Rhyme, 48, 55, 59–60, 62–63, 69, 74–75, 84–85
  scheme of, 74
  types of, 60, 76, 97
Rhythm, 37, 48–49, 53, 55–56, 60, 62, 64, 69, 74–75, 79, 85, 89
  melodious, 57, 62, 68
Richard II, 143
Robbe-Grillet, Alain, 111
Robinson, Edwin Arlington, 63
  The House on the Hill, 63
Romantic poetry, 73
Roy, Arundhati, 104
  The God of Small Things, 104
Rushdie, Salman, 7, 97, 100, 104
  Midnight's Children, 97, 104
  Satanic Verses, 7
  Shame, 104
  The Moor's Last Sigh, 104
Ruskin, 25

Saint Joan, 143
Sarang, Vilas, 103
Sarcasm, 187
Schizophrenia, 9
Scott, Paul, 98
  Jewel in the Crown, 98
Screenplay, 165
Screenwriting, 9
Scriptwriting, 167–68, 190
  five key questions, 171
Self-confidence, 3
Semantics, 46–47
Sengupta, Poile, 157
  Body Blows, 157
  Good Heavens, 157

So said Shakuni, 157
Thus Spake Shurpanaka, 157
Sensitivity, 3, 51, 92
Septet, 75
Sestet, 62
Seth, Vikram, 69–70, 97, 104
An Equal Music, 104
A Suitable Boy, 104
The Golden Gate, 69, 104
Setting, 115
Shakespeare, William, 8–9, 19, 23–24, 30, 63, 140, 148
Hamlet, 23, 42
Sonnet, 18, 63
Sharma, Partap, 152
A Touch of Brightness, 155
Begum Sumroo, 155
Sammy!, 155
Zen Katha, 155
Shelley, Percy Bysshe, 61
Ode to the West Wind, 61
Short story, 101–04, 114, 116
Sign languages, 37
Silverstein, Shel, 31
Zebra Question, 31
Simile, 17–19, 43
Sircar, Badal, 154
Baki Itihas – The other side of History, 154
Skelton, Robin, 48
Slang, 43
Slapstick, 143, 154
Slogan, 198
basic characteristics, 198
Soliloquy, 145
Sonnet, 61, 62
Sophocles, 140
King Oedipus, 140
Sound, 17, 30, 37, 39, 44
figures of, 17–18, 20, 31, 43
Sound of Music, 167
Speech, 17–21, 24–28, 31–37, 39–40, 43, 50, 52–53, 55, 59, 66, 92
antithesis, 17, 23, 43
apostrophe, 17
aspects of
dynamic, 55
rhythmic, 55, 59, 66
chiasmus, 17, 43
conventionalization of, 52
figures of, 17–18, 20, 31, 43
formal, 32–33, 43
informal, 32, 33, 43
male versus female, 37
ordinary, 52, 75, 95
Stanza, 48, 57–61, 63, 66, 68–69, 71, 75, 68, 81, 90
Stevens, Wallace, 4–5
Of Modern Poetry, 4–5
Stevenson, Robert Louis, 84
A Child's Garden of Verses, 84
Storey, David, 142
Story telling, 95
factual, 94–95
Stravinsky, 6
Petrushka, 6
Street Theatre, 154
Strophe, 68
Stucky, Steven, 6
Suspense, 113
Syllable, 55–57, 59, 64, 66, 78, 89
Symbol, 18, 20, 22–23, 43, 59
Sympathy, 25
Synecdoche, 17–18, 21, 43
Synonym, 51

Taboo language, 33, 43
Tagore, Rabindranath, 28
Kabuliwallah, 28
Target, 130
Television, 178–79, 188–92
script writing, 190
Tennyson, Lord, 61
In Memoriam, 61
Tercet, 61, 63, 73
Terza Rima, 61
Tharoor, Shashi, 22, 99, 104
The Great Indian Novel, 22, 99, 104
Theatre, 135–36, 140–41, 145–49, 151–58
The Duchess of Malfi, 143
The Iceman Cometh, 142
The Little Foxes, 143
The Lower Depths, 143
The Sheep Well, 143
The Weavers, 143
The White Devil, 143
Thiong'o, Ngugi wa, 36
Thomas, Dylan, 58, 63
Do not Go Gentle into that Good Night, 63
In my craft or sullen art, 58
To Kill a Mockingbird, 119
Travel writing, 188
Triplet, 61
Troilus and Cressida, 143
Trollope, Anthony, 46
Tropes, 17–18, 31
figures of thought, 17
hyperbole, 17, 43
irony, 17, 27, 43
litotes, 17
metaphor, 17, 19, 21, 24, 43
metonymy, 17, 21, 43
personification, 17, 25, 43
simile, 17, 19, 43
synecdoche, 17, 21, 43
Trust, Mitchell, 7

Universal art, 8
concept of, 8
Unusualness, 3
Updike, John, 111
USA, 7
African-American community in, 7
Black writers in, 7
University of East Anglia (UEA), 13
creative writing courses, 13
Usefulness, 3
Utterance, 46–47, 159

Valmiki, Omprakash, 7
Verbal abuse, 33
Verne, Jules, 100
Verse, 61, 66, 83, 88
Villanelle, 61, 63, 74

Webster, Jean, 98
Daddy Long Legs, 98
Weirdness, 178
Wernicke, Carl, 37
Wernickes aphasia, 37
Whitbread Award, 119
White, E. B., 46
Wilkinson, H. E., 85
Topsy-Turvy Land, 84–85

Williams syndrome, 38
Wodehouse, P.G., 19
  Uncle Fred in the Spring Time, 19
Wolff, Tobias, 101–02
Woolf, Virginia, 97
  Mrs Dalloway, 97
Words, 39, 44, 46–49, 51–55, 57–59, 66–68, 72, 75–76, 78, 81, 83–84, 89–92, 189
  arrangement, 53, 55, 57–59, 61, 92
  connotation of, 39, 44
  denotation of, 39, 44
  meanings of, 20, 39
  selection, 46, 58
  use of, 40, 42
Wordsworth, William, 4, 22, 24–25, 49
  Composed upon Westminster Bridge, 24
World War II, 97
Worldwide Web, 178–79
  writing style for, 193
Writer, 17–18, 22, 31, 36–38, 40, 42–43, 45–47, 52, 77, 89, 95, 205–06, 208–11
  African-American, 7
  career graph of, 103
  creative, 17–18, 33, 40, 42–43
  Dalit, 7
  experimental, 111
  fiction, 113
  goal of, 47
  regional, 115
  screenplay, 159
  script, 191
Writing, 3, 7, 9–15, 17–18, 21, 30–32, 37–38, 40, 42–45, 47–48, 83, 89–90, 92, 135–36, 142, 144, 147, 152, 157, 158–59, 177–81, 183–84, 186–93, 195–96, 200, 205, 207–15
  act of communication, 45
  act of faith, 46
  advertising, 179, 185, 193, 195–198, 200
  anecdotes, 10, 12
  art and craft of, 17, 42
    formal and informal usage, 32
    style and register, 32
    tropes and figures, 17, 18–19, 31
  artistic, 17
  creative, 1–3, 6–15, 17, 45, 59, 73, 77, 95
  drama, 8, 9, 11, 15
  economics of, 103
  editorials, 10
  everything-is-permissible philosophy, 46
  fiction, 9, 10
  for children, 10
  form of, 181
  imagination and, 6, 10, 12, 15
  Internet, 178–80, 192–93, 195–96
  journalistic, 9–10, 15
  kinds of, 1–3, 9–10, 15
  language, 45–55, 57–59, 66–68, 73–74, 78–79, 81, 89–92, 95, 99
  literary, 45, 52, 58, 77, 81, 90, 96, 99
  media, 177–81, 186, 188, 192–93, 195–97, 200, 203
  needs and interests, 47
  non-creative, 9–10, 15
  non-fiction, 10
  non-literary, 52
  orality and, 38
  poetry, 2, 4–5, 8–9, 11, 14
  preliminaries for, 45
  process in, 47
  readable, 46
  reader's knowledge, 47
  reviews, 10
  revising in, 205
  screenwriting, 9
  script, 168, 179, 188–92
  self-exploratory, 9
  social act, 45
  styles, 47, 67, 92
  subject, 46, 48, 51, 53, 58–59, 73, 79, 83, 89–91
  use of language, 47, 52, 53

Yeats, W. B., 28, 78
  Sailing to Byzantium, 28
Young readers, 88
  verse for, 83, 88
    problems, 49, 53, 72, 89
    ten commandments of, 88

About the Authors

Anuradha Marwah teaches English literature and creative writing in Zakir Husain College, University of Delhi. Her research interests include contemporary fiction in English in India and the pedagogy of creative writing. Also a social activist, she writes scripts for activist theatre, and as Secretary, Ajmer Adult Education Association, is currently running literacy and all-round development programmes for rural children and youth in fifty villages in Rajasthan. She has authored three novels: *The Higher Education of Geetika Mehendiratta*; *Idol Love*; and *Dirty Picture*. In addition to these, she has published poems, short stories, reviews, and academic papers.

Anjana Neira Dev is currently Principal of Vivekananda College, University of Delhi. She has been teaching in the University of Delhi since 1991, first in Sherubtse College Bhutan, and then at Gargi College. Her experience in teaching is complemented by her research in pedagogical practices and the field of education in which she has an M. Phil. from the University of Cambridge. Her areas of special interest include Indian English poetry, the postcolonial novel, and the poetry of the Renaissance, along with the teaching of English for special purposes. Her wide-ranging publications include an edited anthology of Indian Literature for the University of Delhi; a book on Business English for the Department of English, University of Delhi; and a number of articles on Indian English poetry in national and international books and journals.

Swati Pal teaches in the Department of English, Janki Devi Memorial College, University of Delhi. A Charles Wallace Scholar (1997 and 2008) as well as the John McGrath Theatre Studies Scholar (2005) at Edinburgh University, Swati Pal's has published essays on Beckett, Osborne and Mahesh Dattani. She has also published an essay on Thomas Hardy's *Tess of D'Urbervilles*. Her M. Phil dissertation from the Jawaharlal Nehru University (JNU), New Delhi, looked at Ritual and Agit Prop Theatre where she analysed Howard Brenton's plays and those by Jana Natya Manch. Her doctoral thesis, also from JNU, looks at Agit Prop in Britain from the 60s to the 90s. She has presented a number of papers on British, European and Indian drama at national and international conferences, including a lecture at the Edinburgh Film Fringe Festival where she introduced the works of John McGrath.